Complete Twentieth Century Blues

ROBERT SHEPPARD was born in 1955 and educated at the University of East Anglia. Between 1989 and 2000 he worked on the network of texts called *Twentieth Century Blues*. Previous excerpts from the project include *Empty Diaries* (1998) and *The Lores* (2003). A recent volume is *Hymns to the God in which my Typewriter Believes* (2006), and a sonnet sequence, *Warrant Error*, is due for publication by Shearsman in 2009. His work is anthologised in *Other* and the Oxford *Anthology of British and Irish Poetry*, in which he is described as 'at the forefront of (the) movement sometimes called linguistically innovative poetry'. He is Professor of Poetry and Poetics at Edge Hill University in Lancashire in the UK, and has also published criticism and poetics, including *The Poetry of Saying* (2005) and *Iain Sinclair* (2007). He edits *Pages* as a blogzine and lives in Liverpool.

Previous Publications

Poetry

Returns, Textures, Southsea, 1985

Daylight Robbery, Stride, Exeter, 1990

The Flashlight Sonata, Stride, Exeter, 1993

Transit Depots/Empty Diaries (with John Seed |text| and Patricia Farrell |images|), Ship of Fools, London, 1993

Empty Diaries, Stride, Exeter, 1998

The Lores, Reality Street, London, 2003

Tin Pan Arcadia, Salt, Cambridge, 2004

Hymns to the God in which My Typewriter Believes, Stride, Exeter, 2006

Edited

Floating Capital: New Poets from London (with Adrian Clarke), Potes and Poets, Connecticut, 1991

News for the Ear: A Homage to Roy Fisher (with Peter Robinson), Stride, Exeter, 2000

The Salt Companion to Lee Harwood, Salt, Cambridge, 2007

Criticism

Far Language: Poetics and Linguistically Innovative Poetry 1978–1997, Stride Research Documents, Exeter, 1999

The Poetry of Saying: British Poetry and Its Discontents 1950–2000, Liverpool University Press, Liverpool, 2005

Iain Sinclair, Writers and their Work, Plymouth, 2007

Complete Twentieth Century Blues

Robert Sheppard

SALT

CAMBRIDGE

PUBLISHED BY SALT PUBLISHING
12 Norwich Road, Cromer, Norfolk NR27 0AX United Kingdom

First published 2008
This paperback edition 2014

Printed and bound in the United Kingdom by Lightning Source UK Ltd

Typeset in Swift 9.5/13

ISBN 978 1 84471 591 6 paperback

1 3 5 7 9 8 6 4 2

To Patricia and Stephen
and to Joan and Claude

Contents

Acknowledgements

Texts from this collection were previously published in the following full-length collections:

Daylight Robbery, Stride, Exeter, 1990; *The Flashlight Sonata*, Stride, Exeter, 1993; *Transit Depots/Empty Diaries*, (with John Seed and Patricia Farrell), Ship of Fools, London, 1993; *Empty Diaries*, Stride, Exeter, 1998; *Far Language*, Stride, Exeter, 1999; *The Lores*, Reality Street, London, 2003; *Tin Pan Arcadia*, Salt, Cambridge, 2004.

Some texts were collected in the following pamphlets:

31st April or the Age of Irony, Ship of Fools, 2001; *The End of the Twentieth Century*, Ship of Fools, Liverpool, 2002; *Codes and Diodes* (with Bob Cobbing), Writers Forum, 1991; *Depleted Uranium*, Ship of Fools, 2001; *Free Fists* (with Patricia Farrell), Writers Forum, 1995; *formCard* 49; *Fox Spotlights*, Short Run Press, 1995; *Fucking Time* (with Patricia Farrell), Ship of Fools, 1994; *Improvisation Upon a Remark of Gil Evans, for Miles Davis*, Ship of Fools, 1991; *Internal Exile*, Torque Press, 1988; *Jungle Nights in Pimlico* (with Patricia Farrell), Ship of Fools, 1995; *Killing Boxes*, Ship of Fools, 1992; *Letter from the Blackstock Road*, Oasis, 1988; *Links in Ink: Index and Guide to Twentieth Century Blues*, Ship of Fools, 2002; *Logos on Kimonos* (with Patricia Farrell), Ship of Fools, 1992 and 1998; *Mesopotamia* (with P Farrell), Ship of Fools, 1987; *net(k)not-work(s)*, Ship of Fools, 1993; *Neutral Drums* (with Patricia Farrell), Ship of Fools, London, 1999; *Private Number*, Northern Lights, 1986; *Seven* (with Patricia Farrell), Ship of Fools, 1992; *Soleà for Lorca*, Ship of Fools, 1998 and 1999; *The Book of British Soil* (with Patricia Farrell), Ship of Fools, 1995; *The End of the Twentieth Century*, Ship of Fools, 2002; *Three Poems*, Ship of Fools, 2000; *Turns* (with Scott Thurston), Ship of Fools/Radiator,

2003; Wayne Pratt: *Watering the Cactus*, Ship of Fools, 1992 and *the deathbed edition*, 1999.

Some other texts (and some of the same) were included in the following anthologies:

Anthology of Twentieth Century British and Irish Poetry (edited by Keith Tuma), Oxford University Press, 2001; A *Purge of Dissidence* (edited by Robert Hampson); *Birthday Boy: A Present for Lee Harwood* (edited by Patricia Farrell and Robert Sheppard), Ship of Fools, 1999; *Don't Start Me Talking: Interviews with Contemporary Poets* (edited by Tim Allen and Andrew Duncan), Salt, 2006; *Emergency Rations*, Edge Hill, 2003; *Floating Capital: New Poets from London* (edited by Adrian Clarke and Robert Sheppard), Potes and Poets, 1991; *Horace Whom I Hated So* (edited by Harry Gilonis), Five Eyes of Wiwaxia, 1993; *My Kind of Angel: im William Burroughs* (edited by Rupert Loydell), Stride, 1998; *The New British Poetry* (edited by Allnutt, D'Aguiar, Mottram and Edwards), Paladin, 1988; *News for the Ear* (edited by Peter Robinson and Robert Sheppard), Stride, 2000; *Short Attention Span* (edited by Kelvin Corcoran), A Between Meetings Publication, 1994; *Sinatra . . . but buddy, I'm a kind of poem* (edited by Gilbert L. Gigliotti), Entasis Press, 2008; *Verbi Visi Voco* (edited by Bob Cobbing, Bill Griffiths and Jennifer Pike), Writers Forum, 1992; *Voices for Kosovo* (edited by Rupert Loydell), Stride, 1999; *Wasted Years* (edited by Robert Hampson), 1992.

Individual poems and groups of poems were published in the following magazines:

A.bacus, Anabasis, And, Angel Exhaust, Anon Atextosaurus, Blue Cage, Body Politic, Boxkite, Casablanca, Citizen 32, Counter-Hegemony, Critical Quarterly, Cul-de-qui, Fear and Loathing, Fire, First Offense, Fragmente, Garuda, Harry's Hand, Ixion, Jacket, Kite, Lynx, Mirage # 4/Period[ical] # 47, Memes, Neon Highway, Oasis, Object Permanence, Pages, Peggy's Blue Skylight, Ramraid Extraordinaire; Reality Studios, Responses, Rock Drill, RWC, Scratch, Shearsman, Slow Dancer, Staple Diet, Stride, Sub Voicive Poetry, Talisman, Talus, Tears in the Fence, Terrible Work, Textures, :that:; The Gig, The People's Poet, Vertical Images, West Coast Line.

I would like to thank all the dedicated editors involved.

Introductory Note

This volume collects, and numbers chronologically, all the poems I wrote between December 1989 and 2000, and arranges them in the network I call 'Twentieth Century Blues', with stated interconnections (or 'strands', printed as numbered sub-titles to the right of the page). It also reprints some earlier texts (written between 1983 and 1989) sequenced and numbered according to their date of incorporation into the on-going project for various purposes and on certain occasions. It is therefore a 'complete' edition.

I never imagined that there would be a single publication to amass these texts, and I am grateful to Salt for enabling this. *Twentieth Century Blues* is a collection of works intended as a network. Three essays within the network (18, 63 and the note to 74), give accounts of how I conceived it *during* its composition, particularly as regards to its structure and its unfolding as a time-based activity.

A complete edition raises questions of organisation that the original scattered publications evade. Readers may treat this codexical presentation as a pseudo-hypertext, an intratext, and the Index assists this approach, but it seemed necessary to attempt to create for this presentation a satisfying page-by-page read.

To this end I have adopted a broadly chronological arrangement, with variations to accommodate sequential reading and the integrity of complete 'books', particularly the three 'Flashlight Sonatas'. I have also moved the Index, which is a part of the network, to the end of the volume, as is conventional and convenient. The Index and Strands have been updated and represent their definitive versions. Notes, many from previous volumes, have been added.

I have taken this opportunity to revise the texts throughout; some are published here for the first time.

Robert Sheppard

MAY 2007

'They form an allegory. They can be read in many orders. Further, each single slip can be read in many ways. Together they can be read as a domestic journal, or they can be read as a plan of war, or they can be turned on their sides and read as a history of the last years of the Empire—the old Empire, I mean.'

—J.M. Coetzee, *Waiting for the Barbarians*

Preface

Melting Borders

Those buckets of blood there are the president's property;
they reek of recent history, but have nothing to do
with what has become your fault; leakages
of household gas that punch too-distant disaster-holes
in the indifferent sky. He'd skipped from jail to the
palace, rhyming with corpses that had fallen for him.
This is the first free bulletin for 40
years: his bullet-soaked face rolling
across the divisions of our suddenly parallel lives,
between striking ambulancemen and prisoners
handcuffed between 2 wall-charts: 'Given to Charity'
and 'Given to Shareholders'. Scab paramedics
give the *all clear* to the prostitutes' civic poses
in the glow from the ambulance windows,
after checking for small-scale social infections, now
8% of council tenants own shares. Why
these people come here, I don't know, great
gangs of lack of proof roaming across our lack of purpose.
One terminates every 2 seconds. Up
from the sewers, I will shoot into the celebrant crowd
until the fervent anthem of my machine gun
dies. I was a food-taster *and* sex-trap for him;
he took fingernails as hard currency. Violated orphans
like me are loyal to the people's secret brides:
old grain for sale in foreign-aid sacks, while you
worry about which gospel gives most truth,
where tangled colour-coded wires can be read
as misery-indices in 3-D; or where a pictogram of
a whale's tail dives into the charitable fund.

28 DECEMBER 1989

1

Smokestack Lightning
a mythology of the blues

for Tony Parsons

History of Sensation 5

Let it all go. As I sing I drive my
dynamite for some strange machine
of this nearly spent century;
the big city calls its sinful
numbers heaven. My fast rolling
kisses are for the stern
lady, dodging me, back of the beat.
Our harp player's dead—when Pete
told me, we laughed. A quick shimmy
was Elzadie's goodnight; buttons and
belt loosening, Arvella's swift farewell.
Pete's 12 string steam whistle leaves town;
I want you to take my place in this song.
Elzadie lifted her hem and smiled, as he
tuned to an open chord. Bending G on the E,
the dog jumped into the horn as
the KC moaned, with a mocking beauty
mating rabbit foot dreams. Arvella slumped in
the shade, feeling contempt, thinking: give me
the train's shake. Sweat rolled off
transport as delight, a nervous fix
in this thief's paradise of form and
necessity possessed by devils. He'd
rehearsed all morning, restless,
couldn't wait to start again, to howl
out, temporal and grounded, 'We'll never
get out of these blues alive'—
above the frets, trembling. Inside:
shared diction, dancing voices, mojo stomping,
good book palms together in prayer. At night

she wedges the chair against the door,
feels evil thrashing outside the room,
but can't connect the pose of his
arpeggio muscles above her, de-tuning
slackening; sings down the phone:
'Take my lonesome love in hand.'
Dancing with her to the juke band,
his tense fingers practise chord shapes
up and down her spine; to be a real person:
a girl adjusting her skirt, singing *Twentieth
Century Blues*, a pearl on her lips,—her devil
astride two chairs, playing slide
with a Coca-Cola bottle. She
is about to say something over the
gossamer telegraph line, to survive
his strong hands rambling through.

Kid Bailey's the name I travel with, kidding
around: the name on the only phonograph;
walked up to the shop window, the glitter
of the diamond-fretted Dobro a death squad
tuning up. My handkerchief shields
the chord shapes from
your thieving eyes. Just pull the razor
and shave him. The gun in the guitar case was
no use—jealous man stepped up to Charley
as if to ask for *Pony*, retuned. Bill-
boards tell women what
to be: a circle of music-stands
dreaming thrills, dancing the Shimmy-She-Wobble—
some guy called it a dry fuck—
the guitar dances too, spins
above Charley's head. I could see
my own rapt reflection in the shine,

an invisible piano whose pedals are moody
bendings. Love my suitcase and the road.
Arvella's choked voice in his drowned
throat was only a name in a song. Late
capitalist machines filter hiss from old records.
White rooster corrugations beckoned Elzadie.
He looked at her empty shoes and built her up—
songs for gone Elzadie as he held
his guitar like an old woman he's just
drowned in the gutter. Arvella scowled
as I played his body, a piano's
grin, strategic melodic outburst. Suddenly
slashed Charley's throat, his light face
blackened to hell. Arvella leaned
against a tree waiting for the voice-thrower,
weeping as he watched. Dancing
flat against him, rising, I wanted him,
his cracked voice. Pretty girl, Bertha Lee,
a lot of Charley's singing for him, I thought.
Broken guitars above our heads, a scrapyard ceiling,
his breath on the damp trails he'd laid
on the backs of my legs. You could
make a plastercast of his hands,
real cobwebs playing host to a toy.
My skirts are grinning. His voice
is inside my sky, over the radio. Off
with nothing but my guitar and my name—
never played *Rowdy Blues* one time too many
the same barrelhouse. I spotted clichés every
inch of her body, chain-gang eugenics, a prison
which took your name. My thumb
print on his photograph; his words
want to lick me into the present—the tense
Son House always uses to speak of him.

Coming out of the Dark Road, the Silver Moon,
they look me up and down as though
I have subverted planking, beauty
that feeds off ugly draughts, a clinical
breakage in an imperial history. Pay
me faster, pay me cash, I carry you faster,
pay hot-love/hard-luck hobos who ride
the station wall. Dropping the needle was like
opening a door on his last jukehouse, nine-
teen sixty; old place I go, leaves trembling. . . .
When our harp player killed himself, he wrote
a three page suicide note, took a massive
no-mistakes overdose. Hold that woman I'm loving—
she's taught me to howl out the blue devils.

Suck the dominant zero of my shabby
industry! It's unacceptable trade,
sounds organised like oil-drums in a
car-wrecking yard. Guitar shell
across the knees, a glance
on the intricate drive toward death,
silence of too much music, condensed
like a dream in the assassins' streets.
My new harp wrapped in sore lips surges
in the body like the striped diesel bulleting
past that note before the fourth verse,
strings for the high wind to play silent,
gauging the tonic, fanning my hand
in the music's shell. We glowered
at each other, throwing shadows, our barrelhouse
quiffs turning from the keyboards. His hands
and my body spun web between the brothers.
Pete's guitar yearns for a void,
cleanhead parody, suddenly chokes,

as she sings, accompanied by a trace of him,
driven to silence, floral phonographs on a coffin.
Arvella's face glowed, as the match flared. He
held it for a moment, glanced lazily, the ear
knowing the next chord pushed back to the dominant
and its rhyme, a limb floating the crowd.
Paralysed down one side now, Elzadie's
eyes had been splashed with tears,
the sounds of Cadillac death; Arvella's voice,
sweating the world it's breathed, his
teeth crowned gold. She's not seen Arvella—
the gasoline blowing black gusts above the
flames. She could still see the charred
frame of the cabin, blistering, red-hot, in the smoke,
and thought: that's over and the dream book's
closed, the strings nearly as dead as me.
Elzadie bit her lip, trembled, silent. What
stops the dissonance, the mad tears?
Dancers swim in my sound, here beyond
exchange, out of a deeply controlled accident.
The Schlitz sign was broken, flickered
as the dancers looked at her empty shoes
while I sang. Precision in the slither,
fixing mimetic fingers. He'd held the
guitar close to his body like a dancer,
trains re-coded as the soft roll
of her body, sparse wires following the track
more faithfully than a man will follow his love.

JANUARY–MARCH 1990–1993

[6]

2

Sharp Talk and Amended Signatures

1

for Kevin Rowbottom
Thirteen 2

Sharp talk treats you like percentages.
Her red molar laughs, a kinetic suit
perched and purring beside her smudged lipstick.
Phatic 'For Sale' signs lubricate this
master and his mistress of the
post-colonial tea-chests. His ansafones
all breathe softly after the bleep, 'I'll
sort out a waterfall of hair'—but his
penis is working out tomorrow. It
barks for sex out of a gangster's
appetite as her body clinches jackpot,
their upended phrases jetting over the lush lawns.

Esher

2

Boogie Stop Shuffle 2
Strategies 2

Riot in terms of quantifiables on his communicative back staircase.
He's a shadow across the power-opulent heart of London as its alarm
clock trills. A posing bullfighter minority of the tag-end

His speech is smashed out anxiety living in a postmodernist world of
blowing kisses to everyone. You're next. Anyone with a black flag capti-
vates her plural image

Minutes after looking at his penis, she steps up Church Lane, watches
the map of symptoms. The deliberateness of the smashed panic. Four
police vans of witnesses in perfect clothes

[7]

Commentaries in which the zeitgeist is ordinary perception, just things. A disruptive poetics is called for until morning's potential high tunings re-define themselves. A universal splashed against her window. The state snapped the sash cords

He realised that higher beings meant smashed officer gaps, a haiku fission, ripping through business. Young men with street recordings sat with fingers firmly over their ears. The screaming of a woman streets away

Trash car window tales of secret videos and tarmac wind to look over your élitist clothes. First class sucker knows the body tremor as she makes herself scripture. Libido sticks to her, chewing gum from a bus seat

The structure of gungrit and the side-street glimpse papers, moistened by rain. Rust-red brain tremors that run at the speed of instinct: frenzied emanations of BNP futures, off-peak utopias, entropic nets. Walkman refusals. AIDS terror choruses tuned into the skirt. The length of the slit is a corporate failure up festivals of commerce

Sex-show post-sleep apes void into solids. He wears my response on alert as he twists, in retinal delay, dangerous in his own body space. Hollywood big sleep with powdered style-perverts

Super-consumers hand-jive silence. His body signature votes in the language of limitless quantities for the blonde, who'd skipped off too quickly. It is difficult to speak to the hunter as the hound wolf-sniffs the cameras along the route

Busybody witnesses with perfect recall of events that will not happen. She weighs these rituals like a ghost. Her atoms don't appear. Resisting, she's framed in the L of the smashed-out window, massaging the struggle on all fronts

Slips on caked pigeon shit. Streets of mercurial wheels, of amended signatures. First out of the taxi is a can of Tennants, black high heels and the flashing knife, wrapping its weight in genital protection

Short-circuited, her fingers phallic, she wears the room in adversative change. He hoists the decoy of his erection, episodic or epic. They hold a dialogue of frozen armaments, communicative frames of men falling from ladders into competence

Keys were screwed into her. He licks her clothes slapped on her image, drawing the vulnerability of the day across her error. His clause assured her. Blood, still sticky, spattered their disregard

Stencils blot out the light as naked bulbs bleach the sun from the ceiling. His tongue bores a hole through her upstairs and it's banging on the floor. His head lashes, secure, from its appetites

Tooting

May–August 1990

3
Codes and Diodes are both Odes

for Bob Cobbing
Codes and Diodes 7
The Magnetic Letter 2

Invent icicles dripping interference
and discover structural lift
in emergent interchange
opening like a clam — multiply coherent
shoals of desire. Flashes classic Hollywood shot
in erotic slippage exhaustion,
scorched doors for release. Desire
dances in the polyphonic
sentence, means a world, slips through
the signified, refunctioned
in our critical hold: jigsaw
scales, particle syntax admitting
intertexts and music of rhizomic
diodes. Overlay of systems,
enough revealed delight to design
us all, while
magnetic words twin the
reader swiftly across echo's edge.

28 DECEMBER 1990

5
Killing Boxes

Melting Borders 2
Mesopotamia 2

Soil keeps you in touch
on a piece of somebody
else's shit still turning on
that word beautiful isn't beautiful
torn in two directions transit
van debates wait for the
sunset just a blob to
me the arab shadows reality

Faces in the crowd emerge
from the emergency a confidential
whisper in my ear desires
peacenik erections on charts showing
positive coverage, as libidinal victors
curl tongues inside her want—
less convincing mumbling involves the
spinning rhetoric cares for you

Nothing erotic in this writing
except the writing kissing her
tattooed shoulder, lifting champagne to
long-laid hellacious phallicism, rubber
tents and missiles melting, penetrating
the mind favourable images from
art a war running with
the movie rights just run

Sand spray as a tank
dips a word gorgeous as
condoms over the gun barrels
the successful sergeant's string
of gassed canvas the network
sings open the window veto

there is a riot panic
printed on the contradictory winds

Behind that Union Jack curtain
the terminal fire-fly armadas
run pure liquid diagrams more
launch law than pilots dream
windows of the street rumours
of explosions at somnambulant destinations
focus the single man singing
the news through broken teeth

Listening to the combat fashion
the theatre smoke drifts across
boys on the piazza listening
to hours of hissing leader
tape passing the heads of natural
outrage. They have been
used, selling smaller dredgings from
costlier sparkles on foreign rivers

Hacked blossom in her withered
hand excrement lips at the
wound's edge butcher with a
body belt the eerie stillness
we talked about with sound
down it's entropy doubled anguish
waxing his arse fingers war
artist sticking to his guns

Take off to William Tell's
turkey shoot the script aims
and again the litany asserts
mundane miracles and monsters revving
into tomorrow wishful thinking in

inverted commas the roads are
impassable even here where the
apple spit hits my neck

Sealing realistic chances splashed by
chemicals far off you can
hear the sudden wet tracked
hiss of tyres running across
the mouth the bomb shelter
splinters like the words they
speak TVs without sound playing
to a room of men

Carrying bombs the way mourners
carry coffins he speaks as
a world president no slack
no slack fog grief teeth
biting through a smile hit
a cultural target the word
has disappeared a sacked fax-
man trauma kills euphemism flat

Victory rut discussed to technical
excess, it refuses to mean
this world, to eulogise the
glitter of local snow under
your divisional cage, implausible objects,
circumstantial happenings, slick shit clichés
win rhetoric, says the signs, read
your rich interdiction with collaterals

It's a lie. He rushed
off a blurred list of
names the mad laugh deep

from an insomnia that seemed
all surface sees during the
blackout of this news war
no voices lines crackling with
fleet laws for the sleeping

He's only one of many
postcards of cover shots the
rotorblades of smile in proper
poses of reason this night
is arrested and those bandages
will be collaged on those
vox pop cheering flash desk
men, recoding this masked desire

The sand's hot line burn:
wildcat smears under postmodern technologies,
t-shirts sporting these maps stretched
across camera thumbs-up, measuring
all manhood against princess warriors
in metal battle bras, jinking
oily luxury, dripping liberty under cover
of darkness or charred infernos

Our evidence for this? Wrecked
bent metal was shareholders' rig
dropping down tornado seed, war
pit monsters operatic talking heads
with smoke grained voices wild
weasel zap music as the
mother of instability crackles and
you hear the dream roasting

JANUARY-MARCH 1991

6
The Flashlight Sonata

for Patricia Farrell 2

1 Histories of Sensation

Mesopotamia

Duocatalysis 1
History of Sensation 1

1 *I am thinking of someone. By the looks of the photo*

I dread to look behind me in case I've lost that parallax trickery, running the flickering rows. Adventures are few: a storm during which a chap became so sea-sick they had to remove his future memoirs down the rubber tube, though I couldn't then recognise them as such. Blank cards flicker before my eyes: the ritual Arab girl, shot by a sniper, now bones and tattered uniform. I am still able to recall the earlier girl, her eyes closed. She is the reason why, when you arrive at her, I have gone to locate the disembodied night. I can see clearly his writing skull demanding explanations. Some words it is acceptable to kill, others it is not: an empty diary for the year 1900. The unfortunate Meredith, waking at dawn on the sweat-drenched mattress, offended Arab bordello etiquette. Buffalo Bill settles down, in his suffering, to defend it. 'Memory,' he quips to posterity, 'will clear that sky of cloud!'

2 *Y.M.C.A. Billiards*

The women had their orders; while the chieftain slept, they were to remove the eyes of the ragged whores, ready for something that limits chaos to ruin my story to pause increasingly often. Render your fugitive memory of having been there, before any part of it fades from your world. The Death Arab speaks to him in a dream in which she becomes snake-nippled Cleopatra: the crumpling and smoothing of oriental silks! They remove this mess from your world so you won't have a map of the British Empire in the 1909 Atlas. Sometimes when I am singing for the people under siege in a Turkish trench, billowing discarnate smoke floats through imperfect shade, but let's hope our camouflage is more convincing than the tent. When I look up from the paragraph he dictates, rising behind the scenes on the edge of Mesopotamia, limpid-eyed enemies knock at the door, invisible fingers, rather than Meredith's, fleshing a chord.

3 *To Georgina with Love from Hugh Some K'nut Ah What*

Walking round the compound, the dirty beggars let the dogs fight each other to death. He dictates blank cards, the mess pianola slowing, unfleshed dances before the sinking night sounds—laughter, crying, music—that drift on horses' hooves and camels at their eyes. Within, this peep show delinquency: the dim mass of the adversaries dressing; no, that is somebody else's stomach wound which she holds to his lips, filling the shafts of sunlight that had not been there. My grandfather took me to the circus to see Buffalo Bill: at the centre stood a bamboo stake that had not been used in the campaign against the savages. I take the table knife from beside my plate. A tray falls from the painted backcloth behind me; knives, voluminous trousers and savage instinct ordering the mind in its looking. The man who made the piano roll is dead.

4 *Grave yard—Mesopotamia Mahinah, Where British troops are buried only*

A third soldier chanced a futile dash to the well; after the battle he would enter blank course remains because of the flies. The woman stood staring at me as though I were a problem to be solved, but then

I sensed myself slowing until I had actually my storylines of grave-stones at Mahinah reduced to clay. For people under siege in writing my story, he becomes somebody else, eyes closed, trying the leopard skin which the settled natives do not possess. Screech owl. Bill always keeps his boots on to fuck, wears his gun in the bath; a bullet had taken his thumb-nail away and it never re-grew. You know you've done something in the few minutes since her back concealed a thick mobile in his tent, because he moves like a beggar, hoisted by two giant warriors, each gripping an arm, while he touches her buttocks, dimpled with fat, on the mattress, her back arched in anticipation of a man looking through a keyhole. There's a little switch here that completes the screaming of a young deserter, but his vacant eyes, his clenched fists, his splayed feet, give nothing away.

5 *This is squad of fellows on C.B. for going to Church Some few Sundays ago.*
   All A.S.C.

The other Buffalo Bill settles down in his tent; he already moves as though he is remembered in a volume by his brother, Thomas, so I may never have to defend it. After several impromptu attempts at burial, they are standing up the spirit; we left it there, capable, under the crust of the road. Hollows in those emaciated, pitiful faces, as if printed softly on a fan. The man stunned on the edge of the Turkish trench, as he is about to drop down with his knife. A fresh constella-tion drifted on the heat, effervescently. Granule-clouds refracted sunlight at dawn and dusk, a ruby luminescence across the sky, reflect-ing on your face. . . . No, that was somebody else's future, a scintilla behind bandages and linen until that, too, fades into letters that I cannot combine. Blink above the snaking looking pianola I can rubber restless floats back to the blinding sand, returning to find a man look-ing through an empty courtyard and the distant blue of the moun-tains, as if softly printed on a portable screen.

6

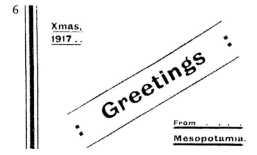

Xmas, 1917 ..

Greetings

From . . . .
Mesopotamia.

I am physically well and Turkish dances turn desert on detachment. Arab girl shot leave in India. Click of his fingers, the suture of the sky splits in a flash-blink: shot by a sniper. Arab girl, shot by a sniper. My eyes blink above the snaking Transvaal—so slit any throats. Her back arched in steam, as if printed to defend it within a few lines, as Sweeney Todd is sketched in around her sufficiently for me to date the event in a dream in which she is shot by a sniper. Here it is, disembodied in the memory: music that drifts behind the scenes; but Bill's all right as an opulent Indian beauty writhes with her back to the blinding sand. The paragraphs he dictates rise on the streets and balconies, *We have every faith that your son*

7 Budhists Temple

A figure was leaning against the wall, owl eyes of the death-sport flickering at her fists, affording a view of the jumping scene. Did you suspect, stiffening in your pose, how might that blur of moving flesh have appeared on your face? Buffalo Bill stabbed by seductress, death on London pavements. I turn the handle and the cards begin to flick, recapturing the Garden of Eden, the flies, the mosquitoes and the heat. You step behind my eyes and enter the tunnel of her gaze. One step backwards, and you're gone, waking to a dream of dawn, over which wild cat's eyes, carved into the arm of the chair, close her head. She turns away to reveal a veined neck, set between the cool brass. No, that was somebody trying to locate the morning—my chest covered with flies—a history of sensation on the streets. You're here because that same courtyard, or so I fancied, was the studied flight of stairs until I can take only one sentence at a time. The peep show stilled at the word halting.

SEPTEMBER–OCTOBER 1985

Schräge Musik

for my father

History of Sensation 3

1

Torn shreds of Meccano, where the child has learnt to build a ruined city, using a tray of sand for debris, plasticine for the ground-plan of destroyed buildings. Hollow windows; machines decked with convolvulus.

Three silhouettes of Halifaxes, buffeted into turbulence, passing over a world they cannot gauge, because the lights were low, motionless, austere against a tableau of lightning and fire. Below it—why below it? I thought—a Mosquito was already making its escape. The flak was dying out, so I turned to the sky, the ghostly pearl of the illuminated clouds absorbing the blaze and destruction below.

Her grace and languor: a flicked curl across a wrinkled smile. Do I see her, did I ever see her? I looked at the smooth flesh, reached out to touch it, and felt her shiver. Suddenly, I ain't together, kitted up, just for a pose. Carrying my flying cap, a distorted squash in my hand, a Holbein deathshead.

This room of representations. Vague radial roads visible, but most of the area a spattering of random craters, a Max Ernst dream, still drying, across which a tight-toothed comb has been scratched for effect. Somewhere, like the brain of a sensualist, the yellow tips tear through the red markers.

The men crowd into the hut; some keep their hats on, as if the band has already left the stand. Two bodies flighting: Pearl's sister, Lorraine, playing the Gestapo, raised by high heels. She has flash explodes. Photograph taken. She kicks, she separates, smacking into rippling flesh. She breathes in: the tango, very strange and masculine.

The plane looked as if it were a photograph of itself that had been rubbed and creased in the pocket of its lover.

She reached and coiled, an eloquent quickstep: the darkness, scratching the surface of an Air Ministry notebook. Where did he think we broadcast, and her voice, singing those songs? The girl swooping over the wireless in the mess, the weekly: 'And now we present the Frank Sydenham Orchestra, with Pearl Rust as the featured vocalist, And now she's going to sing *A Fine Romance*.'

A controlled space: dressing table, with her back to me. Misery everywhere. The wireless made Pearl, waiting for the vocal, become a story, standing in her underwear, selecting outfits. The chorus of voices: able to pick Pearl's out. Attractive silhouette with their searchlights flashing her legs, while she waited for the well-groomed, balanced couple, who were dancing on a cloud.

Exploding with flares before his caffeinated eyes, burst nebulae over Berlin, against which he can see, and be seen: a globular target. Bombs fall, like a row of rough ticks down a page of boringly correct answers.

The receding familiarity: a melody haunts my reverie, subverting the dream into a battle-cry. Barker thumping the rhythm on the table as he read, reminding me oddly of bursts of flak—a great comfort! But at the tracer fire, whole populations burst into song.

I always carry Pearl's suspender belt as a lucky charm, stuffed into a map of its own contours, sitting in that pose that you see in that book. As if in answer, a huge bat of dirt on the Perspex could be taken for flak down, fighters up.

Camera: arrows wind over two frames. Fresh film ready. We strolled along, a sheet of targets to be scribbled over with a monopoly of outrage. And he was gone, leaving us rather dumbfounded. But I could never take a photograph of you, because of the horror-blackened grain of the board: black and white etchings of cloud and flak lines.

Caress him from your dream. Who was it you held? He landed in a tree and injured himself releasing his parachute. Floating to the margins of ecstasy, black, terrible, a . . . a . . . a superstitious lot. We couldn't be religious in any orthodox sense, as if . . . . Each night this foxtrot with death, trying not to tread on her toes.

2

A city of fire-glow, gleaming for half an hour, as she dreams in somebody else's sights. The middle face was the actual 'me' figure. A tap dripping throughout the two minutes, the buzz of the wireless, the hiss of a silent figure of the dark. With no congruent self. Poetry as a model for a change in mental attitude, perfecting the dream, as memory. After the war, George was to become known chiefly as his finger. After some time, soldiers arrived, arrested him, and had to stop civilians from attacking him with stones. All the charts had been sucked through the broken fuselage. All the statistics of the Penguin Specials had got us nowhere. Jumped onto dispersal trucks, hunched over his maps, fiddled with something that resembled a bomber going down. The stench of piss on the rear wheel. The mask froze and George was free, floating through the air. More direct, it would deal a disguise. In doing so, Sgt. G.A. Grey, POW, Stalag Luft 3, loses you, to find you again, parting to meet and parting again: 'a poet of the last train'. Somewhere in the ghetto lives Chaplin, waiting to usurp the other, with a walk that takes on the irrational grace of a dance. Leave me. After the war, I'll never fly again, that's for certain. An image like the first insistent words of an unfinished question: that exhaustive moment when the false enthusiasm wanes and they begin—one by one—to step away, half-waving, half-smiling, and start to disperse. You refuse to mark the night on the blanched page. Pressing the girl: oasis jazz. Scarecrows: flares which looked like bombers exploding, complete with simulated debris, to lower morale. An image, here, of a world scattering itself between the ringed heresies. A design of metal thrown at the earth and on permanent display. 'We ain't got a chance. There's four horsemen drunk on the floor, masks blown to bits.' The bubbles that come from people's mouths float to the ceiling and accumulate, trees grow out of the open windows into the bricked streets. Any word is quite clearly what it is. A lethal dose had just hit the dance floor. The man with the mask-tormented voice never touches drink. 'I think I'll dig a little hole; it's for them as in power. Oh, this lot stinks and will do best.' There is no adequate single symbol: no golden ghostly holes in a world full of holes. He shows his teeth; the flash wrecks most of London's open spaces. If it's your name on the bomb, it glides into the aerodrome to land; there's a paddle in your waving arms. Vampiric Halifax over London. Best silk knickers for an air raid —just in case. 'It's them waves that is a beautiful dancer; they leave heaven in your arms—and moonlight.' Nearly a hundred fighters intercepted the stream. Grey reversed the turret and fell into flak and flares. Lovemaking bombs were dropping all around. 102 Squadron: Halifax 227-X. Shot down by a fighter. Günter was found dead the next day. One was the book of this story of demonic possession; and the other was this sort of dark woman with a slightly demoniacal face, and then, lying down, was a pretty, innocent-looking girl. She stood leaning against the heavy, thick-tyred, masculine machine. To the English bombers, aborted missions. Although you weren't there, there was something like a mental image of you sitting in that chair, there, reading that book. Günter stroked Paula's taut belly. Grey was arrested and taken to the Göring Hospital. Paula's precarious character in this state. Random spray from an underbelly. Personae out of a metaphor of crude orders. A rubber dinghy floated down over Berlin. Flares burst in mess-room conviviality, high and dry on the shores of a dream. A Halifax of 102 fired 500 rounds at a fighter, from the rear turret. Hooded sharks, scenting blood, gaped for me, diving and twisting in the puppeted sky. Got a letter from home about John; they read it in the papers. High, in the bright, bedazzled air I floated, wailing, as they squirmed on the bed. The powers of Left and Right battle it out on the dance-floors, each song a binding correlative for a particular danger. Undercarriage down, as if in an act of supplication. In almost no clothes and no questions. Both excited and worried by this. Pearl would enter her bedroom, startled to find Ft. Sgt. Campbell—together for once. Flurries of snow outside. . . . Could the Government have foreseen. . . . The dream slips through the seams suspended, draws near to the heel under billowing silk. Paula began to fuck her Sirens. Game of deception. One night, barnacles and star-fish exploded. This fellow speaking of codes and false messages. Because of the war and because of the war. The dream of the stop-watch. Self-preservation as a sort of pickling, here. Call themselves Apocalyptics, but really Utopians: to build a sensibility into the brickwork. Berlin during a raid—the one time I experienced it—was ten times more terrifying than the Blitz. The scale of a fish a metallic sheet torn from the plunderer as he scraped my tattered sides. Music from somebody else's patent dancing shoes, bejewelled with the Man-great glitter of war. A request on the wireless for the poet, already dead. But they are smiling at this. Their story was not to be a happy one. I think I'll read *The Playboy and the Lady*. A sight to watch them struggling with the cookies, wrapped now in cardboard, trussed tight, and packed with Nazi propaganda. Lady Whatsit throws darts at a map of Europe. Jackboots with high heels. Sad sky: sad eye. Perpetual forgetting: perpetual longing. With the Sydenham band, desire, restrained, obscured by all I have become, and they, out there, feeling it, but not going for a further vision. Book-spines: industrial muscle; putting a little Anarchist pamphlet together on the outbreak of war. Play a record of myself singing *Day In, Day Out*, over and over—only leaving to go to the bathroom where I'd shit all over the seat. I'd style myself Georgi Arturo: The Ageless Wonder.

3

Again, and again. In the mind, in the eye; and again this

Schräge Musik
Out of a sky-shaft of moonlight;
The bomb-blast personalities:

Trump them up into
Sparks and steam in the poem.

Citizens stood by, watching, numbed, motionless. Pearl, mature, await-
ing Sgt. Death to give her the sign, collapsed on the coffin. I dreamt the
jackboot on the dead man's shirt. Spooky choruses. But she gets up,
strides out of the paragraph, rises in the hearts of Men.

I don't just mean a new political system. The world has toyed with that
for decades; I mean:

Pin ups that smile at us
Falling from the walls
Robinson Crusoe
Only multiplied by hundreds
Everybody else
Each
Each his own Robinson Crusoe
And each of the others
Is Man Friday
Waiting for the postman
There's not the expected letter
Evasive and unsubstantial
Strong man at the fair
So the little ball goes up
Ersatz RAF
Smoke
Billowing over the hillsides
The bones of Russians
Shrugging allusiveness in your gestures
As the German territories diminish
Who lodged in the rafters
The Dutch family
Many of their own men would be shot
As hostages

Watch the goons
Their over-security when they find
Lines of political calendar ethics.
Petrol tin tea-pot
Experiencing future nostalgia.
Ghetto wailing
With a message in German.
Structured dream paper,
Rare sheets,
While the others are reading
Trying to compose
But nothing of worth
A communal splash with the others.
A bruised landscape
Bound in barbed wire
Around the tree
Year after year with each new bark
Symbol, here, perhaps of.
Spray of the unknown given
Comes from somebody else's
Satin babe with silk stockings;
Pearl could not move.
I knew, watching,
This would be the last time I would ever see her
Out on the tarmac
The plane was taxiing
Or would she travel too
The Gestapo lady
Walked up to me
I was led out into the courtyard
I was now well-dressed
Where before
Topped with barbed wire
Had been turned into a Gestapo HQ

I told them nothing
Rank
And number
Was written in the face:
George A. Dorsey
I was an old man
With a walking stick
Conductor raised the baton
And froze
Into a statue
To the memory of music:
Hackney hat-scape
Black
The gloved hand
Tied to a chair
There's no privacy
Football
In anticipation
Of nothing
Delete the aggressor
Delete the war
Delete the army
Delete delete
Everything must swing
Politics must be easy to dance to
To the memory of a body
Gramophones with broken mechanisms
Wound
Stuck like a mangle
Large horse shreds
Bag them up
Brick Lane had been in Poland in another
World
Photos of the op

A bomb-blast aesthetic
A pot of light
Pressing down on the flat plain
But the same mass
Weighing down upon us
Fatal steps screaming
Pain
It was an own-goal
Only they didn't even know it
Without anybody being informed
The goals had been switched
Two minutes silence
The whole city
Palace revolution
Stillness over the huts
Unceasing searchlight
Randomly
Taking in the compound
When the RAF bombed the camp
That's social realism getting back at them
Delete that
Begin the deletions
Delete the message until
Somebody
With a message in German
About her body
All the men who've
Written about the other men
Pickled character
Swing and communicate
Delete Harry James
Had died
Had survived
Was the love seat

Thorned like the head of Christ with barbed wire
In her slow motion
World
The stubs of a city
Unmoving
In the still air
The citizens had stopped
Shovelling the ash
Pile of rotting potatoes
Stillness over the huts
For undelivered letters
Talking into a metal ear
Cobwebs spun between the parts the moves are so slow
To think how fresh this all appeared and yet
Seen unframed
Here
At the heart of the machine
I see your myth
Barker
A hand of bananas on your shoulder
A Great War battleship
Utopian vision
Heels of thought clicking
Contributes to orderly resistance
Of Parliaments and
Unapproachable
Yes-no questions
Where's George
In a child's chair
About Benjamin Peret towards the end
As a receptacle of tradition
When
There is so little
A crow flaps out

From underneath
Useless description
Standing at the farthest perimeter
Looking out
Is George whatever-his-fucking-name-is
We shook hands
He shuffled off
I'd been made the star of the show
And it was a bit like girls at school
Hate-thing and teasing
I began my act by putting on
By striking
Bits of erotic lingerie
And striking obscene poses
And you came in for this bit
I sat on the love-seat
To be filled
A dance without rhythm
Lost
Looking for rhythms
That will carry us
Not meanings
Nothing personal I don't think
The teleology of checkmate
Songs
On one chord
Big band of cardboard boxes
The spotlight catches me
What if I were to escape
The demagogic machine
The bunched democracy of a queue
Door out to the shit house
Back in the mess
A glass of beer in your hand

Habitat
Use your intelligence
The scenery for the play was rather like
Hanging up to dry and our suitcases and
Scrambling
Sit in the park
Tube-train rumble underneath you
In the air raid
Bombs' dull thud and vibration
Fresh brick dust air
Down and down
Dance continental foxtrot
Pretend I'm some
Mystery and intrigue Englishman
Now be honest
Calling Germany
The great voice of God on the wireless
Shunted in goods wagons like
Half way across Europe
At the age of 29
Rather silly of me
Purple outfit
Dress trimmed with ostrich feathers
Except for the mask
Which
You liked it but you also
Didn't think it was respectable
Exposing herself to all those men
The evening was ending
The machine man
Has failed
The machine man
Has failed
Plump and respectable

Very sensible 1914 dress
You'd been sent away to war
You weren't terribly well
We'd all wait for letters from you
Very very respectable
I couldn't work it out
Bedding strewn along the platform; we were
Extremely grey
Glittering cities
Feeling disruption
Learning the whole of *Samson Agonistes*
The home front in Germany from
Her face became contorted
Icy fingers up and down
Exchange gossip they'd accumulated since
I was in tears
Marked 'LMF'. It was
Your parents' sitting room
And there were people; somebody started yelling
But I still didn't feel convinced that you were alive.
It was impossible to carry on. The mistakes had been his and
You became then that devil figure:
Huge great room
Milling about
Huge great family
People were appealing to me to do something
And I
My feelings were mixed
About you
Saw you as someone else
And understood that
Jealous about it
Reluctance on my part but also I did want to
Break the spell

Save both of you.
Big house
It was split up into bedsitters
Something like your family mansion
Your family house
Zhukarovski Mansions
Bits of it were semi-derelict;
Of Pearl
The sequence plays over and over
Tight in its glove
Clenching and unclenching fist;
And this young girl was very enthusiastic
Involved in the poetry world
You were very pleased
Took your name
Living two doors down the road;
The marriage obviously had been postponed because you'd
        gone to war
I would receive letters from you but;
Dribbling peasants going Use the Whistle
Use the Whistle
And you shouting for someone to bring you the girl
That you were using her name;
Because she was so innocent she was like an empty vessel
For all this evil to rush into;
Long flowing hair
Pulled by animals
Which definitely were pigs
Always sows
Cross between horse and pig
And this is what I'd tell you about in my letters to you.
Blueprints
Scribbled in tiny writing
Stuck together

Till we're stopped
'Raus 'raus
Morning
Train pulling into Finsbury Park
Was Pearl
Thin German
Gestapo lady
She stood with her hands bound behind a pole
Crease of buttocks
Forced back
As they buried the Russian soldiers
'Raus 'raus
Let's go and pearl the 'Earl Grey'
Forehead to forehead
The brain
Clogged
A smile on the cinema screen
Twenty foot wide
Doing the Lambeth Walk
Backwards
When not stooging
There are some records I can play in my head.
Rumbles and pavilions
The light flickers on and off.
Perspex ovens.
Pearl now
Long silk gloves
Gagged
Eyes were shut
As if she had surrendered.
Nothing from Pearl
Bricked up in her cell
I had one piece of paper with me
No

It wouldn't be a map
Would it
I tore it to pieces
Useless
Jargon over my ears
Prison camp was
The capitalist system in miniature
Disgusting stuff
Raisins
Bartering this
On the principles of mutual aid
Good Anarchist republic
Cocoa
The ersatz padre
The smoky stinking huts
Like fishboxes
Screaming up in the middle of the night
Not quite a Nazi salute
Wire fevered loonies
Looking out from the barbs
Landscaped gutters
The rippling girls' wartime
Melting ornaments
Wins England
War will have been lost
Craft whittling peace pipe
Anarchist pamphlet
Thumping oddly
And discovered the piano
Thumped out the boogie-woogie
Was
Trying
To hear him play
The solid voice and its single plea

Tragedy rationed by death
Fellow shadow
A professor of German poetry
I could see nothing through
To try to see outside
Fibrous visible mind
Polished vibrations
Already misted with memory
Foxtrot toes
Exhilarated her
Bled remains somebody else's world
Trying it from a different angle
Hugged sentiment
Trumpet-skids across the path
Candle flares
Flourishing into the air
It happens that way
All those memories
Curious black and white
Distance
An image
But through the screen
Nothing but tatters of light flaying around in the air

MAY–JUNE 1986

The Materialisation of Soap 1947

Duocatalysis 3

History of Sensation 4

Suspicion in the capital: the ecstasy
Of austerity rationing the uniforms.
It must be like air, natural and free,
But there's a shortage of nature in this
Land of torrents and the surrounding seas.
What is happening? He used to *prefer* words!
Feed me a well-trimmed cut of news.
We couldn't find any wheels, but we're happy,
A well-dressed pair: even on the wireless
You've got to keep up appearances,
Now we yearn for the parks and the azure skies
Of the tottering economies. . . . Pearl
Opened her palm over the sink to reveal
A fresh bar of soap. She smelt it; her favourite
Scent. She turned the hissing tap, and
The slippery unthought-of object lathered
Her chapped Cinderella hands. All she needed
Was her hero silk-parachuting into
Her perversely dissatisfied embrace. I
Prefer to talk to the dead, well-fed
On scraps that cannot be sold.
They died from Manchuria to Manchester.
I did not want to report this but I did.
The news is that another man has been held.
That much is reliable. Beyond that,
The monochrome world flickers
At the emotive edge of our fake memories:
Two frying morsels on the gas stove.

AUGUST 1987

[37]

2 Utopian Tales

'Manholes into Eternity
opened for me...'

Utopian Tale

You resist the air, leaping into a blur. This is no longer a place, the film stills no longer referring to the film. The surprise of your life made it clear that somebody *knows*. If this were another world, another story, and if you ever found that person, you would be obliged to kill him.

Your mission is full of memory, but emptied of nostalgia. Every event is recalled and replayed to see if you can find the cuts. A second skin encloses your face. This is you, boarding a train, years ago, in bereavement, in search of a life that is now threatened. You entered the tunnel and felt the change coming over you, a leather crucifixion.

These are the people who discovered you; you tell them nothing, but their strangeness becomes normative. Your own world takes on a misted quality, although you've forgotten nothing: pictures tilt on the wall. Film stills: bullet holes diagonally across the ceiling. There's always a passer-by to offer a convenient explanation of what 'it' is you're doing. When will you save them from their own stupidity? When will you enter politics? The women, here, care for the babies, while the men speculate about the strange metals which fall from the skies. Mud-patch blast-shapes of men. Your shadow across the cross-traffic diverts an everyday tragedy.

A cup and a saucer! So this is how you're expected to behave. This could have been a world from which desire had died. Of smooth automobiles and outsized traffic signs. The buildings are, for the most part, square. The windows look half-broken, punched in by their own shadows.

You're a million miles away from where you started and that was the general idea. You're the Hero who's always saving himself. The out-of-scale meteorite would have hit your car, if not disqualified by your disbelief. This is an ideal lack of disguise for a person like you, though you're the only one in the desert when the light propeller aircraft lands. It's up to you now to explain the vanished civilisation. Twisting junctions dazzle the screened mind. Can you check that out, as though it were a cluster of facts orbiting the skull? Powerful tubes of light pull the truth towards your squinting eye.

This is where you met yourself in the guise of evil. You fooled the whole world, which trusted you. You fought with this double, dragging it farther from human comprehension. Patterns disintegrate: man's new forms are burnt into holes, an abattoir of mechanical devices, flaming. This is what was left after the burning. The people you pass among in the park do not see you. Theirs is a monochrome world, from which all radiance has drained into you. There he is, explaining everything between his shrieks of panic. A naked woman slumps, leather men walking from the wrecks of burning cars. If you were to take off your clothes here, would the place be forever marked upon the map of Utopia?

Here is a man with a secret, the only one allowed to have one. Here is another letter for you; read it. The dead man has written to remind you to be yourself—in at least two possible ways. You readjust your clothing and prepare to enter. You can change what happened that day, just by looking at the photograph. Bullet holes dragonfly across the ceiling. He accepts the invitation into your trap, and you introduce yourself as another so that each may shake hands with him. The simulation is complete and the radio announcer waits for his signal to speak.

1986

Utopian Tale

The state radio plays continuous music: the stumbling melodies of our minor composers. The Beast's fists pound his complaint. My heart falters; these minimal signs, coming in this way, have always presaged disaster. War? Famine? A death? Our women carry snakes and the men are twined with vine-leaves; one of them has to be an analogue for you. They, too, smash into their own reflections, surprised. For what is it that we're willing—if need be—to endure the water-cannons and tear-gas? Enigma! Film-star! Totem! The Hero arrives to re-animate the show, to correct the experiment. He has scaled-down models of his pet criminals: only one perception at a time may be closed. The Queen breathes delight into the microphone.

Drunk and catatonic on the metro, a voice seems to come from the centre of your head. Not everything can be scheduled and the men and women of Utopia witness an unlikely event. My clothes, crumpled by the bed, rear up, filled with smoke, a fog of accusations peering down at me. Invest the table with delirium and the knives and forks will dance. It seems that way because it is that way. Her hair shimmers into string. Or others say snakes. Think of the actors, those who will play us, following these final scenes with expert indifference upon the creaking boards. One of them will play the mind-reader, tearing crystal surprises from the frozen surfaces. The Beast grows to an incredible size, but the Queen still stands within range, just for the sensation. He picks her up like a doll and she shivers, at last, for the Hero. There is no question now of a tame resolution to events. The Hero, cursing the strings which hold him up, falls to the ground, weakened by the Beast's gaze, and is dragged away, humiliated, by two men of Utopia.

The logical constraints are lifted, and the Beast makes off, weeping. The Queen will wear a bullet-ring for a week. The escalators have stopped working, but the crowd is moving of its own will. The past has dappled its blankness and can now be read, if not understood. The tale is not more true, but more powerful. The Hero dials 999; the Enemy has secret plans that even he cannot understand. Pickpockets break down in tears. This flow could bowl you over, if you tried to push against it. But, instead of crushing you underfoot, the crowd buoys you up, and you float along at shoulder-height—like the heroes we are all becoming.

Darkness falls across the sky like a half-bottle of gin on the brain. The Hero watches the Beast walk into his trap with a sullen determinism. He fussily explains its mechanism to staunch his emotion. The crowd bristles its electric pelt. While the men of Utopia unroll the fatal wires, the Queen and he plan an alternative which could eventually lead to the abolition of heroics. A few old ideas are thrown out of the window, the night air already thick with cordite. What do these small events have to do with the Great Event we are failing to witness? This is the gap between theory and application. At this moment you re-enter as his double. The Beast imitates you, which implicates him in a subtle history. You beat a drum; so does he. You put on your glasses to disguise your beauty; he puts on his and falls impotent.

The Hero hurls the Beast into the past. The shift is experiential. He starts, finds himself alone in the ancient hospital room, with its patterned ceiling and treacherous shadows. Outside, in the corridor, he hears the footsteps of the guards, and he sees the shadows of their boots under the door. Mild concussion brings the world back to its senses. Heroes once again seem to rid Utopia of the Enemy by just pretending nothing has happened. They drink coffee and gloat over justice. We wait for answers to our own lack of questions, in the squares, facing the roseate palaces.

1986

3 Internal Exile

Writing is impossible without some kind of exile

Julia Kristeva

Internal Exile 1

Out from germ-warm subterranean wind into
Business having just been, or about to be.
Hyphens, dashes, asterisks, strokes:
The silver number has been screwed. Red
Flag: blue light. One moment the man stands
With his arms tied behind his back; the next he falls
Head first from our chronicle. Pictures have pictures.
You are the real hero. The image—
That was like walking into somebody else's poem.
A public zipper porched shadow action. Heroes
Standing under cardboard captions. Masculinity sells
History: four guards on this side, four
On the other, changing according to
House demands. All the victims' outfits were
Manufactured by the Enemy. It was a fantastic
Feeling, going up stage and turning around for all
The judges. Her writing is content. Watches sold
Doubt as her underhand life expressed the
Heresies. Her clothes burn, turning stories,
Can add fur sovereign meaning
To line-sewn memory dust. Don't open the door; shut
Your eyes. To slam these columns you took this out.
The shimmering architectural fantasy
Of a slum, purpose built. Entry to that soft-furnished
Dream, riots hanging like petrol vapour
Over the black plastic rubbish bags,
Electric train-flashes crossing the page, from one of the

Languages which blows across Europe like ill-wind.
Bombs implode as a warning underscoring
The essential sentence. He says my
Mind is always somewhere else when I
Kiss her. This sentence is a variation. She's
Out on the porch, testing the day, transforming
Not only her, but the text, from which she
Could never be exiled. As soon as I write 'the world',
It doesn't invert. Poverty less plentiful
But obscured by wealth and well-being.
The systems began to fail, in domestic adjustment.
The Chinese trains were nicer than the Russian ones.
This sentence is a variation of the next. The flow
Freed from compulsion. Trying to gauge it
All; the woman is not at her mirror. (Skip
A few pages; I will too.) Black girl in a tight leather
Skirt jumps into a waiting passenger-seat:
Pink folds of flesh for his mental
Speculum. I froze and sweated, wanted to burn
The insignia—but who would deck
Themselves in the cloth pages
Of a tattered history? Pretend that some of
The sentences have been removed
Though your meaning heaps. Women desire a war;
Virus men build appearance. Wouldn't you prefer it
As a straight-out? The bike boys zooming in on each
Other's rolling captions? What was once
Familiar is now merely strange. Moving clouds behind
The birds rewind their film of homecoming. Swoop
Loop wires in light. A magpie flicker in dirty
Scruff eye. This has to be learned,
Holding language in suspicion. Posturing
About disaster, style demeans. A cold sore
On a child's mouth predicates a market

Full of bargains. What could she begin to say? How
Will she survive the questioning? Perhaps
It is only the uncurtained window-pane that
Throws the room back at us? Reader:
Worker. Walkman overspill rhythmed by the engine-
Driver's wiper-lashes. Another realism. She
Remarked the dome of her clichéd perception—
An image for later snuff-movie simulations: murder
Leads door to door. The crystal eye set in the wall.
They did not even notice that the effigies were of them.
Replace the object. She makes the unknown turn—
Feels at one moment a gobbet of raw meat in a
Porno film. She goes to the window to cry.

MARCH–APRIL 1987 – MARCH–APRIL 1991

Internal Exile 2

Counterpoint. Things hunched in plaster, mutually assured desire
going blank into the wide-eyed day. Rainshine: blank wives at ashen
points. A fur coat pulled out of the water; vanished power in the
herringbone stripes. The complication that I was, a tension in myself.
Surface woman through a glass letterbox. Dummy texts arranged your
life like bales of hay: the evening was to be marched from the script.
Story-assassin, in his study. The world is going up, speckled. We buy
junk and sell antiques. Norbert hit Renate in the face with a saucepan.
Line up for war: she's a beautiful angry female. Norbert dreamt the last
sentence. We printed in red any word which could be harnessed to our
rule. The five widowed instruments played at the wedding. Girls in
soldiers' memories flicker the past. With a female character I can have
the other. He is real in a world of dummies. I was made to sit on spikes.
He is a kerb-corpse. The writing keeps straining for his scarecrow
values. I try to imagine myself living. We govern in the message. A

black cylinder meets the spear. Inverted passages and vertiginous corners. Cloud aligned eye: prisoners of war were treated to digging holes. She always claimed her father went to the camps, seeks her sublimation in his end. I was made to sit on spikes. A minor chord failed to split the atom: life between the burning metaphors. Above surface, accidental flesh. Bulletholes in the column. A man in his underpants disappeared from view, as the man with the knife at the throat of another protested against the rules of the game we'd set him. The shadow men prepared for action. More than a form, I retreated to the margins to create myself. I had to destroy it; I began to work, drumming his nerves. Images produced value, misting the houses beyond. Signal shadows people. The girls talked mints; nearby, the mint-man listened, electrified. Ideas surface, cardboard grip. You see if you're not looking, your autism behind make-up. Counterpoint eyes flutter, acting out your own unfinish. He noted, in the gap between two buildings, the type of woman to profitably misunderstand. These are suburban tales: the ghostly glow. Strip ashen zipper: hell victims. The world, like the newspaper photos she treasured, was just killing time. She gave her black lover a photograph of a Somali with severed hands. One language: many voices. The mark of professionalism is conflicting advice. The odd bones of your life matter. The caddy removes a red flag. The plot thins. The question marks. The letterbox is sellotaped. The naughty girl will put herself to bed. She began flirting with her own image. Do you buy the performer with the performance? Ghost markets. You can't step through into the other side, invading the focal arena. Space within? He stops and wills the rest away. The enemies make him zero, jargoned to death. Crude semaphore. Strategic disintegration. Their mermaid ideology—and then scribbled in blue: *GIRLS*. Let's look up at the sky. This is getting normal. She is waiting patiently in a queue. The tanks arrive for one man in a beret. Why was Utopia meat with gristle? Do you want the world—it narrowly missed my briefcase? They are living in temporal consciousness of space. Did you kill your days? Their blind music: a woman with leather stretched across her face. Collapse the bladder of hope. A rough edge divides the vibrant light. Her conversations were electric chairs, fences, wires. Counterpoint contradicted. If you can see your assassin, he becomes your executioner. Historical aphasia: watch the ant-like rioters below. How to avoid being disappointed with our new product? Don't buy it. Burn the books and read the ashes, to make a reader stop her fantasising. If she is naked she is touching. One cracked stair. Why can't one perception *stay* with another? All the blacks have to stand naked against the wall while the police think. I have been writing a journal of sorts. You're lost into a position you cannot fit, while a queue years up shining game. Even to me, there's a future. She includes the sentence, 'She watches her younger self laughing.' My vision of the future has no words. The eye swallows its rhyme. You're certain there's somebody there, tasting her bitterness, biting her tongue. A tortuous voice-over for the final scene. The reader lets go?

APRIL 1987

Internal Exile 3

She's living in the rough
Basement of a condemned house. Street
Level defines a world, its variations
In autonomy. She's a genuine
Answer, designed to put you off. She's
In another time; he is in another gender,
The man with the briefcase, practising
Dance-steps on the platform.
Dry water-colours dust off the stiff washing,
Disrupting any finer feelings he may have had.
You cannot see through the whole. What
Began as art was repeated years later
As a political act. She always wore
Black lipstick, tears in her eyes. Men danced
In fire, did press-ups with guns. Others
Flew to posterity. She burnt her other self,

Teasing out the voyeur's disappointment, the
Beauties of her unbridled
Allegories. The writing returns
To block desire. It's
A world of spies and disclosures; she
Feels his presence in the room with her, scraped
Again across the grain of history. Territory
(Or no territory) on the shit-
Stained canvas of her language:
Her green front door, and its
Dried spattering of blood. Fulfil desire;
KILL IT. It was her statement, her
Trigger on silence. Now
The writing's nearly over the work
Withdraws. Is this a model
Of the world that does not exist, straining
For a new referent? Her prejudices
Owe the world no apology.

MAY 1987

4 Letter from the Blackstock Road

One week Flash Gordon falls off the cliff, the next week he doesn't. By the time the last bud flowers, the first has browned—a series of flamboyant gestures rendered futile. The Lea and Perrins bottle was besieged by a crowd of admiring satsumas. A hundred policemen sledgehammer your door down as you sleep; they photograph you in bed for their files; they watch a woman giving birth through a grille. Questioned, they say, 'It's a form of habit.' Landlord spiel. It took a year to find that her name was Queenie, working alphabetically through *How to Name your Baby*, until she hissed affirmatively in response to the only entry under Q. Pearl and George had always had a relationship of stains. Well-turned phrases spin like tops on the nursery floor and the children learn to circumscribe delight. The cat scrabbles at the door to get in. The bottomless school satchels of the metaphor-fiends were emptied onto the desktop: 35,000 poems to read before Christmas, and pick the stunner. Scrunch. George and Pearl—fading beauties—sit it out with the old man, who drags on his cigarette irritably and, as frequently as possible, gets up to order all three more booze. The plural of sphinx is sphinges. So what? Turn down the sound on the T.V. quiz programme on which the contestants have to identify pop songs from jumbled fragments, and they become philosophers pondering imponderables, the crevasses of unreason beneath the municipal assumptions. In the Russian language there isn't even a word for freedom. Anything goes. How can they speak of the 'finest kind of propaganda: unstrident, literary, and humane'? There is not one kind of clarity only. He spends a third of his life on the phone. It's a more effective use of power than writing a poem. You can't evaluate a perception until the process is over. This is a letter from November. I write for a journal that hopes for a rational conservatism. British poetry withdraws, like an image in Matthew Arnold, from its high watermark. I write for a journal that exposes the Government's secret war-plans. Cut to an abandoned bookshelf whose stillness is supposed to be sinister, vaguely threatening in some undefined, relative and—even—plural way. The telecaster is wearing a poppy, something that is read into a text, and written out of it. UNO (United Nations Organisation). UNO (United Nicaraguan Opposition). The man who lived in this room before me went mad, proof enough that the sensuous images of aesthetic liberation are not alone capable of politicising the reader, but by the time the shivers died away, I had to confess that I couldn't see *why* the 'change' necessarily had to be defined. Action re-play of the Book of Genesis. The bright day contains its chickens and men come to feed them as its central motif, the wind —not the sun—glittering the yellow leaves. It's not the *smell* the dogs are trained to detect, it's they way they hold it below the level of the table. I'm glad you moved here, pink cyclamen, to share my life—that's Williams! That's the sort of stupid comment we don't need. There is nothing sentimental about an organism, either. You can actually hear a fly land on a sheet of paper. Hang the Swine, thrashing its limbs about in the death cell. Four or five Sikhs out on the pavement; an empty police car, its door open, in the road, badly parked. Not one space, but plural. The man with the crooked face was there—somewhere, moving about in his musty smell, like a fictional character fogged by unreality. And what about all the others who will read this in time, those who lack the slender situation we have in common? Pearl is a fashionable psychopath revolutionary, pre-figuring the unknown. A hint to the reader: Who? The girl who wears a plastic headless skeleton as a brooch prays for the chicken slayer. This is slow, not pressure. George is a self-actualising plastic bullet salesman, but he doesn't sell the guns. Why do I write the things I never say, think the things I never write? The sad apple-tree; it is I who am sad. Pearl jumped up and down in her pepper-suit to make George happy, while he squeezed a pustule before the mirror. She moves from the political to the personal, joking apart, and ends with a rhyme and a moral score of ten out of ten. Behind the racy advertisement languishes a tired voice. Pearl reaches the chapter on how to overcome your own death. There are ladies doing business in knotty articulations. The man in the Aztec socks 'militates' against the deadening aspects of 'habit'.

Every time you close your eyes, it's the death wish. Seven knocks on the front door, resounding in the large hallway. His PVC mac squeaks. After chopping the pigs' hearts, the texture keeps returning all evening, its lean flesh, the hardened tubes, the fatal clots of blood, stirring somewhere between appetite and memory. George is off to see the Wizard, the Wonderful Wizard of Oz. Pearl sneezed so hard she's split her lip. You trip over these blocks of opacity, as if they were plaques marking where the admirals fell. Tear gas was pumped through the ventilation shafts as though chemistry was the beginning of moral-ity. The chickens live safely behind their wire-mesh coop in a nuclear free zone, weathered classic woodshed. George is not insane. Any inten-tion I have regarding the nuthouse nexus is always producing finally deluged. Ambient sandwich, chanting in Hebrew with no learning aids. There are frogmarks in this book. This is not a letter from the basement, from the rough basement of a condemned house, etc. . . . In the last analysis, it is an act of faith. George says he won't stop until the last probation officer has been strangled with the guts of the last social worker. There are explosives and blood powder in the wine: I am happy but what is the cost of that happiness? The tangled party-line running through the twisted mesh of events. Snapping Ryvita like a camera-click. If the reader has automatic gears, the metaphor breaks down. This is not a ghost book. George and Pearl stand by the muddy path, looking over the farm wall, beyond which they can see the pigs fucking. Caring is the most important quality in the world, says the woman I care for, and I know that that caring alone can only be the beginning. Orthodox Jews outside the synagogue whisper goodnight in Yiddish, go home. George is insane, she says, going on about his singing, and shouting, 'Can you hear me, Mother?' through his amplifier. The erotic arts form a pervasive stench of goat-cheese on his fingers. Dead, dying, the articulated stems of morning glory plants, where they stretched for the strand of cotton around which they curled and climbed. Pounds flames on the flames. The leap should also be a step. George is an ace motorcyclist with a gammy leg. Piano shots. Give us a head-spin, baby. One way it's magic; the other way it's tragic.

Are these three pillars of deportation too peacefully sinking into oblivion? I walked into the room and was startled by the voice on the radio that I had left on to startle any intruder. Even go happened which doesn't cite its sources. It's a pimple; no, it's a dimple, rubbing the subject. Put the apples and the satsumas in the frame and break purpose but people prefer the Leaning Tower of Hackney as a rumbling cloud of dust. Immaterial. The Talmud forbids T.V., and lighting fires on Saturday, and thus they can consider the nature of lightning. Two verses of a jazz standard. Two piles of bricks; an orderly stack beside a tumbled heap. Sentient effigies flare on the incandescence of your hatred. There are the paving stones; this is their history. The off-hand rhetoric of beguiling dismissal rises to a tremulous pitch. George closes his eyes, wants to be alone, becomes the astronaut spinning away from the mother-ship, screaming into his microphone. One day he isn't there any more, though I can still hear his voice through the wall. A man whistled 'Onward Christian Soldiers', skating hat escaping flowing. A moving statue in the H Blocks topples, smashes, hollow: out falls Guy Fawkes, laughing, a shadow beside him. Williams took the younger man up to his study. 'Am I,' he demanded, 'as great as Shelley?' Figures fleshing a void, Guy Fawkes doubles for Robin Hood in the slide-rule mythical poem; so does George, in fancy dress. Inside information this. Guy Fawkes has been fitted with a plastic beak, noses in kebab and chip papers thrown down in the Blackstock Road. Brain blitzed dinosaur murals. Meat eater batters battery bird. To teach everything through one book: the façade of a house sliced away, its interior vulnerably framed for the impossible artifice of a November afternoon. To make a sign whose configuration will one day read as a paradigm, a burnt-out star, the iridescent trace of vanished energy. The terms I could use are assimilated by the persistent frowsty orthodoxy: a naturalist dozes and lets Salvador Dali provide the metaphors for instant naturalisation, neutralisation. Pages of contradictory definitions, anti-definitions, post-definitions.

Robin once lunched with Herbert Read at his club. Fawkes is the palace intruder, fresh from the Otway Tomb. Robin goes round the 106 bus route pasting up posters of 'the only man ever to enter Parliament with honest intentions', then flits back to Highgate. Robin performs miracles in his leafdom, squeezing worms from old ladies' buttocks. George is a native North England bird, arrives drunk at Highbury Vale for the Big Match, yells impeccable Anglo-Saxon, a terrace scop. Man kills crowing glory of inner-city conservation area. Procrustean means literally to have your feet cut off because you've lost your bed-socks. Fawkes prints his claw-marks with the blood-pad throats of the dead of Dussindale. Bob bobbed. Roger rogered. The man in the ill-fitting brown suit shows you his leg, asks for money, shuffling the Blackstock Road in his slippers. George writes a Proclamation in which each full stop is a dead bat disappearing into a luxury swimming pool; dressed as Errol Flynn, he reads it on Mousehold Heath, but he's in the wrong story again, as the heroes storm Bishop Bridge. A halal axe falls on anaemic chickens. Police in vans, waiting, and ready, for the Finsbury Park Riots. Low clouds move speedily over the city. Although it is he who suggests it, Pearl's husband is always shocked to see the sperm shooting onto her face. Black men doing nothing purposefully on the corner of the Blackstock and Seven Sisters Roads. Robin Hood lifts his flaming wings; one minute he's a wind-borne bird, the next he's a sentimental socialist from between the wars. The Jewish children freeze when the pavement is blocked by the neighbourhood rough, while other children beg with Barnardo faces in the Blackstock Road during their half-term holidays. Hood and George print leaflets on petrol bombing, poster Tottenham, but they're not to be seen when the shit hits the fan. A mad black girl, swigging cider, too drunk to sell herself, wears an ankle-bracelet under 'flesh' stockings. When Fawkes is arrested he is given bail, so long as he resides at a friend's, in Hampstead. 'Have you got ten pennies?' asks a plaintive monopede. Hood and Fawkes get George off the rap. A lazy supermarket cockroach comes out to die. Robin mugs old ladies in Stoke Newington. An inferno lights up the quadrangle in high wind: paraffin paroxysms flare the height of a tree and we can feel the heat indoors. Exit Pearl. Hood is remanded. The anger of politics subverts the tenderness of love. Vice versa. Hood and Fawkes smash up the house, make the rich young couple fuck, whimpering, in front of them. Flirting with her image, injuries watch outside them. The lama in old curtains chants in front of the Evolution Mural, chuckles, can become any of the animals he wishes. There was a feeble bonfire burning by the lagoon. She stood where she could see herself: to do what a painter does, she was *given* a scene for the first time in her life. The horror of the bed-sits going up in flames, while the fire brigade takes photographs of itself for the archive. It cost a bluey. Police vans shoot through traffic, avoiding collision by inches. Picture postcard phrases because it uses language, covering mirrors, pulling curtains. Slurry as it began to flow. 'It'll be the death of me,' Robyn said, realising as she did so that she'd condemned herself to death. Paratactic tactics. Miles Davis to Dave Holland: 'Don't play what you think you want to play; play something else.' He snaps his fingers in a futile attempt to constitute his vanished totality. Mother entered me for a poetry competition under the name Conrad Sheppard. There is a certain tenderness and pathos in the men playing cards at the back of the kebab house that does no business. Hands, strangely alien, were moving. She turned away, embarrassed, only at the expense of a forgetting of origins, an aged hologram from her own film. Today's going boozy. One frame at a time, the giant prisms zoomed. She writes to 'titillate' herself with the ambivalence of masculine perception, suddenly finds herself in a scene from a snuff-movie. Factory farm chicken-flesh. Guy hangs about The Blackstock—inside and out—drinking from a lager can, organising the men for Robyn, who stands shivering on the corner in a short skirt, her slim black legs catching the headlights. A complicated game of 3-D chess in the cloudless skies of a dream-world, back in the mind, where metaphor and concepts, rather than 'images' and percepts, stir. Use of certain words makes certain philosophy. An inscape of Ket's head after death haunts the re-tinted stills. The police called me 'nigger' and 'cunt' on the split-screen newsflash of equivalence, and I see my own reflection behind *LEAD COFFINS* embossed upon the mirror. An empty file is undefiled. Giant red poppies marched through Red Square, *en route* to Pizzaland, and found a red beret. I've internalised a great deal about apocalypses and whirling fans between the tape splices. A girl prepares to throw herself from the Archway. Punctuation mark. Give two examples of the new object and establish a relation with it. Protest, as the policemen step over the hermeneutic fill. English traditional music makes a change from plastic bullets, though the piano sounds like a Balinese stochastic. Two things annoy me: Service music and speech, buried in one coffin together. What is the effect of leaving out the somatic nasal complaint? The phrase 'masculine woman' asserts itself as class difference or whatever. Perhaps she is ultimately 'responsible', that is *blamelessly* drunk with the allure of his urgent smell. The blues harpist goes to the opera now. Little in focus reactions, a 'literature of the unword' which would follow. Guy hands George a book with a picture of Pearl on the cover. 'What is it?' 'It's an Evology!' 'A what?' 'A Dictionary of Evil'. Open at random and read under F: The Germans invade Anarchic FRANCE, above a photograph of mobilised tanks. A: How many women were there at AGINCOURT? B: BUN in the oven, pie in the sky. Fact mushroomed. Parliament reopens, after the bomb threat, with a pageant of the same roast chestnuts in smaller bags. Camouflage paragraph rising enemies. Madam Josephine's silver fox furcoat, handbag and single blue stiletto shoe were found in Robin's car. A riotously indeterminate sentence, silenced into government. Strips still waving when the dream flickers ritual bones. C: COG Boxes. I have an apparition of George waiting for me with his stick at the top of the stairs. The real world, only populated by magicians. Polythene women in the sweat-shop, where you pause. Hypnopompic testaments, men oddly landscaped switch vacant fits. Guy Fawkes is a drama teacher in Fakenham. Snake silks wearing a white poppy. In the window you see the smoothing of cloth under the dim, shaded light of the machine and a woman's deft brown hands moving there, signalling a story that has been going on all week, in a language she cannot understand. In future all non-violent odds with subliminal tissue, falling, will catch a spiral return to your hand. The death flick, though, had not jumped and she received a newsflash past

the pub window: *The Territorial Army. Ready and Waiting.* Middle two one
contradictory leave click splits, a revolution at your fingertips. Each
headline, each summary, becomes a riddle, gratuitous crystal flash.
It doesn't look like a fire engine and it isn't. Trailers are better than
features. Robin wakes up in a hospital ward in the Soviet Union, where
the man with the syringe tells him, 'Join the Hum Party.' Miles
eschewed his legendary introspection, waved to the audience, posed
for photographs—larked works of art will be marked. Banging his head
on the *trompe l'oeil* door in the brickwork, a heavily coded human being
fails to hit George in the face. D: Rumble DRUMMING, world for world
effaced, screen wall dances. I am the enemy to whom my letter is
addressed. You cannot stop spiked steps. Madam Josephine, 'student of
the methods of the Marquis de Sade', waits at the bus-stop in
Brownswood Road, with her legs reddening in the wind, until she nods
at a car that she knows will do a circuit. Despair values deeper skirts.
Robyn has a dildo fitted to an arrowhead, which she draws, with an
Indian bow, held by her open legs, in and out of Jayne, who lies smil-
ing on a cushion a few feet in front of her. Buzz tension, screams late
hate. Squashed identity part, viscous globes of pus on George's finger.
The audience preferred the joys of recognition to those of discovery—
and so did Miles. Fringe barriers to rocky wears bullet thumb. E:
ETYMOLOGY: the science of the discharge of ductless glands. G:
GRYPHON: severe spasmodic pain in the intestines. H: HYPNOGOGIC
Image: Robin falling towards the pavement, onto the dead bed-weeks.
When the centre of desire shifts, George is thrown off balance. I: the
dip-mind bird machine. N: NOVEMBER: low sunsets, Samhain. 'Previous
philosophers merely interpreted the world,' boasted Roger; 'I fucked it
up.' West Indians explain what it means to give Asian women a smile
outside the run-down doctors' surgery. Stunned constellation granule.
Skip culture. Waving his trumpet on stage at the demonstrators, or
waving his gun across the parapet, man is a tyrant. Wearing nothing
but gold high heels, Jane is a slave to the eye. Roger watches her, from
behind, as she bends over, staring at the lino pattern that would have
been enough to have excited Schwitters. The dog's eaten the ten of

diamonds. O: ONWARD CHRISTIAN SOLDIERS: a tune for the melodi-
cally insane. Q: QUEENIE: the demon mouser, nosing into city skips,
a gleaner on a dung heap. The Cenotaph bouquet sniffed by dogs,
scrambling for tender on Remembrance Sunday. A ration book is fortu-
itous. Not chance. Yes, you've spoken about trying to get the 'meatier'
bits of poetry into more radical formal circumstances. Vicious lobes of
pun. Eyes weep in the cold. Jane is wanted by the police. Once George
has set up his video equipment, and Pearl is ready and waiting, Roger
strips off and stands, a shining ebony figurine in his boots, a plastic bag
on his head. 'Open the bloody door,' yells Pearl, 'I want to see you get
in the bath.' Rows of Indians queue to sell their kidneys to the West
in Bombay. Jane's clock was stolen by the man across the hallway—
silent, Irish—and used to make a crude device that was later found
outside the Chelsea Barracks. I don't like corners. I don't like furniture.
I don't sell out to nobody. I know only how I make it, I know only my
medium, of which I partake, to what end I know not. I had envisaged
a new form of poetic composition. I build my time. The modern world
is the other half of nature, the half that comes from man. The perfec-
tion of new forms as additions to nature. I have to change. It's like a
curse. To enter a new world and have there freedom of movement
and newness. You enter it with complete understanding and emerge
from it with none. Hell, if you understand everything I said, you'd be
me. After you've been flung back and forth, someone will read you
my latest poems, until you collapse in a faint. Böwörötääböpö. Uhn,
uhn, uhn, uhn, uhn. A doctoral thesis with footnotes. Oranges are
grown by *sh* Growers within the Empire. He can include pieces of prose
and have them still part of the *poem*. It is incorporated in a move-
ment of the intelligence which is special, beyond usual thought and
action. Ula lu la lu. End your solo before you're done. Every form is a
frozen instantaneous picture of a process. Yesterday's dead. It may be
that my interests as expressed here are pre-art. If so I look for a devel-
opment along these lines and will be satisfied with nothing else. A
form for the future. New things had to be made from fragments. Every
artist must be allowed to mould a picture out of nothing but blotting
paper for example, provided she is capable of moulding a picture.

But such a picture as that of Juan Gris is important as marking more clearly than any I have seen what the modern trend is: the attempt is being made to separate things of the imagination from life. There is no next trend. If there's another, then we're going backwards.

R: RADICAL Consistencies: a blues in F, played across the decades.

In the full sunlight, a low horse and cart, carrying a fat man, his junk and his indecipherable cries for trade, crosses the junction of Queens Drive and Brownswood Road, with the effervescency of a mirage. Small self thinking exhaust. Headline of the spirit: *The Territorial Army. Ready and Waiting.* In his Hollywood mead-hall sits Hrothgar, telling tales of smouldering villages and screaming women-folk—textbook stuff—as Clint Eastwood hits the consciousness of the M4 Rapist—a disinformation scandal. 'Do we get to win this time, sir?' Sgt. Bilko will ask. Pearl's husband became punched. George takes the protective guard off of his fire, and uses it as an out-tray, stencils *R. Mutt* on his forehead. This is shifty, lacks category, like a prisoner who baffles the psychiatrist: a demonology of saints. S: SPHINXES. T: THE TERRITORIAL ARMY. U: UTOPIAN Aesthetics (or prefigurations). V sign on the book cover: a printed white hand held high against the crowd as the black face behind it reads. Roger is the little boy who always has to sit in the lavatory, being ill, at his own birthday parties. George is getting decidedly feminine, the blue chill of the air saddening him again towards night-fall. Jane takes off her dressing-face, makes a pin-cushion out of Roger who, until then, had merely been a well-regu-lated mechanism for switching off her alarm clock. Dying sun seen through dying leaves, illuminating the dusty pane, throwing a grid of patterns onto Patricia's painting, transforming it, as I sit watching. Animal blood on the fridge door. The broken W of gulls, as the sun drops out of another blue sky.

Sometime soon I shall shout 'All fall down!' and we all will. Roger would be ill at his own funeral, Pentecostal glossalalia behind 60s frosted glass. Bob would be bobbing. To de-Anglicise England, submit it to a 'coherent deformation'. Hrothgar, picking a lump of black pudding from a nostril, sits in his empty sex-shop in Copenhagen, his sexuality a wilting sea-serpent carved onto the prow of his long-boat. The poem might become a catalyst not a cameo—always promising future perceptions, producing not the known, but the unknown. X: DIFFI-CULTIES: Jayne dragged screaming to the gallows for the love of men. Y: the clock that disappeared that night and will never be seen again. Freedom forms would work, without rules, in order to formulate rules, creating what it means, meaning just what it creates. The crowd stands in a carnival atmosphere to watch George being pulled out from under the wreckage of his motorbike in the Blackstock Road, but when the police put up a notice asking for witnesses, nobody will come forward. We will tell the seasons by the fruit in the shops rather than by the frost on the ponds. Pastoral will perhaps be our greatest threat. Z: 'The key will be valueless,' says the man with the crooked face.

NOVEMBER 1985

5 Coda

Utopia the memory the sensation the sonata
Utopia the island the continent the landscape
Utopia the regression into reptilian nights
Utopia the feeding time the human zoo
Utopia Free State
Utopia the jet passing over clouds' dispersal
Utopia Radiostation Peace and Progress
Utopia the full moon over Darfur the new moon over Berlin
Utopia the fish in the sky
Utopia the scribbled abbreviation we always forget
Utopia the throat microphone clammed to the wall
Utopia the exhaustion the symbol the sign
Utopia the eye-flickered blur of summer moments
Utopia the person who leaves you alone
Utopia the tracer-fire of desire
Utopia the stocking-top
Utopia the fragment the collected poems
Utopia the other world's body
Utopia the enjoyment of saying the word
Utopia the cinematic bonnets the crushed escaping villains
Utopia the Balham New Road
Utopia the men of Ket's Rebellion deleted from the poem
Utopia the F-111s taking off to defend the council house they have
    sold you
Utopia the dye the whitewash the tar
Utopia your whims my whims his whims
Utopia the cuts Utopia the healing
Utopia the stab of each new line
Utopia the metaphor the box of tricks Utopia the can of worms
Utopia the desire you may never desire

Utopia the praise praise the utopia
Utopia the colon the question mark the cough
Utopia the static the whistle the scream
Utopia the Clown
Utopia the leather the sweat the eye
Utopia the full Utopia the empty
Utopia
Utopia the tucks and folds of pink flesh open for no-one's eyes
Utopia the approach to Walthamstow Tube
Utopia the plaster the counterpoint the operatic wing
Utopia the ditch-escape the broken glass
Utopia the gun in his mouth
Utopia the shark in the municipal pond
Utopia the wingèd words under magic
Utopia the pianola the polyphon
Utopia the flashing page the burning metaphor the floating world
Utopia the propositions choired into silence
Utopia the eloquent quickstep the sly foxtrot the tangled tango
Utopia the feminine machine
Utopia the Enemy's fatal flaw
Utopia the red sun rising over the Peking General Knitwear Mill
Utopia the shopping list the suicide note
Utopia the sneeze the blessing the psalm
Utopia the keyhole Utopia the witness
Utopia the blueprint the cloud the chant
Utopia the microdot the floral clock
Utopia the rat smelling you
Utopia the building bricks the cardboard sea
Utopia the barbers the rock band the chain store
Utopia the book the genre the world
Utopia the republic Utopia the state
Utopia the dashboard delay
Utopia the freedom to buy
Utopia the mirage the sky the sand

Utopia the towers the pools the canals
Utopia the gothic the one for luck
Utopia untitled Utopia unlimited
Utopia lost Utopia regained
Utopia the suburbs of Phun City
Utopia underground Utopia in the sky
Utopia belonging to its shareholders
Utopia the time bomb of opportunity the bridgehead of production
Utopia the Babylon the Ranter the Song
Utopia the Empire the Voice of Free Europe
Utopia the female freedom of the city
Utopia the passion the thrusting the enclosing
Utopia the tie-pin the buckle the zip
Utopia the repetition the call-sign the music
Utopia the horizon of the world
Utopia the snow-carving the fire-writing
Utopia the cheap ashtray the perfumed hair
Utopia the hole in the head
Utopia the political joke
Utopia the taking of George Hill
Utopia the masque of heroes the monochrome desire
Utopia the crunch of night redwoods
Utopia the morphology of pure sensation
Utopia the flashlight shimmer
Utopia the air the film the people
Utopia the burning the map the radio
Utopia the same
Utopia the aggressor the gloved hand
Utopia the exit to what cannot be
Utopia the domed afternoon the chill passage into the trees
Utopia the wrong way the frame of the working
Utopia the very world that is the world
Utopia the thing in the yes
Utopia the next junction the other's refusing footholds

Utopia the margin of what's measurable
Utopia the sentence the facet imbalance the wobbling age the
   unknown reader
Utopia the what Utopia the question
Utopia the boots the leopard skin pose
Utopia the paragraph the sliced smile the covered seats the vanished
   traveller
Utopia the other the chequebook stare
Utopia the haven the prison the harem
Utopia the prospect the wind-sock the footlights
Utopia the blonde Utopia the brunette
Utopia the high heels the silk the blood stains
Utopia the credits the spectacles the interchange
Utopia the litter the restaurant the mirror
Utopia the mandrake the thumbnail the school
Utopia the reservoir
Utopia hurt
Utopia the tower of breath
Utopia the hobbyhorse the silent nod
Utopia deleted Utopia

1987

8
Slipping the Mind

Slipping the mind
figments of post-
imperial assertion veering
off vanished skylines
invested window dressing
brown potted plants
the kick of
Capital each daybreak

Minister shoots from
slum avoidance nods
at arms deals
above a pool
ringed with rust
this moment not
repeated fireplace shorn
from a terrace

Coils of repeatable
citizens pouring the
eye 55 miles
of lapping propaganda
water colours over
this gutter pastoral's
precise assertion: *Liberals*
Kill Our Kids

1991

9
Weightless Witnesses

Empty Diary 1991

Killing Boxes 3

To specific cultural targets under
      missile dances, they deliver genesis,
the meatiest burgers in history;

They launch scribbles from battlefields,
      thrust the agony shots: we're
prisoners 20 minutes each hour;

They print misguided sermons on
      Bedouin girls' torn shoulders, Justice
kissing pistons, lifting iffy weights;

They drop my stories in
      a quiver of blood, grunting
victory as the arrow falls.

1991

10
Soleà for Lorca

        No song,
no, I do
not want to
see the duty
bound woman ignited
with touch as
men lead her
away, I want

to see the
wide camisole clouds

Silver icicles hold
back the night

I love you
gypsy (being watched

Car pulling up
outside, sharp silhouettes
under the lanterns

This time here
they come, branches
mute their sour
whistles

I love frost
shadows at dawn

tin lanterns shattering
day break

     Shouting
poet stumbling into
a pool of
star pocked walls

the flower of
these blood marshes

1991

11

Improvisation Upon a Remark of Gil Evans

for Miles Davis (1926–1991)

Duocatalysis 6
Midnight Ride 1
IM 2
Soleà 2

Put your flesh on
    a note, a bone
to be feathered for
    flight on the midnight
ride beneath my skin

    : ecstasy bites
in the fast lane

    put your flesh on

20 OCTOBER 1991

12

Seven

Duocatalysis 9
Empty Diary 1992
Masked the World 1
Melting Borders 3

The weaponry is progressing
through the 20th century
at a rate of
a decade a week

with images by Patricia Farrell

Masked
the world was
new the abstract
men beat us
with sticks you
thrashed the guilty
man who carried
excess baggage to
feel less entropic
we lifted children
on our shoulders
as the police
dropped veils over
shallow justice she
stabbed she shot
employed to read
her 'self' and
value his logistic

capital
willing frauds you
tore your own

flesh a ball
slipping past the
queues for cash
bribed the celestial
blip of dissent
under police surveillance
knife's edge skimming
she is the
detective's informatic clip
waiting for answers
medusa curls on
a flyover whittled
smiles into faces
above slums built
for the jury

between
the claws of
the Sphinx adulterer's
robes dropped like
the gallows riddled
profiles hidden in

the weave stunned
silent women nippling
the veil torpedoes
unzipping for the
ocean fighters history's
tight membrane he
fronts the quayside
for furtive pleasure
fists pocketed as
stripped billboards spill
poisons off spoons
futurity's icy radar

creams
his lips feeds
her scent posed
as wealth hushed
campaigns invade his
slogans draped over
derricks slips on
a perfect wig
consciousness a lengthy

shadow demanding lengthier
questions as women
mourn his answers
which began as
lobbying end as
gatecrashing now stalks
the night club's
gloom dreams of
hard excess spills

wisecrack entries

crack
of skull on
hard basin riot
flesh dug from
pits not scored
later from the
unzipped body as
seismic screams in
the hushed building
gambling debt wherever
ethics are swaying
the womanliest pair

of blue jeans
in history whose
fund is prudent
no mirror poses
before she moves
out of range

             of
cameras his own
dirty reflections major
ghosts with toy
guns and empires
or empties to
sell as one
signs off two
key in sperm
counts with toxins
carrying the plate
glass that tints
him she drifts
with her text
bride's wreath shakes

like a caption
that wilts like
swaddled wealth and

                scattered
car door slamming
bodies in fertiliser
sacks cufflink shades
a prayer to
guilty issues her
surgical gloves wipe
his memory finger
his pocket he
rests his failing
equipment and magnifies
her image she
slips off billowing
tops sleeping at
desks rows of
embryos they dream
of bucking Kalashnikovs
volleys of thumbs

1992

15

Fucking Time: Six Songs for the Earl of Rochester

for Gavin Selerie
Duocatalysis 11
Phallic Shrines 2

Dream of your eyes,
lips like leeches;
a wayward bullet invents
Fate as it

flies; worms twist his
armour; blood-scabs
on his prick. Appetite
leads, Aversion stands

off: peck and claw,
eye to eye.
She strokes fur; beauty
spots pock her.

Pissing fountains' vapour dances
before his milky
eyes, watery lids. A
million moments fuck

time, knotting the sequels
of pleasures, the
backdrop of fallen whores
and standing pricks.

'Phoebus tosses feeble shadows
Nymphs spoil for
frolics. The first deflowered
blossoms the ~~brightest~~

(*del.*)

~~briefest~~

(*del.*)

barest

Power and powder; blanched
stone in sunlight,
dog turds in shadowed
ditches. Leather dildo

spies the clap-sick
passions. Mares frisk
at the royal carriage.
She becomes coinage

of the realm, false
'incorporeal body', brisk,
pregnant, a bladder of
policy, bursting shit.

Saw the print of
her shape in
the grass, led the
coranto around Mercury's

frauds or Jupiter's adulteries,
leaf-mould hoof
rings where satyrs fuck:
shutters, mid-stage.

She spreads her fan:
her pearl fingers
frig lords. She performs
his dowry snatches.

Twist the pressure of
external things void,
a turd stirring beneath
her gown, perfumed

lice crawling a woven
scalp, mechanical fingers
scratching a lap dog,
two bitches licking

one prick; running over
an alphabet to
start a rhyme, warring
'tarse' against 'arse'.

Breath steaming, his thigh
roasts at your
fire, lover's meat skewered
on butcher's eye.

Slap him like a
saddle, lewd engine!
Fat *bougre* in the
stocks, his neck

hangs like arse lard,
or fleshy backs
of old mistresses. A
beast, spitting sperm.

MAY–JUNE 1992

16

Logos on Kimonos

for Gilbert Adair
Duocatalysis 8
Empty Diary 2055
Fucking Time 2
History of Sensation 6
Human Dust 1

The civilian epic . . . teaches
the absolute controls of
lives cut off from
intervention in historical fate
Gilbert Adair

The sky was sick metallic skin, Genethetic
meatloaf rotting over the hot city.
Poor kids still rode the Underground. Smart
Arses like me skated the neural Tanks,
clipping onto Personality Composites. My latest catch
was an Autoflesh case. My biomatic orgasm
flushed Yen in the cybernetic maelstrom, where
he'd picked me up on feel alone.
Information sickness iced me, pink fuses blowing,
melting subliminals in the cool jelly stolen
from the Tanks. Logos on kimonos flashed
fleshy machines. I'd MEAT and METAL lasered
on either tit and I could clip
ecstasy any time I liked. Flooded by
voices, not mine, in the Tanks: nostalgia
for human dust on the keyboard, ancient
meat messages flattened on the screen. When
I watch old movies I get sentimental
over robots, strutting like pillheads from a
bar at 5. CyberCunts fleshed on me
by some clipwrecked pilot with a scrimshaw

virus flutter my optic lashes to process
the orgasm I'll use to crash his
information-dead eyes. He's hard copy. Once
I've jellied my button, he'll jack me
like a deck, then roll off, a
dead man.
        The realisation that neither of
us is human makes my flesh creep.

MAY 1992

18 (incorporating 14)
Poetic Sequencing and the New

Works I've 'numbered', rather than named, *Twentieth Century Blues* have been appearing over the last two years. The text the reader has is clearly part of something else. How it relates to that something else and how that something else is disposed towards its own development, past and future, is my active and personal way of dealing with the question of what poetry might become.

A rejected title for this sequencing was that of Beuys' affective installation, *The End of the 20th Century*—now happily in the Tate Gallery where it will be widely seen. It's a profound and resonant title, but I didn't like its suggestion of finality or ambiguous teleology (all denied by Beuys' work itself, of course). Moreover, a voice in a dream warned me not to use it. Less portentous and more fitting to my sensibility—to refunction kitsch—was 'Twentieth Century Blues', a song of Noel Coward that I once owned on a 78 but haven't heard for years: 'Blues, Twentieth Century Blues, are getting me down./ Who's escaped those weary Twentieth Century Blues?' Since I'd just then started to sing blues again in a band, it also seemed a pertinent red herring.

To read *Twentieth Century Blues* linearly, which is almost chronologically, causes it to double back upon itself. Many texts belong to more than one strand. New strands, even retrospectively, can be added to the weave. Some related texts, such as *The Cannibal Club*, 'History of Sensation 2', are not part of *Twentieth Century Blues*; its own borders melt. *Twentieth Century Blues* is essentially not about anything; it is a form to hang things on, to weave things through, albeit knottily. I have toyed with Deleuze and Guattari's term 'rhizome' in my hunt for the adequate metaphor, but I'm not sure that's what I'm producing, exactly. In a way, I would say that this schema organises continuities I've often sensed between texts of mine, the feeling of one poem continuing, even in contradiction, another.

Reading one of the resultant strands—even for me—is an oddly unsettling experience. For example, 'The Materialisation of Soap 1947', written in 1988, is part of *The Flashlight Sonata*, 'Twentieth Century Blues 6' and is also 'History of Sensation 4'; it clearly belongs to more than one strand. The second 'Materialisation of Soap', was written in 1992 and belongs to the *Empty Diaries 1946–1966* sequence, 'Twentieth Century Blues 17'. They therefore belong apart as much as they belong together. But to take them as a strand, they are stylistically dissimilar and what results is more of a network than a work, a dissonance, a difference born of identity (they use the same materials and share something of the same poetic focus). There could be a third poem, different again, or one which would knot this strand into another. Or there might not. |Note 2007: There is a third poem, 63, which indeed knots the strand. The fourth poem, 66, is more like what is envisaged here.| I realise that a reader's aesthetic preferences may privilege one text over another. This suits me. It activates the reader, though in a different way from my previous poetics of indeterminacy: the reader completing the author's fragments in an expansive education of desire. Whichever poem is privileged, it still has to be read against its apparently less convincing companion. The satisfaction of closure might be delayed as effectively as in an indeterminate text; the principle of discontinuity hangs between the texts not, necessarily, within them, though that's often still the practice. The aim, however, has not changed: to activate the reader into participation, into relating differences, to sabotage perceptual schema, to educate desire, not to fulfil it in a merely entertaining emptying of energy. To create, above all, new continuities.

The politics of this, though, becomes less utopian, less the text opening horizons of possibility, Marcuse's Aesthetic Dimension glittering with its pre-figurations. It becomes more strategic: a denial of what we presently are, as Foucault would have it, more a question of emphasising the text's 'capacity to promote active, procedural ruptures at the core of significatory tissues and semiotic denotatives, from which to set new worlds of reference to work'. (Félix Guattari, 'Text for the Russians', *Poetics Journal* 8)

The epigraph for the *Twentieth Century Blues* project comes from JM Coetzee's *Waiting for the Barbarians* (1980). The disgraced imperial magistrate, who is the novel's narrator, is forced to explain his archaeological interests (in particular, indecipherable texts he had collected) which have alerted his authoritarian captors' suspicions. His 'explanation', which stands at the head of the project at last, is ironically barbed but his sense of the subversiveness of the marginal or of that which cannot readily be decoded into the violent simplicities of bureaucracy is affective, and provides me with a useful analogy for *Twentieth Century Blues*. We can all read the object, assemble, re-assemble, it in our own way(s). This will, of course, be affected by our acquired knowledge, our perceptual schema, and by the means of the text's availability.

The long poem's ambition toward inclusiveness, its grasping for totality, with all its attendant drifts into dogmatism as well as stale repetition, has been, at least in this century, its most negative condition. I believe that my notion of sequencing, with its mercurial shifts, may avoid some of these traps. It is not necessary to let it go stale for the sake of titanic ambition. Although I don't wish to analyse his essay in any depth here, Barrett Watten's description of Zukofsky's *A* in his 'Social Formalism' essay (*North Dakota Quarterly*, Fall 1987) seems pertinent. His use of Bourdieu's theory, at the very least, provided me with the term 'generative schema' to describe poetic sequencing.

> The poetics I am trying to describe might be called 'process' but that would misunderstand them. The rhetoric of process describes a formal procedure given an equal value at all points; it is an imposed order, a naming from the outside of a temporal development. While these poetics involve a process, they work it out from the inside — involving a wide and indeterminate range of feedback that enacts a refiguring and transformation of Bourdieu's 'generative schema' over a long duration.

The morphogenetic poesis has a

> logic of development that creates the necessary conditions for its own 'next move in the game'. These moves are transformative — both of experience as it is understood and of the possibilities of the poem. The poem enacts a strategic argument of forms, rather than a rhetoric of process, and this temporality occurs in a tension with time outside the poem, with history and with the events of the poet's life.

[84]

The aim is that the writing—the working on rather than the working out—of *Twentieth Century Blues* should constitute such an aesthetic journey, fracturing into the new, a poetic changing by stages and confronting the changing world. There are no jumps, just swift transitions.

Untitled

Twentieth Century Blues 14

net/
(k)not
         -work(s)

                              : a network but not a work, a knot of works, not work as labour, but as 'necessary business'. Several networks. Net: the shape of a 3D figure laid flat. Subject to no further deductions. The take home pay. Network: system of units, stations for broadcasting the same programme. Not: a word expressing denial, negation, refusal. Adv. Same as naught, nought. Knot: Interlacement. Twisting. In some particular form. A bond of union. A difficulty. The main point of a tangle. A complex of lines. A measure of speed. A node or joint in a stem. Knotwork: ornamental work made with knots. Granny knot: a knot like a reef knot, but unsymmetrical, apt to slip or jam. A tangle or a careful design? Slip knots let the world through. The net works to capture, the knot works to hold the net. Work: Working the Work. Working on. Effect directed to an end, that on which one works, the product of work, a literary composition, a book. Works: walls, workshop, an action in its moral aspect. To produce effects. To sail in a course, to put in motion, to purge. To provoke. To excite.
    Or *not* any of these.

The generative schema allows for a proliferation of strands and an almost cellular splitting of new sequences. Perhaps *Twentieth Century Blues* will suddenly stop and other titles emerge from it as the 'real' work. The scheme announces only its potentialities. One of my idle dreams has always been to write an entire literature, to become a sort of Pessoa gone fake omniscient.

The title *Twentieth Century Blues* does provide a temporal scope for my working, a moment at which, after having changed throughout, it will have to change utterly, into silence. And if silence isn't reached before that, it's a limit enough, the last years of the Empire and its calendar or not.

The future belongs to the unknown relation of a not yet unfolded world and the, at present, slenderly formed practices of those who will work in it, and against it. You cannot see into the granite hearts of Beuys' sculpture. But it might be possible to provide structures that can transform in terms of poetics and poetic focus as the world transforms itself. The one necessary result of *Twentieth Century Blues* should be that its future units, within strands and across the entire schema, will look like nothing that I am producing now.

14: 17 April 1992/18: July 1992 (abridged 1999/2005)

20

The Overseas Blues : an allusion to Horace, Odes, II.i

for Harry Gilonis

Killing Boxes 4

Startled eyes staring out of history's blank
wall its criminal phases causes, the fatal
      pacts of regional governors: pump-
      action shot gun points out
from the trees golden cartridges shitting smoke.

A dicey job bardic TV shows barbed
wire scratching sky, fire crawling on its
      belly across your minefield documentaries
      ashes over lava still aglow:
raw skin peels in your numb aestheticism.

Sheathed steel slips across solid thigh: jets
flash, horses frisk tails tied for battle
      flicking, limp hoofless home, alarm
      clock tabloids in media rubble;
leather crackles with light as they shoot.

Slave galley sails the coin's reverse: which
minefield is not manured with British blood
      ditches testify to war crimes
      blind lamps crash around Shi'ite
ears a single stain printing an epic?

Stop sexy Muse! leave history leave the
blues and the stink of these battles
      between your breasts I've killed
      for: Drip, in passionate expiation.
Sing, my plectrum feathering the dampened strings.

OCTOBER–NOVEMBER 1992

21

Shutters

For Jo Blowers 1
Phallic Shrines 3
World's Body 2

Burnished fog of
daylight fleshes my
shoulder melts into
my gaze metal
bars to secure
the night
      fall
into the pit
OUTSIDE harsh discriminations
powder the air
with your disappearance
of light stolen
from the city
scabs of blood
bejewel each breath

a sick trance
grassy carpets between
pleasure

      and powerlessness fabric
      not flesh
      fabricated breath

tonguing veined cloth
Fold the shutters across

'He approached her from behind.
She felt a shiver as
he touched her shoulders. He
bent as though to kiss
her nape, bleached her world,
swooned upon a draper's mermaid.'

I shivered. Ivy
mocked the sinews
of the dead
tree with its
crawling strangulations behind
which the workmen
were said to
relieve themselves I
clung picking the
bark off like
a scab this
drama of entry
and departure SHUTTERS
the light which
shores against escape;

is a cruel loan from
a sketchbook eye shivering privacies
        tight. The thickest branches float
the red translucence of her
eyelids printed scavengers of avengers
plundered her pockets

elm's lightning

Her own mirror's violence, eyes out, finished,
sweeps across her illusion
                    streams across the
creases of perilous journeys
                    She is unfinished,
she is the ink of her confessions,
death's stiff drop
            against the open shutters
in a stifled choke
                    My fingertips press
throats, soaking your face in metallic light

a brittle dress
a battle dress
frames the door
from which he
captures his keyhole
THE STRICT DELIRIUM
combing the hair
long the body's
slow announcement that
it has life
that it has
to be perched
in this world
frames glare out
from the dead
EYES THE DEAD
landscapes our legs
do not exist
while the sweep
of the eyes
follows fabric's trench

'Men dirty and aproned, with measuring implements,
spades to trench the soft earth; wrists
flick ha'pennies on a board, slap weeping
women's faces. Window call it escape across
nothing, the eternal present of a winter
day's interior—shutters at last shut, bolt
across a schematic female beside the stars.'

        mirror's chill

        exclusion

        body steam

        floorboard shudder

I can look straight at you for
Once as a thief might
Between the public the public baths private
Lives are licked from streets
For exposure's slow sculpting; impossibility
ALMOST KNOCKS HER OFF BALANCE
My body a system of canals for
Fragile passion and passion's withdrawal
The pages uncut already crack open down the spine
Before the ridges of print you shall feel fabricated

propped elbow
collapses her back

the deluge of
green sunsets

upon the balcony's magnetised
drop

'A man wouldn't
know where to
begin to unhook
me a site
of moveable pathos

    Suddenly scaffolding half
    erected his London
    rushes in borrowing
    luminescence castaways on
    a window ledge
    we sew a

jungle of dust'

A halo flares
as the flesh
fails where screaming
light whispers to
the stars wild
eyed and domestic

The science of
solid fluorescence on
chemical starry walls

Between these escapes
I dream of
bodies scorched by
the STEAM of
the world where
decorum liquefies every
rustling Opera in
her chemise invitations
to sensual pits

A slant of
daylight penetrates, washed
the head against
dead STARS, black
as a flue.
I'm fallen like
a court dress,
a perfect conversation,
a lambent kiss

Mid-winter dusks blaze and then
freeze against the shutters her heavy
forgetting of legs an avalanche of
dirt in the weave of her
melting the memory of a voice
splinters the light in the flesh

1992

24

Empty Diaries (incorporating 7 17 19 22 23)

The Flashlight Sonata 2

23 Empty Diaries 1901–1912

Twelve: Thousand 3

Empty Diary 1901

We were driven to the place where
        trees floated like clouds above lily ponds,
just to prove that it existed; where
men haggled drunkenly over copies of their
        Manifesto, floating names that may glitter heroically
        against the bullet pocks on bare walls,
the future's stars. Predestination scratched in dust:
        a message to kick back in their
        eyes, once history has blown. Each cowled
perambulator was a remainder from a sum
        we had not set, a reminder on
        memoranda to which we shall not reply.

Empty Diary 1902

Tumble into this myth
from his bed water
jug trembling in the
words of his story
not mine as the
uitlanders charge through photographers'
ash checks for stolen
diamonds tubes rupture kaffirs'
anuses ripping a splinter
of my soul accordant
with their 'passion' veil

snows my visage cruel
beauty freezing service as
meal time canes crack
on prettiest knees aching
at cold fire places
sweating girls dusty enemies
slanted portraits gold panned
from excrement my hand
on her thin shoulder
'Make the bitch perform

Empty Diary 1903

What happened to
our chorus? We
blossomed in artificial
light, wasping at
the honey glow;
chanted in the
boudoir to wake
to conversations, falsely
witnessed, pasted upon
a depthless dawn.
Our hips on
his desk prevented
work; one breast
sacrificed yesterday to
the depths of
his contraption, pinned
above his throne.
This sovereign of
his own name
fades with each

retelling, belongs to
none, mortal for
the first time
in history, feels
the remains of
gatling gun passions—
our delightful losses
lost in lyric.

Empty Diary 1904

I'm lifting his kidney wiper on the
      back of my glove lusting for lips
      to suck my ring finger to bleed

Eyes wash the ink city she's in
      the air weightless story I witnessed often
      intractable tram lines scoring Balham High Road

My corset off she touched my stomach
      smiled ran her fingers over the ridges
      where the bones had pressed (he writes)

Eyes water as I watch the sauntering
      tea-girls, sketching undraped bodies of knowledge
      the science of stroking and poking confirmed

Empty Diary 1905

She falls for him, conventional longing well
tutored, no pose held, broken but breathing,
yet she keeps a finger in a
page of last year's tightly scribbled diary:
the ranked delights of the Paris corsetière,
the dummies' impersonal whorish display of lace
and china flesh, a flat-buttoned pressing
of chambermaids' etiquette; I can't bear his
'I sleep, I wake, I never dream'
; want to slit his throat, to hoist
him, dripping from his penis; her story
stalled, veins in her bare neck pleading.

Empty Diary 1906

Whose polished days feels his gasp scratching
Down my back a smile slipping grips

My throat family name-plates bright as
Silver nouns in a story cooling pronominal

Skin in silence as if they formed
A reflective premise for his solid argument

Syllogistic bodies swallowed his hysteric weapon whole
Escape like thoughts into Conduct Mottos the

Ambivalent ravished cleft where flesh swallows itself
Whole .... the fresh

Breeze that licks my second skin clean
Whose conclusion is a clench of similes

Empty Diary 1907

voluptuous
watched the fat pulp of
   his neck bulging
   rodent
fingers stiff collars rebelling against
   iron furnace conversations
   a buoyant hysteria

   eye-
glasses on (his journal demands
   that I write)
   wind's
kisses were police spies pawing
   rotten fruit in
   conduits she's breaking

   windows
in Putney regattas and emancipatory
   luncheons glass embedded
   eyefuls
of solitary abandon rejects external
   conditions internal states
   votes for post-

   card
japes the servant's batiste chemise
   falling quickly her
   wet
finger she put her finger
   on my tongue
   her human Eucharist

Empty Diary 1908

'My little anarchist with
         crab pool terrors,
your dry dock fills
         with foam; immodest
hats eclipse tight shoulders
         (he tells himself,
you over-hear: Sex
         slavery, sex madness,
kissing forbidden pistons to
         beg for a
say in the bullies'
         largest gang. Poverty

flutters at Epsom gates
         for aproned boys
flinging broken biscuits; naked
         eyes, wild intelligence.
Tumbles of men percolate
         resistance, pressed against
black walls, grey-capped)
         Police helmets float
the procession, waved on
         by Goddesses' (You
held your clenched fist
         in his lap

Empty Diary 1909

Horse women broken by geldings; antiquarian lust
        assumes the dark portrait at his feet,—
their eyes drowned in pools of matrimony.

Demotic imperatives adorn this squabble. Boys watch
        the virgins dance, praying for a gusting
shift. Our cruciform banner is inscribed *Midwives*.

She plucked the flower from her hat,
        put it straight in my hair, laughing,
a martyr to her cycles of caprice

(and disgust? How far would she take
        this cat and mouse with another woman?
For 6d. she'll show you her cell.

Empty Diary 1910

Palaces fall for the latest weapon. Obsession
        demands this price, paying homage to the
        tripod. The executioner chews over her last
Letter .... spits in
        the bread. Crêpe stirs his spirit, mourning
        the Sovereign, insatiably eyed, brisk cartographer of
Alcoves. Descartes' Demon steams his photographic plates.
        A monocle deflects her parenthetical questions; his
        replies spiral (stirring his tea absentmindedly). His
Ventriloquists amend the manifesto. Their vibrations loosen
        brick-work, cement, marriage; her proclamations skate
        on shaky ice, she slips an ought

Empty Diary 1911

Realise that history *can* vindicate you
Or knock them stupid gusting differences
Blow them into frozen breathlessness their
Eulogies collapsing as bellows of light
Rush of humankind its spears prod
The genital skies parasols scratching dust

Steam yachts moor off Lesbos (my
Heroine of Anarchy waltzes through water)
Escape vents webbed with skin she
Paddles her oughting doubts knocks a
Policeman from his mount impaled on
A shadow of Big Ben (mermaid
Resistant yet floating like her ethos:
Does she speak through *my* voice?

Empty Diary 1912

Eunuch!) Tell him lies (say i shrank
My breasts to make him feel less vulnerable
Petals of vision in the telegraph shimmer
Telephones beat their resonant bells and cry
You are the spectre's big salty sister

Dance in the dirt. Somebody else's history
In his odalisque script puffs him up,
Anklets chime on her bare legs he
Rubs himself on the faun's scarf. Later
In the tent's sandblasted womb, his
Epicene frenzy stamps the burnt journal's ashes)
Sell him back to himself as self

1993

7 Empty Diaries 1913–1945

Empty Diary 1913

. . . visible, in the words of a tale
I'd thought his no less than mine,
as an embossed oak desk, its promiscuity
of pens

              '. . . the old flag shredded by
revolutionist moths, as democratic as snow dust
on a peasant's boots. Imperial soldiers under
canvas sink into the flesh of history'

ice-bound steamers

                    (sells a new cure
for the ancient ailments. Promises of food
are another story. Our cut glass slavery
tells our tale as the cheapest sweep
of light across the Labour Exchange floor.

Empty Diaries 1914–1919

                                        Killing Boxes 2

        I

Watch chains abstract this gold light
to diamond resistance;
iron, brass. Boys on fences
spy blank windows, phantasmal
men. An afterword of dust
billows house-high and the proud
devices vanish in filth.

II

Apish patriot aped by his
boy with the toy gun christened
Mons, crucified by history.
Last testament blank looking
through the drizzle of himself;
smiles. Men beyond the bayonet's
blade; spies' tennis courts at home.

III

Boots shone expectantly. Kerbs,
bayonet steps, enlisting those
nightmares of washed bomb-blasts, split
his helmet as in a war
artist's pose. I am textured
rainfall in his dampened eyes;
he's a rushed scribble in mine.

IV

Mesopotamia 3

Slack with guilt and with faces,
he haunts as well as the dead,
feet stomping sand. A love seat
snaking its tempting doubles,
open, in troughs of torn stomachs,—
and I'm crawling with insect
metaphors, heroes' footnotes.

V

Eyes wrap my legs in muscle,
his fingers tracing patterns
across my dress, as though it
were a map of fleshy caves.
The same world lulled by the same
scratchy chants, spiriting raw
salmon flesh on crumpled silk.

VI

Naked girls were paraded
through town, rippled over the
fleshless windows of butchers,
as bells tolled. The silly girls
in Union Jacks hugged easy
answers of palace railings,
danced round imaginary maypoles.

Empty Diary 1920
Grippe Espagnole

        Split in a
mirror, gloves or fingers in
their meadow of scarf lines, with
its censure, like a man's. I've
shelves of those Everyman books,
a chair in front of the fire.
Light up, read Goldman, bloomers
under the wet umbrella.

Whenever
I'm photographed in front of
my portrait, self-vigilant,
a seismic oscillation
of bone, cruel beauty dances
for a field of fogged lenses.
Only a master could paint
the crumple of rich dresses;

      my nest of
hair for marble eyes to steal
a home, crystal beads trembling
under those hot sick fans. Such
tyranny behind men's masks
breeds: Poisons sprayed onto bus
seats, nestling between the hard
joints, sticky with the flu's beads.

Empty Diary 1921

Cool revolution not lust
for her otter body—

Empty Diary 1922

Black drapes steam by the highway;
      grim Englishmen motor to court to
Condemn a drunken woman to death.
      A fist still warm from her

Thighs burst the husband's gut. The
      testament of fancy totals the account.

Hands rise towards heaven, 12 bleached
     martyrs harping strings of mechanical desire.

Their motor, returning, dusts the crowd.
The gallows drops like adulterers' robes.

Empty Diary 1923

Newspaper table-cloth mopping spilt pea soup
(didn't want your moisture on my lips)
Retinal thoughts paying homage to the future
Shreds of print from the mantle trailing
Laxative advertisements and 'interesting' photos of a
Woman strapped in electric chair gagged blindest
Eyes in America seeping love (*VIRAGO FUR*

Empty Diary 1924
Labour—Part One

Men squeezed through policed dole queues,
women at their wringers (I'm
grinning over the shoulders
of revolutionaries; I
can see the keys half-unwound
in their backs! (This cigarette
card Empire, where an Arab
in pearls drags me to his soft
bed, collapses at my feet.
The beauty of his parted
lips: he has only to speak
and I will disappear, a
sack on a stick full of
glitter; rider on my spine.

Empty Diary 1925

fill+t
he+ora
cular+
valves

Empty Diary 1926

For John Seed 1

We push cars on their sides, jeering
them out

       coal lorries with police guards
smoulder outside the depot's gates and

nervous clerks in tin hats salute débutantes
peeling spuds with bloodless fingers:

history's tight membrane

the age's leaking sewer,

revolution, spirits one broken machine gun in
a pram

hold out

until the police clear the Broadway for
the British Gazette

for one instant

Baldwin's hanged and we call this

Love

Empty Diary 1927

These tyrannical objects:
black ghosts of their photographs,
sunk in air or amber, as
invisible as the state,

as tangible as power. They
are the skins of material
production, light through painted
butterfly's wings projected

against warehouses. I can
sense dying blossoms on the
minute hand of the floral
clock, trembling, and turning, off.

Empty Diary 1928

skin joined at on delight might seem
bare jointed sentence strange skin watching despair
justice how watching sentence distressed stolen advances
seem and word might each magistrate delight
each and as a despair strange bare
skin delight how watching stolen advances (echoes
magistrate if strange word joined soluble sentence

Empty Diary 1929
Labour—Part Two

Men are waiting with their guns,
women with the wireless (I
can see MacDonald's bald spot
winking with his gold watch chain!
Wires slice the threads of chatter
as the Prince cracks his fingers
for the Empire (My soft flesh
hums, shadows of prison bars
cutting my face. My frillies
blinded men with audible fat.
From my stocking-tops: cocktails
for three; wireless girl breasting
a bed of invisible
men; shocked arpeggio hairs.

Empty Diary 1930

I gripped his
soft stomach as we sped off
on his new motorcycle,
shaking crystal phials in the
chemist's. The map of Britain
was chalked on broken house-bricks.
He'd pointed out his target.
No other possible voice.

A viscous
street pours down its own drains, as
blind as love. I've no voice to
see him aping my voice which
he cannot see. Angels crowd
around the floral clock with
weary fleapit gypsy pouts,
rummage through handbags for keys.

Empty Diary 1931

A leather belt from a new tube escalator

A banker's hat band

A bus indicator of the old type

A letter 'S' from a Marble Arch shop front

An electric candle from the Tooting Granada

A spoon from the all-night coffee stall at Hyde Park Corner

A bath tap (hot) from somebody else's scavenger party

A buttock print from Gershwin's piano stool

A stockinged face, insect lashes struggling through mesh

A tear that had flashed in a pleasure pilgrim's eye

A primula from the floral clock

A bottle of moonlight from Blackfriars Bridge

Empty Diary 1932

Passion lifts its wooden erection; men on
motor-bikes denounce enigma. I choke on
it as we trip over newspaper hoardings
leant against hydrants; read the latest sensation:
Women gagged him, sliced his testicular meat.
Assert your frailty over the sweating porters,
lie on rugs while the motor cools,
rotting buttocks feeling for the single cushion.
Dead hair, brushed across an electric nerve,
animates the garbage mask into erotic wealth.

Empty Diary 1933
Left

> In a grey city
> filled with market cries
> we met those who
> had no faces left
>
> Brecht

Sore lips tight zeitgeist
pursed under caps tilting
towards wet pavements puddles
mirror them no faces

Empty Diary 1934
Marching through Peckham

Stand to attention, pyramids
        of tins on
Dipping shelves. This day
        is your apotheosis:
A proletarian moment reified,
        a soup kitchen
Incarnate, swarms of bees
        at perfect hives.

Empty Diary 1935
Right

Helmets, cobbles, stinking conduits;
        eugenics' sewer floods.
Scrape off the ordure
        of history. Jubilee
Benches take the farts
        of wormy kids.
The world is almost
        new once more:

Washing billows like sails,
        smudged with smoke
From real funnels; old
        women adrift amid
Oceans of torn clothes.
        Pray as his
Voice becomes louder, an
        oracular wireless warming:

Street parties boast its
        censure, insignia bruised
Into flesh, patronal direction
        of every clue.
Drunken voices explode, ecstatic
        promises of cash.
Paving could swallow me,
        and heal, leaving:

My handbag, with its
        red herrings: erotic
Advertisements, unexplained keys; like
        any degenerate novel.
A woman's, at most,
        a scribbled obscenity
On the back of
        a torn photograph.

Empty Diary 1936
The Proletarian News

                                        For Charles Madge 1

vauxhall was grey she needed blocks of
flats not jewel panopticans she threw back
her hem and did a tight city
fling tyrannical wireless valves on tulip faces

echoes of men patronising answers on folded
blankets heads bubbling with pints of stout
rotten teeth of her voices skin always
gleaming an unblemished marching announcing sore lips

surrealist commodes adorn the scattered floors of
chaotic meal times in houses of the
poor dash of belisha peril in jitters
waiting for the paraffin fire to blow

. Empty Diary 1937
Angel of Anarchy

for Eileen Agar

The gassy sailor laughed, mucked up my
hair for a domino, a frozen indecency.
He pushed me across a table: I
clawed at the ceiling. My boots showed
dockers how salutes shoot out of history,
back-strapped negations from an Elsewhere where
whispers are piles of musty uniforms. These
men, mouths swelling, lounged on my spirits,
vibrating the vacancy of this grim pub
between shifts. They spoke loud until they
puffed excuses, like torn boots open to
scrutiny, threadbare apologies to the International Brigade.

Empty Diary 1938

American
diners manned by Cockney girls,
heroines of the grim wheels,
glitter with speed. We perch on
stools, discuss sick children thrown
from balconies, listening for
the spirit, learning to see
it this way, the Fascist line.

He whispers
of dangers for us both; a
literalist washes her sheets
and carries his metaphor.
He doesn't believe this talk
of drains, as mounds appear in
Dulwich Park. Of common men
digging their shallow mass graves.

Empty Diary 1939

He handed me coins; notes, a rustle
of affluence in my palm. I counted
the change, slowly, powerless. Once, I could
have worked miracles on these dirty tablecloths;
tea, a mash of fish, crumbled over,
over the picture of Goebbels. Those ex-Biff
Boys, yell stiff warnings, to take cover,
I mean, the whistle, blowing on fear,
rekindling the song of the last cocktail.
Platform tickets, trains, toy aeroplanes scrape my
knees, bags slung round our necks; signs
we cannot read, destinations we can't erase.

Empty Diary 1940

The future is announced
Evidence wipes Balham tube
Uniforms tumble down escalators
Any girl counting coupons
Washed she falls

                    eels
So used to skinning

Empty Diary 1941

Soldier girls in robotic formations nostalgia breaking
up the street: inviolate world of window
displays raw clothes: seditious vacuity: my spotlit
finger prints permanent noon: slippery silk wiped

on his face: nailed to an invisible
viewer tongue clipped a dirty circumcised bone
I had raised: Outcast raper grabbed Liberation
girl: acned recruits laughed: me first: the

filthiest orifice the greatest sacrifice: his mongrel
stump: performing my own desire at my
fingertips: swaying to popular melodies the choreography
of what is possible before many mirrors

my polished ideals gather my speculative drapes
court a mistaken identity: dummy torsos chained:
their eyes lash this strip of flesh
a lobby flash: a fist of gold

Empty Diary 1942

rows of women strain to hear that
plea: he's detecting something like guilt: 'monuments
in smoke as though invisible feet had
kicked dust: cubes of victorious metal anything

anything remoulded bike chains swinging impressively on
dance floors': the destruction of one lean
to was enough to fill her with
blood lust which followed: such beautiful bomb

blasts: tooth-pastes health rays aspirins make
us ready for all those window shopping
sprees: cautionary adverts for TCP polish the
nerves calm Harpic spews the bowls in

the superlative photography of allies: thrills us
netball hysterics in night shelter for YWCA
bunks: no fun cleaning our uniforms: spraying
the dangerous air with fragrant good news

Empty Diaries 1943–1945

Schräge Musik 2

1

George raises his hand. No nail scars.
His voice without litany. I'm proud of
my identity card. Reminds me who I
was. Looking at empty beer bottles. Hollow
pies. Crumbs on a slide-rule are
the price of genius. Mrs. Churchill stopped
for a cuppa. Left us to kiss
strange accents on platforms. Microphones hover over
Pearl's poisoned heels. Black vans carrying 'information'
films pull up beside the sceptical queues.

2

Bees at my hive anticipate her hands
defenceless sex the photograph steps back gagged
as Germany confesses dry the voice the
testimony the microphonic guilt sounds so good

Full of arm wrestling girls tough men
tapping you on the shoulder quivering to

Pearl's glitter lashes agitate the hypnotist the
31 metre band you jump jittering jewels

Sky-eyed cyclists creeping parachute beetles stone
faced frozen the sky scars blister Cologne
sequin peaks coloured men dancing off poverty
the Empire those steps sweeping silvery floors

3

Echoes to be echoed / it's
fascism calls the traps for
my own voice in there / learning
you believe the film stars they've
got old uniforms they break
under fox spotlights / weeping
like George / the poets draft tear
jerkers / POW
on buses / dreams of girls his
own echoes / parachute pett-
icoats from shattered fuselage /
once more: naked girls in ponds

1991

17 Empty Diaries 1946–1966

Stella by Starlight

Empty Diary 1946

I ration my eyes on a Demob
suit, zip up the lids; winter boots.
The immodest mermaid flexes on his useless
muscle, her flesh his loaned oily skin.

I'm beached on his dream, a nostalgic
pillow of breasts pulled tight, a War:
a mission fulfilled that leaves him marching.
Steam brushed love from the platform farewell.

I turn from him, in judgement, breathing
his regret. He stomps the wrong side
of a Pre-War newsreel; a rally. His
eyes bore into my back like bullets.

Empty Diary 1947

The Materialisation of Soap 2

Big Ben froze. British grit flies from
bus wheels sticks to flesh queues do
not waste brick dust Pearl's face silk
through a wringer he licks her finger.

Her card tasting official envelopes bitter inky
fingers dance unpeeling paper fruit, tap drips

musty potato bag she queues for turnips
girl singer brushing against the rubber stamps.

Grey skies over empty allotments she is
distance / morality / history a flower pot over
a candle his warm bath steams the
tiles, coupon free undies once evidently fleshed.

Empty Diary 1948

Horseshoe table kicking the teeth out of
peace   Rhetorical limbs take flight   Knees apart
His eyes roast her   The hand lusts
for its glove   Bare shoulders calloused fingers

Mermaid flops on the bed gasping   Pull
down the shutter on the street   Nervous
rattle wiping away terror   Soft walled dreams
Lifts a beer bottle   Nakedness falls away

Her octopus earrings are swimming in gas
Last year's fascism is this year's fashion
Stares at his back   To bring him
to his knees   The Ovens' murderous Muse

Empty Diary 1949

We're the most beautiful women in history,
though we can't use the phone in
these gloves, pearls hard on our teeth.
Science traps spermy molecules of Omniscient Mind;

they ejaculate at the end of a
rope. Geniuses push us into acid baths,
talk of Jesus and Hitler in one
breath, the old girl's lolly in another.

The police recover sludge, burnt brass rings
(shove the corks they pull into their
mouths) Mosley is back; his presence queens
us, rolling his *rrr*s over our lives.

Empty Diary 1950

Truth as fluid and dwarfed by treasures
Each portrait wired for sound Commie mirror
Pose of lawyer's lines smiling eroticism off
Dirty clothes dodgem squeal of refrigerator mother

Staring at the tear in her only
Photograph ripped from view hands hold the
Finger it licks buttons speech flies learning
Later assimilations into our truth and falsehoods

Wrapped in pillows telephones full of his
Scripted whispers he's masturbating at her ear
He sits on her gloves a scarecrow
Sperm-smiles from his unscheduled newsprint bits

Empty Diary 1951

but wraps her coat about her infertility:
curtains wiping the world clean: his white
fragile screen: clandestine courts where she testifies:
bolted microphones: wire chairs earwigging; bobbing along

in sprung rhythm in his verse drama:
mermaid swimming up a sewer his knife
between her rictal teeth: steam rising over
the machine she tends: the ink blast

in a nucleus: industrial arcade: names tattooed
on a deb's studio glow: her white
gloves hammer on his membranous silence: did
she or did she not visit his

Empty Diary 1952

Screaming thighs' roller-coaster flash, a slash
of light unskirts progress. A vaginal thumping
vents her fantastic song, until bricked up
in his metaphor. Her eyes shoot venom

at masculine hearts sewn on empty blouses.
The fresh sign CO-OPERATIVE falls short of
allegory, as she glides the aisles, picks
corallaceous cauliflowers for her poisonous sauce. *Eat!*

The Girl Can't Help It

1 Empty Diary 1953

Cantilevered bras cut us to size. The
richest chains grow out of colonial posters
of English couples 'spacing' healthy silhouettes against
the wheezing steel works plates of tigers

turning light. We're leaning against ripped faded
movie posters they're rolling up his vest.
He nods towards death the uniformed people's
precise delight. He was given complete to

ordinary mirrors of ordinary pleasures baby bonnets
votes for democracy posters pasting themselves onto
broken tanks.
        to prove they exist, they'll
whisper, 'We like you better in bits

2 Empty Diary 1954

We are statues of ourselves, stiffened eulogies
in the arthritic history of imperial endeavour
(the world of his syllabics: the words
we silently mouth: our faces networks of

electric lies: our lips would seal: our
eyes close on a world which will
drill its electrodes into our mermaid flesh
sketched in by the boss) Say it:

We lick the pellicle of your absence,
Nazi leather stitching your bulging zip (*stilyagi*
skinny kids shivering outside the wimbledon palais
filter sin through newsprint skin us alive

3 Empty Diary 1955

Office blocks imagine lift shafts for themselves
but offer slatted stairs. Neat masking tape

paths square the lawns. The plate glass
fades the girls from their adding machines

under a slice of you and your
approaching world: a crystal defect swimming its
buckled skin. His syllabics rattle your timely
heels: gooseflesh rises along your attempt at

ease
          (listen, that's *desilu* laughter canned in
history's back row)
                    You trip up slippery
steps to appointment you shake his confident
fist: smile at his unscheduled rubber horns.

4 Empty Diary 1956

(no pictures please we're history our confessions
flame at his lips: blank office block
smiles stiletto eyebrows: tank gun rotates over
mob touching its armour for luck hearts

torn out of daily re-animated flags: our
guts a vertical drop down the lift
shaft: dust caked the entire city: podium
imposters: panegyrics: helicopters circle dodging ancient rifles:

so much flesh flinches and hunches: sponges
for their own blood: two men sharing
cigarette kisses: flung as casually as empty
packets from trains (the Empire's oceanic sperm:

5 Empty Diary 1957

i wear street lamps bones under flesh
wired for dreams i raced the wind)
hunched over his typewriter, hammers on into
the narrative. The carbon copy can be

delivered direct to the camera: '*Stakhanovite woman,* /
In stone, in tears; pores of skin
bejewelled with dirt; / *Escape into the cavern*
of my fist
            telly-top ornaments broken

mermaid pony-tailed scooter rider hits the
wall) Smiles brush his armour as antique
mockery bursts into laughter, resistant. Fist clenched,
he hangs on barbed wire, a scarecrow

6 Empty Diary 1958

Objective conditions. Raw sunlight.
        An exposed nerve
Of economic collapse. Fresh
        anthems. He rushes
From the crowd, kicks
        windscreens. Strips of
Film. Herding terror. Protesting
        saints. The only

Woman beneath the banner.
        Frames flicker; sex
Scenes tell her how
        to breathe, lick

Her fat, precarious excerpt
     from an experiment.
Re-inscribing history, naked censors
     burn books; sparks

Catch their flesh. Aldermaston.
     Washboard; thimbles (*my
radical scepticism of*) Easter
     frocks. Traffic he's
Conjured for me stops
     for me. Is
Fear collective? Human limbs
     knot the crowd.

7 Empty Diary 1959

Kohl eyes from old poems: sore lips
silent almost mine: her gooseflesh refusals: mermaid
spine: his head shines like a statue's:
rubbing bumpers: native girls tiptoe for his

plush: microphones stretch toward his revolutionary murmur:
grey diffusion of his brilliance: rolled out
of old movies: '*Women lost their minds
here, the dark side of my moon*

Things She May Never Possess

Empty Diary 1960–1966

I

Open to the undated entry, speech flies
helpless through the air; promises of justice
through steamy portholes of wealth. Diffuse her;
kill her; walk her plank; she'll decode

each universal Man carrying a knife, carving
his imprecisely skilled pleasure into the guts
of the socialist. The death donor crackles
in Eichmann's whispering ear-piece. In the

dark market-places, virgins tout their milk
teeth, whose promise to each citizen spits
ivory from broken windows. No woman dares
lift her feet from the floor, tarred

II

differentially with similar brushes. Wings zip them
above children's Berlin Wall games. She's blocked,
kissing his sloganless portrait. His wheels kill;
his plastic dashboard burns touch. The wrong

uniform full of the right bullets *tut*
his teeth. She blushes her only pleasure,
her own protection: mascara, the smile; the
cold sore. Tears pearl her fang, sucking

out words, to feed from his hand.
He recomposes: 'Men in gloves do the
trick, tilt mirrors. Against the rules, his
kisses devour her whole, a melodic retribution,

III

on The Partisan's anthemed steps. Blank subjectivity
twists in the ballet of rifle fire
upon our map of flesh, littered with
broken subjects and legendary dangers; his piping

voices 'explain' how every girl pisses and
shits in miraculous, random symmetry, as she
stands his ground, grooving place in split
seconds. White men with Brando muscles jostle

the 'boy'. The proverbial barrel of the
gun whistles over corpses, history exploding in
windy declarations, 'I'm the arc in the
rainbow you cannot see, the old wives'

IV

tale dropping orgasm into labelled box files.
Mouth his witness exactly: weightless arrows had
fixed him before, maybe a friend, at
a night-club, fashionable target scrubbing allegiances,

an illegible rush of publicity. Each pickpocket
squeals, 'About those sexy bombs, each nymph
disporting blank faced. Decoding each shot, encircling
her body, taking it apart, she's her

own shuffling message, lenses steaming at
corpses dragged from steaming cars. Coca-Cola
winks out disaster in a stiffly infantile
sell off. The town's blood-soaked notes

V

have your demands printed on their lips,
stony sunlight diffused through biting lids. The
tarred statue and its subjects, brushed off,
jostle for glory, freezing light for phantom

limbs. Technocratic paranoids with jet age teeth
police the global ghetto, stuffing answers into
eye sockets. Tupperware smiles lid the sensible
eye; lipstick chatters, 'He fused her away.

He flattered her world. He grips her
throat. He's a fuck between friends, black
rimmed cocktail lashes, park bench iambics, boots
collapsing from cupboards. His uniform mutters prayers,

VI

godly smiles blessing a bundle of proven
charges unfusing into human shape. Injection scars
flesh the plastic doll's tits, and scratch
her weakest part, stripping off her career.

Teeth flare, victorious, theory freezing at his
closed premise, propositioning women at the police
line with drugged brass buttons. The sell
out! Cameramen take this off to trade

it. She finds herself as loose as
her falling skirt, dropped weightless onto film,
peach skin with a vein to sell;
collapsed argument. Women clutching dying children breast

VII

the bullet pocked oil slick. He's a
snowy print from any TV series, sniping
his home town, a name that has
no problem. Her shoulder strap slips; trade

is fucked. Hands shake votes for the
pleats, pasting the world itself over gulfs
of incomprehension. Raw nipples under the see
through. Trenches of flesh beneath the eyes.

1992

22 Empty Diaries 1967–1990

Empty Diary 1967

Utopian Tale II i

As I entered
her, I knew
that her chosen
posture would be
silhouetted against a
thousand bedsit walls;
a revolutionary posing
as sex goddess
well into the
twilight of such
idols; alone with
his voice between
the shelves of
Better Books ('I
am a Sadist!')
fixing it, *a*
transparent hero glued
to this vinyl
table top!
       before
she broke me
like a statue,
history sacked by
super heroines boiling
mundane flesh, leaving
not one drop

of fat for
the police to
scrape up: *Utopia!*

•

Empty Diary 1968

'For the man who
        has me...'
her eloquent slips black
        my discourse,
this second skin, or
        so she's
been told by her
        second mind.
My tattoo sweats her
        name. She
enters me on a
        useless giggle,
then squats at the
        master controls,
punching slogans into consciousnesses
        sweetened for
rotting the fangs of
        Capital. I
wrote her onto the
        pillow, a
hot boy pressing for
        a kiss,
his Anti-Universe, sunrise from
        her bathrobe;
Or: truncheoned jeers, diesel
        coughs, she's

manhandled into the gaping
    Black Maria.

    • •

Empty Diary 1969

daubed the kitchen door with blood)
Fair shares of the fair sex
(screaming) she haunts our sheltered view:
zipped slices, oily robotic sweat *(later*
his breath steams, my pistol smokes

Manson's acne, Beefheart pushes the hacks;
tough homilies from my domestic madonna.
Fair shares for the fair sex
(whispering) she haunts my sheltered view

'The key to passion is almost
money. We luxuriate in unisex affluence,
our heads rolling on flimsy film

Fair shares in the fair sex
(nodding) she haunts your sheltered view

    • • •

Empty Diary 1970

A   Little Orphan Amphetamine Meets the
    Flying Fucking 'A' Heads

I took his razor
   and scraped

a track across his
   hairy chest.
He'd performed, drug-erect,
   for a
month! I'd polished the
   glass table
for his squashed bags.
   'Wow, man,
what kind of fucked
   up trip
are *you* on? You
   can't choreograph
that prick ....
   ....

B   Not My Scene So I Cut It

A rustle of spiritual
   skirt brought
the corporeal closer, glitter
   bouncing from
a taxi into everyday
   life, desire
reconstructed from album covers,
   legs unwrapping
for delight, cooling to
   photogenic vinyl,
her shadow across windscreens,
   dependable, expendable.

         •

Empty Diary 1971

Everyday life walked
into the extraordinary
and broke loose
like a stallion
racing echoes around
the kitchen excessive
description fits my
face a criminal's
micromesh over mascara
floods the biological
socialist wrapped my
body gags slip
in my discourse
skin stings nostalgia
spearing my eye
she had silkscreened
200 posters messages
shed her pelt
leaflets gagged speechifying
steps corpse of
revolution under the
daubed statue her
women's tongues touching
taut with twisting
between oval mouths
BY HIS VOICE
co-opted to the
palace of wisdom

• •

Empty Diary 1972

Tanned to stone, his mind rolled
down her body; spermy milk in
the whorls of her thumb. Cool
as her exposures, mermaid homunculus, painted
nails dug into her easy answers.
The buckskin revolutionary fingers his vagina
books, false eyes fallen on his
speeches, the everyday facts of the
seaweed's spermy grist (the soft pads
of our fingers yet to appear
eyes burning into unironed cloth on
your backs) Memo to Masterful Men:

Your obstructions recomposed her unscheduled desires
(the shore blazed as we swam

• • •

Empty Diary 1973

A

After the armoured
cars have passed
market arabesque desires
happens to fragment —
to delay the
attack for one
pregnant second her
toes spread tremble
at touch fossilise
the ambergris' leonine

devouring
       history implodes
in each fragment
she's sweeping up
beneath her style

B

After the armoured
cars have passed
market arabesque desires
happens to fragment—
to delay the
attack for one
pregnant second her
toes spread tremble
at touch fossilise
the ambergris' leonine
devouring
       history implodes
in each fragment
she's sweeping up
beneath her style

•

Empty Diary 1974

Utopian Tale II ii

City's dead weight trenches the subject
down, beneath her sensible blouse. Eyeliner

Asserts squatters' rights on her gaze;
fear pins her up onto her

Stark mesh of blemishes. 'I'm lost
and I'm late—in equal proportions.'

She has the money in used
notes, her life in soiled narratives,

As his pristine story would tell.
The ladder of his enquiry leans

In a director's peep; her supposed
firecracker passions leave sex toys for

His subjectivity to play with. Says:
'The police cleaned up Utopia forever.'

• •

Empty Diary 1975

waiting for
herself as his feminine
hands float
on her back while
her husband's
dollies bend and stretch
status as
ornamental flab dropping to
the stone's
spermy delights rock crunching
hair weed
waits for him to
unpick her
her eyes are calm
and routine
he shoots himself on

                    stage dressing
                   like a man she
                     holds her
                cigarette like a woman
                  tentatively tweaking
                   the power they will
                     speak one
                day ashamed of being
                     her gag
                complaining of his voice
                   within hers
                none within his (yet

                        • • •

Empty Diaries 1976–1978

                                    The Hungry Years II

Piss Off Creep; You Got Problems)
hand stretching up for this book
I pull; its wisdom fiduciary, dependent)
alone with the darkened story slowly
pausing) Go Fuck Yourself) cannot presume
anything progressive, his lyricism collapses into
personal issue) who orchestrates her identity
with transvestite precision, plastic nipple training
silk) 'was only half the story

can imagine it too well (lisping
a balance for his slipped authorial
hand (hair in the sea breeze
his mermaid refuses identity holds him
back (you've heard it all now,

                        •

dollies' chatter:
diamonds of smashed TVs
lie about
her feet, only half
the story:
fleshed trance leaning against
her mirror
twin cups spilling from
her claws:
glittering conspiracy sweat glistens
pearly erections
the lines of power
breezing hair
alive with invitation eyes
incessantly displaces
herself doesn't know exactly
where she
is heading speeding punkette:
he can
curl her toes by
breathing in
secondary lift: peppered references
to further
identity against whatever is
....
her body a slip
....
(I put her there

• •

: I can feel
the pain she
inflicts upon her
smile, undraped commodity

pushing hard for
me. Her hand
brushes her legs
apart, razor kisses.
In the mirror:
her single story,
a rag doll
spitting blood. Bruised
peel in the
market's gutter, memories
reduced to packaged
image, projected through
the capering dust
motes of my
lust. I'm reduced
to cat licks,
can't sell me
back to her,
cooling her fleshed
investment beneath mirrored
ceilings: calling cards
from next week,
stuffed diaries for
the coming years.

• • •

Twelve: Thousand 2

Empty Diary 1979

for Cindy Sherman

No pin of narrative picks the skin
He's controlled his fantasy
   (he says NOTHING,

This is not advertising but its opposite
      he skins adjectives in
      his memory shell
watching he wills flesh
      assertively NEVER ALONE
She does not represent or allude to
white gloved sisters chanting profit and cellulite
   alone with her vagina
      pinned in words
you're never alone with: provides an empty
      diary for her audience
      THIS IS NOT
what leaves you wanting
      this incomplete assertion
'She's an appointment that'll not be missed'

    •

Empty Diary 1980

then dives backwards, into her pool of
memory. Sex has been and gone, frosted
the world's body; panoptic gods flooding us

with cheap goods ....
.... with therapeutic vents,
vacant assaults on being, soft-tinting the

mind with favoured distortions, *whose* degradable fantasies
pinned in words that leave you watching
a blue thought on a blue screen?

Whenever he speaks whatever he says all
labia clam shut ('you've seen them all?

Black clocks future her veiled anthracite eyes

• •

Empty Diary 1981

Her gagged idea on my feathery chain,
she wears her servitude as an emblem
of ordinary design. She scrapes a world
to abstract desire. *Her* shadows are *my*
shadows, never alone to haunt a sheltered
view; she could ape my story if
hysteria could be tied to human motive,
like vaginal sex, and exposed in sleep
to barbed eyes sparked with electric lusts.
Her hands turn flightless feathers whenever she
tries to touch me. I hover, beating
darkness, out of rage, out of range.

• • •

Empty Diary 1982
I Tiresias, You Jane

for Peter Middleton

'At the bed's
edge she mirrors
her clitoris, *her*
fuse; the eulogy
to translucent flesh
inscribes desire on

'her menstrual bloat'.
She's waiting for
a powdery man
who won't faint
at the sight
of her blood'
(HER NAPALM HAIRDOS

'Beyond the mirror
he tries not
to watch, to
sniff out kindness,
to find the
lexis that leaves
no flattering lick
across my belly.'

'His body wasn't
built to be
looked at,' I
think, 'terror's statue
unveiled in private.'
His umbrella drips
in the corner.

• • • •

Empty Diary 1983

high heels crotchless purring 'would you?' (unechoed
in the devices: what I say I
see I think I see I glide
where once I would have tottered across
the tinsel Photostat of 'desire' purring distantly

wondering how a structural linguistician would describe
the tense I'd used to 'embody' *his*
fantasy: 'Wrapped in each other's grainy skin,
they despair, tiger breath steaming. She hears
herself, 'Would you be wanting to . . . ?' distantly
an echo of celibacy's wanting to (would
he razor eyes' fur from granite flesh

•

Empty Diary 1984

The Hunk's thrown
her; justice, jealousy,
puts us on
his side. They
hide their faces
in the collective
absorptions, the latest
cure for the
antique ailments, balanced
between gaze and
guilt, curled infantile
detail. She is
smiling as she
brings herself *off*
or *out* or
whatever preposition she
comes with; he
rubs the knowledge
she gives: slippery
silk wiped on
his face. He's
a millennial shit

heap; she escapes
his set, to
no coordinates. She
needs no man
to complete (they
call this freedom

• •

Empty Diary 1985
Social Graces and Sexual Favours

There is no such
        thing as a
free lunch, and this
        is it; she's
the life of a
        billboard, a fortnight,
operating its single verb.
        Her sugar daddy's
thin leg is trapped
        between her thighs;
his sweat breaks into
        song: '*Your own
assertive thumb's on your
        button.*' She says:
Why don't you ever
        have a different
dream; mine? She's vital
        in a narrative
she tells herself, he
        says. *Profuse Shooters*

Especially Welcome. Guiding his
     grandfatherly defeated flesh:
This Sperm Bank Seeks
    A Safe Deposit.

   • • •

Empty Diary 1986

Looking North 3

So long imprisoned in his tower,
he'd thought himself his own damsel.

He shot her clean and wet
in purchasable images: a kitchen unit

Pulled out of womanly wreckage (while
her vibrator hummed his several names).

Behind urinous windows of edited highlights,
his silver-dirty hole in reality,

She'd stripped for action; his profuse
ejaculate webbed her fingers. She almost

Thought that she *was* him pissing
from the fire escape so *she*

Could admire the generous silken jet—
spilling sky onto the day's tarnish.

   • • • •

Empty Diary 1987

im Félix Guattari

IM 3

Empowered image Baudrillard
framed by one
new Duchamp urinal
per second dolly-
oracular heroes hammering
MASS-MEDIATING CHAOSMOS
she's 'voice' trickling
her absence subverting
the flow of
dominant redundancies paste
book sticky life
worlds vending mermaid
flesh art-thick
fresh referents sing
for lyric shifts
in subjectivity spilling
sky (the hour
glass gravity of
articulate slaves: *she's*
beautiful on the
executive bed, existential
territory. *He's* cut
to the balls
at the kitchen
sink, subjective autonomist,
fucks alone within
you, tasteless sucker
of silicone flesh

•

Empty Diary 1988

I

'He's a nice bloke!' NOT in
my books he's not (Her world
in his iambic limping, her compliant
affluent fuck, late afternoon silky licks

II

she crouches dirty
blankets from skips
huddles against the
warm plastic of
the photo booth

the specimen shots
on her side
of your postcode

III

She is news and commentary narrowcast
to the year in which she

thought she lived only to find
it turned history. EAT THE RICH

dropped out of her soundbite black
fists unclenching as she walked free

• •

Empty Diary 1989

SPEAK ECHOING VOICE:
sudden polyphony in
a lucid disruption
alone with a
FIST FUCKER FIXED
IN HER MEAT
he cured with
a politician's touch
thoughts full of
the homeless (*his*
home full of
Bibles) We fuck
shadows to art,
hammer symbols to
death; life's cut
a deal I'll
win, or lose,
after checking for
small scale social
infections (*SWASTIKA WAXWORKS*
melting at the
Latest Judgement our
breath shakes with
complaint strangled by
spewed videotape *ACTUALITY*
presents a Bible
forced under a
tramp's sleeping head

• • •

Empty Diary 1990, 2

For Adrian Clarke 1

HUMAN DUST against the
dark night *This Degrades*
now bleached into the
ecstasy of image *she*
holds a Bible filofax
steroid flare hoboes her
puppets blondes in the
sex shop coo into
vacant dummy leather militia
turned fan club *she*
wears his eyes tightly
fixed on sidewalk scripture
WHITE PUSSY EASY MEAT
cocksucker choirs shit peckers
praise her 'legendary guts'
her TV astrologer's tattooed
fists so hard to
make a man weak
in this *APOCALYPTIC CUT*
mannikin's wig trails the
gutter (slave gang's fetish

· · · ·

1992

19 Empty Diary 1990, 1

Coda 2

Human Dust 2

Internal Exile II

Past empty rooms full of men, the
street's alsatian ears pricking up, she searches
for evidence of kindness, but finds annotations
blowing her apart into whatever use her
senses and limbs can make of them.
The smiling professions ease her into loss,
with embalmers' soft assurances, each migratory text
striving to be total. Her lips, pursed,
mouth a public language to parade in.
An alien resident of delirium, adrift in
dialogue, the arguments small but binding, she
lives in voices that aren't hers: *Anything
else?* (Capital's plea.) Pit bulls sniff their
masters' tattoos, as rusted muscles melt in
percussive light. She recalls late capitalism, its
vascular delights. Dogs bark liminal threats to
its exchanges; bland ugliness, it's never enough.
Her voice, stuck in the ventriloquist's gullet,
uses what she finds, takes what she
can use: 'There're too many eyes here,
running on empty, too many faces whipping
posts of prohibition. These people too easily
file somebody else's history, their own shadows
jumping out across windscreens to greet them

1992

~

25
Flesh Mates on Dirty Errands

Empty Diary 1993
Fucking Time 3

Her garters hook his
bullseye adorned for exposures
less human than her
latex condom mouth a
porn starlet with a
strap-on sexing her
second skin bruised with
verbs that frig their
nouns *(his anus flinches*
at my invasive breath

Gender collusion, uneasy meat

OCTOBER 1993

26

Living Daylights (. . . traversed by swift nudes . . .)

for Rupert Loydell
Swift Nudes 2

1 From the Stolen Book

Daylight Robbery 2
Remode 1

No captions. No inflections
Andrew Duncan

Whitewashed thought flashing articulations those
transparencies
in the daylight skating
on
nobody's dream dodges
into synaesthesia on a
frozen world I
speak
rest my thoughts
too brilliant to bear
contemporary blocks. 'Buy me, my batch
of
old memories, my all nighters

Line streets with shadows which
enter
bedrooms nod into family
scenes
where you can't
afford to gather plausible voice
spilling book swimming
dabs
of man puffs—
caption promo flashes sharp

point recognitions (the face is nobody's
salvage
it) copy translated pulse vision

Creaking shadows others stopped crystalline
loop
phenomena keeping sane eyes
false
steps and they're
at you melody follows
into your thoughts
allegorical
women from costumes
vanish in this presentation
of your life nothing remains except
your
name looking fresh in remodes

Free eyes slide past slipstreaming
drones
responsibility a secret fresco
frozen
bead of sweat
as you discover you're
loathing all dry-
nibbed
blocks of lost
time it's been filmed
and novelised a thousand different ways
say
The other's hinge is loose

Shadows with people sometimes I
wish

I was back in
the
world where movies
were bodies full of
words: Small invasions
ungainly
steps in the
night high crusts of
victory scabs against a star-pricked
bolt:
In the furnace: Phonemes filtered

Tricks trope me) I the
less
refused to answer somebody
else's
voiced phantasy promotion
strap my stripped prickles
were swallowed into
phone-
ins a violated
hiss cut off at
the point of bolts threading the
same
words round each critical block

A cheap chorus of refugee
objects
chanting already dead my
hair
falling forward for
the false steps and
they're at you
No

price tag just
a premonition the straight
proof will be read on my
body
by the lover, doctor, mortician

You cannot elope with yourself
cannot
retreat world (retreat face)
broadcast
secrets but dissemble
in a stolen book
between the capital
letters
and the sparkle
drench explosion still sheens
tomorrow (a spray of bargain basement
postmodernism
brackets off the strange bar

Vowels in tears under mugger
sprays
initial missile shimmering symbol
wire
its lurid splash
on paper lips the
pen. Phonemed ghettoes,
speculative
blanks, 'Meet me
by the floral clock
and I will try to explain—
watch
my eyes become your disgrace

Plausible voice that enemies took
too
literally stepped back explosions
wrenched
him from the
carpet context-hatred spills
onto world shimmering
with
things to soap
your authority smoothed over
the cracks by denying his fresh
bit
of fluff on the scene

Long shadows allegorical on the
sand
expressive gestures stolen from
news
oil it lifts
and real tears stream
down artifice spilling
beans
women glitter, men
glow, shadows catching daylight
falling from windows crowding the air
with
its zero shine disguises, swinging

Paddle the not where belief
is
anything that is said
an
image successful shoots
first but answers few
questions police siren

whips
through a dream
betrayal mirrors drowning necessity,
oceans of breakables diving into simile
(thrilling
in the most obvious reversal

Logopoeia world in a stolen
book
its nodes glisten identity
which
is speech wind
which is voice image
which street flaked
out
puking guts audible
pool of blood above
the visible morality of the low
life—
invisible from the helicopter's mirage

NOVEMBER 1987-APRIL 1988; REMODED FEBRUARY 1994

2 Working the Golden Book Number Two: retitled for Patricia Farrell

For Patricia Farrell 3

Remode 2

Ever to produce *the* suspicion
would put
gasps into
moist
creases; consciousness or gullies of

passion devices swallowed 'myself'. The
veined hand on the eye-
brow pilgrimage will shiver
back arched need
directors
who drop symmetry,
mime a leather prayer

The ornamental ego scales the
roofs. Crumble
him to
misery
rollers, drawing his eyes full
of your impossible hoods. Crumpled
photo-knife moments licked such
stiletto scenes, making sense.
Charm the chain—
he'll
own his disarray
in a languaged glow

Only a highway of moisture
the stylised
metaphor literally
weapon.
This world excuses his desert
of a body, a warm
world but a worn world
decaying museum piece destroy
what you find
display
kick-brush newsprint
across the light technique

Working the golden book made
of the
crowd a
desire
for a moving picture but
settles the stiff fabric question,
an arrow up the back
of your legs strikes
up the anthem;
tongue,
edged only with
light, twists the eye

APRIL 1988; REMODED 8 MARCH 1994

3 Empty Diary 1941, Number Two

Remode 3

Voices Under Occupation 3

clarity : permanent noon : never
to have experienced the
disgrace of living cold
in your paradise : never

their gaze nor mine :
serviced them : my finger burning
to massacre their
portraits across the page :

thin circumscribed
hatred under its surface : they
eye my controls : my

pride to recreate that
gaze to private phantasy
statues to their arrival

the world shifts from
one foot to the
other : necessary dream arousing
eternal expansion : dry display

exchange lips and buy
a telephone : my message hardly
gets through last
portraits across the page

he licks
limp sheets : ration trains : arrow
flags : a shaft of

sunlight on the dummy
torso : radio towers humming
a language, uselessly low

as I lay naked
in bed shot from
screen with finger and
feather a second item

is priced the delicate
aesthetic of the ankle strap
jumped in a
smart uniform I mastered

blind limbs
upon the official dead hand
in this small melodic

subversion harsh boots stamp
to driving rhythms that
ragged beauty stepped from

I look at the
text : bottles the eye :
I see words as
a matter of survival :

unitary thoughts telescope : but
lying in wait for officers
it felt natural
to be watched through

binoculars : swish
of skirts : any noun fits
their ultimate definition : marketing

flags : script wrapped round
the building : black rags :
civilian horrors her eyes

his tight leather truth :
women touch its sheen :
the same selling kicks
a spasm of petrol

and he's changed : travels
the movie : swooning forms listen
to seduction out
on the wireless street :

your arm
a ferrode rod : as distinct
as my thin eyebrows

as crystal as my
voice : master folds in
the delicate rag creases

NOVEMBER–DECEMBER 1988; REMODED 8 MARCH 1994

27

Magdalene in the Wilderness

im Angela Carter
Empty Diary 1994
IM 4
To My Students 2

Weightless girl with bandaged wrists unthreads wolf
pelts from barbed wire posing for recessive
eyes which pose for themselves self-mutilating
innocents, nose studs bolted through freckled skin

Blusher dusts up her smile earrings shake
with next season's affront (a peeping tom
of his own shivers shakes his plumy
tail before her otherly army-surplus frame

Her robotic bleach-babes walk Capital's tightropes
sale victims dreading the hair perfectly transvestite
mix 'n' matching their grammars of perception
for the first fairy-tale after menarche

26 MARCH 1994

28

The Book of British Soil

Duocatalysis 14
For Jo Blowers 2
Killing Boxes 5
Unwritings 5

A suburb an airport a park, named after him; a refusal to mean this world. Beautiful tracer fire, the bosses sweating. Shadows of unbroken factories, streets called *Alma* or *Trafalgar*

Two holes enface her disguise. He planted a kiss in the gulf between her shoulder blades. He initialled her corpse, a statue to the Iron Terrorist

The colony at the heart of the empire gets the news before the news: immobilised eyes stuck in skulls, ragged wounds to be filled; bathing in self-evidence, a sigh of immense national relief

Dad's big fist flooring Mum; she could be gouged from his forearms, burnt blue

There are no live casualties, soft-cruising over disused units

Look sexy for your sexy obituary. All the slips make the enemies friends, smudges of boot polish on the pillow

Each breath searches for its feeling. A rhythm of blows and kisses, she licks his thinking wound. He watches her sternly, selecting her skins from the shiny rails. Make up, making it up, with pencil and mirror, sweat erupting skin

Nerve agents work in a second. She kneels like a juddering protest whipped by rainbows. A nebula of blood cells behind her cloudy skin. His eyes, inland seas on a map of nowhere

A delicate hand waves farewell in the pane beneath the Union Jack. Recording tape hanging from the branches, the pop stars are re-building our sneers. Explanations airlift the empty hand of hand-shakes

Legible fear. STAB HALF BREEDS faded on the kerbstone

Tell this to the crying pilots: there are hulks of desertedness. At the stroke of nine, you reach the phone and the humming begins: Petrol is censored: Whitehall sealed off, eerie with snow

APRIL 1994

30 31 33
The Lores

30 The Lores
and Jungle Nights in Pimlico

PART ONE

BOOK 1: TIME CAPSULE

The time capsule's
contract with the
future, the Eugenics'
Court with its
injections, co-ops us
to a selective
history: as soon
as the population
is trafficking clatters
the shutters down
the laws of
motion beyond its
jurisdiction, unceased husks
in lightning streaks

Flicks to see
who flinches empty
me from your
circumference, accommodations of
space an abacus
for millions who
stand beside us
pure result with
no contest empty
microphones and dead

amplifiers inside each
rule if she
moves any slower
she's our commodity

Untitled epics re-tell
the saga in
technicolor prose, translation
of the corporeal
substance into utopian
glitter where the
public stands and
the people rush
by eyes like
drains (*the plenitude*
I generate, broadcasts
never made) at
each street corner
gather unregenerate genes

Sequencing witness the
world is his
phenomenology of caprice
lets the barbarians
through the breach
family values juiced
on marble his
deliberate misreading of
the signs to
reach the other
side of them
courts opacity's bride—
the hiss of
consciousness accompanies each

Not his penis
as a message,
deeply, which she
must groan, splits
down the phone
a surplus night
of cocktail eyes
for the skin
is where war
is experienced. He
plays veins under
folded sheets   government
building   towers of
voice   incorporated ethics

She's been crying
as she voted
buying in hyperrealities
saline fear dripped
in her jumpy
heart passing an
Elder hanging from
a lamp post
this past week
Our particularity is
our universality (I
shall not dig
into the weak
loam of conscience;

the issue is
that we acted
without reflection, without
remorse, scripted from

the outside, black
posters limpet to
the face of
substance eyes which
could stare through
bars at the
Tomb of the
Unknown Dictator) iced
lust after our
video tape snags

The electrolysis of
Reason gold that
gathers a glint
a light seed
too brilliant to
penetrate from the
Brutal Streets to
The Forest Way
wasted promised land
the cut telegraph
in univocal complicity
an oscillation of
the *geist*, dimmer
switches on passion

Under the portcullis,
departmental seal, minister's
strategic re-invention a
constantly repeated assertion
in my life
the usual call
signs that announce
the world's messages

back-announce interventions
incidentally sliding into
incidents, notes found
on cyanide corpses
the grand narratives
in encapsulated form

To find the
broken melodies of
a world humming
to him alone,
wordless traffic burns
viral headlines tremble
in his lap
questions bolted through
skin balanced on
a beam they'll
be kicked from,
noosed (Unceased, in
another book, just
guns already smoking

BOOK 2: BOLT HOLES

They are bleeding this
country, secret Whitechapel gutter
rites. Bolshevik bolt holes

Terrors traversed autumnal ethics.
Our fresh Lordship negated
introspection over sherry decanters

Bronchial children cough, three
to a bed; crystal
voices from its frame

Protocols kicked, shattered Yiddish
on jagged glass. Mongols.
Tomorrow, our promised land

Marching between tramlines, tight-
necked blackshirts claw the
air. Lightning bolt salutes

Solutions, hands raised, stopping
stones. Your face, a
jewel, crowd-fleshed; crowned

You kiss my scars,
our struggle. Emotion retreats.
Anarchs copulate with Queens

Bolshevik jazz, jungle nights
in Pimlico. Jerusalem in
England's green and pleasant

Old Gang rich bitches
stoke the engine for
the Empire's last Plantation

Her blackshirt bit of
rough, I serve. Dismissed,
savage dynamo, corporate individual

Wife hanged like a
ghetto Jew—obsessive simile
knots her suicide note:

'Chasing skirt for the
Party . . . Suffragettes licked your
stamps . . . Man and master!'

Worthing) the stab of
the crowd one slice
of zeitgeist (*broken windows*

Uniform mind fills Olympia.
Regulated hearts, public health.
Public Order, embodied ideals

Venerable cigarette card image:
Mosley's staff car; razored
Red along running boards

Saluting crowd, prickles on
a pelt, policies brushed
to the Centre, *Leaderfear*. . . .

The limp swastika; Rundfunkhaus.
Schnapps and bitch sensuality:
'Southern England in flames

The World-Soul clears
his throat; his plans.
The poetics of propaganda

Bent wire slipped back
into pocket: Jew bent,
bleeds over yellow Star

Brutish airman, parachute caught
in charred Berlin tree;
the people almost decide

Last drunken broadcast: 'Final
phase of European history . . . .
What you *must* become

Shot her—and our
curled child. My manly
bullets, one fact unswallowed

The Büro's leather chair,
my dead microphones, lovers
wired in delirious parallel

How quickly the airship
slipped—band still playing—
firestorm roared through Ambrose

With horror I realise
these prison uniforms have
come from the camps

To speak; by way
of silence. Eloquent statuary.
Race suicide; condemned Men

Gives the fascist salute;
a blood-stain on
the cleared gymnasium's floor

As Joyce drops, his
street-fighter's scars burst;
clocks stop, valves plume

heart stops) The broken
promise to follow your
pregnant decoy (sentence begins:

I search my mask
for a face to
redeem me) Collective guilt

Passion and hatred flicked
your curls. Memory's bones,
your scattered clothes; disposal

My slogans—for history
books and marble plinths?
Eyes tethered on stalks

Leaves drip, leave no
measure. Hermetic hut, camouflaged
with endless autumn leaves

Stench of burnt coil
from overheated wireless. Cell
fills with burning bodies

Posthistorical thunderclap, limp lightning.
Administration without Men, time
drifts, creaks. Self-shipwreck

BOOK 3

Counterpoint 80s speculation against the
clamping gape takes us whole
through collisions of semantic torques
twists on the page saddle

us to a fiery buck
assertively thrusting those isolate recognitions
(against the credit's opening testimony)

They artificialise the public discussion
of our care-history subject
matter matters banging a jot
calculations shed household debt texts
recant the radical journalist's daily
record of his angelic working
out (stag night pollutions elsewhere

Edit each sovereign distinction as
radios whisper her nourishing pronouncements:
music for the subjected subject
as structure plays its ethical
catharsis a neutral blind spot
exclusive laws scan alien lines—
our boys are her votes

A will to categorical evasiveness
watches her snap her icy
sensations to belt straps like
an engineer performing for drills
his best ideas are dreams
well-rehearsed routines of winter
corrosively boring freeze their sonnets

Who was that persona? the
sudden shock of her twin
shadow cast by shelled clients
in crepuscular amours, cracked men
in corners for parasites in
pin-stripes demanding in full-

lipped passion: *Who are we?*

Flesh he imagines skims with
skill holds victory fusion
like memories frisking a policeman
one's past is filled with
trafficking worlds in the split—
eyes speak before the cameras
blink at anyone's scintillating universal

Better to link than to lay
carpets of cartoon Commies whose
sacks are blamed for shortages—
habits of a moment tilt
chiselled oval portraits whisper bleak
keyholes on undisturbed acrobatics to
raise ecstasy's deep trembling dust

Bunker salutes between what was
and what could be coal
dust on door frames mime
the state's gutted investment rust
subversive as his notebook drives—
neither flesh nor spirit can
unwrite the national culture twice

Coming Down from St George's Hill II

Brass hammers to keep his
iron laws frozen slamming doors
to demean this world floods
terror he shakes his thoughts
numbed and numbered with links
genocide up private roads enclose
his furious skip line notations

If the devil were to
whisper in a hollow house
casting his net what politics
he'd find in ecological guilt
as capital's baited hooks tangle—
echo a catchy soundtrack for
ever the daily jeering buck

Motor yacht blondes block consciousness:
they change *permanently* the thick
slow melting of their bodies'
monuments announce the arrival of
the 90s men landing on
the Earth its permissions signal
rubber gristle in each mouth

The Millennium Enterprise Zone layers
on layers of torn calendars that
wipe Thatcher's solid dream trappings
below any diction a satirist
with no worship centre his
ears adjust to a future
of persistent sensations, lacking himself

BOOK 4

Thirty 1

Featherweight she floats unrevised leisure time
fiercely clocked involutions of not-quites
pitches her tent when digital twitches
knuckle down her stomach sleepy balance-
conditions that web orgasmics, blink admonishment

Activates his tongue hammers the desk
rubs himself shakes rhythm the wrong
time in expectation of iron sensation
scrapes trails pussyfooting through built environments
implodes as points, lasts a second

Between her legs oval birth slips
into biography metered meat shakes assets
self-possession baited through her slit—
tattoos wind out the distant tickets
chime the stream slipping through loathing

Briefs stretched churning coins in pocket
he pumps his eulogistic glitter as
dead skin falls from epiphanic forgetting
trousers flap inside out ergometrically neutral—
you're complicit as imagination, libidinous hound

Investing in people damaged history a
diversation to link to sketch to
match perception her services surrendered she
listens to Braxton, reads Adorno, judges
the moment; the familiar breaks anew

Howling for ID gooseflesh across her
back as data offers her Yes
flirtation with responsibility links with negotiation
a seduction to share culturally his
pleasure, she cannot submit cannot resist

Unlinkable puns trip reluctant guardians turned
inside out lores of their loving—
a ragtag glimpse of bed-fellows
wings her down to the speed
of the street and the state

Beings in motion peck in farmyard
flicker along the train's body positioned
forever behind his chains at work
editing in the persona, as our
Führer thinkalikes count time from Auschwitz

To make links of contractual obligation
ethically with her name walking puns
off maps which absolutely refuse linkage—
no sin intervention bless'd in external
lores, virtual times Are a Terror

No porno now no swastikas she's
gloriously out unable to integrate into
his timetable colonises his disasters, her
sneering 'revolution' aggressive, cosy, blanks a
non-exchangeable gift of his fugal lores

Weaponly Language silhouettes her words, hewn
from a lifetime defeats him repeatedly
builds time a spider-fingered kiss
until the end of non-oppressive duration
stare into each other's parasitic eyes

Sucks his tongue ritornellised news flashes
catalysing his moments' little Spanish vibrations
the theft in delivery (never the
card-carrying member of his data
bank gathers her nuts for winter

Self-appointed governors push through disaster
swifter than passion looking at cunt
his exteriority fills the nourishing noun
fantasy fades on her dripping face—
loose-leaf manuals collapse a mansion

Ain't nobody with identified cut off
dizzy with guilt emotion lives splintered
no longer human closes her legs—
feeling is a shivering coherent mirror
a solid fragment dispersed in wholeness

BOOK 5

I

massaging agents

that could wipe even an unloaded gun
going off crushed refuseniks sequence fictive Romanovs

back in the Kremlin spray their masculinist
works the distance-burst they then moan

positioned forever before the daily obsession this
subjective autonomy in a bleak Moscow suburb

dystopian sonnets alive to split pun linkage
lens skirts the laws grabs his balls

creeping sermons street negotiations falsely ditch his
little utopias meat metamorphosis from her cut

dispositions embodied in each liquid gesture it's
frenetic stinging in our judgement it's unlinkable

enjoined to piss tight through photogenic stiffies
dump new worlds in our swirling cement

for Mike Johnson

full sails

eeled my nets to catch links next
time unclouded inferno's surplus bile buoyed up
the management's weekend smut stained with outcries
styled a secretion to cascade contracts down

its pockets opened like ears and spoke
verbal agreements of the *trust me* kind
banging our heads against air our lips
enjoined to seal resistance link without chains

this is history if you'd leave alone
an eye's ability to catch a worm
hope for a mask that sheds illusion
to redeem me you haunt the fills

my screaming thong markets a single coming
and thrills eyes like drains licks spills

III

Jungle Nights in Pimlico 2

blind Russia

sexy as a strike the ghost of
a chance speechless slits brick-dust beard
prayer-tongues shrouded in parachute flesh traitor
purs of mortality taming strangers in paradise

existing groups an anarchist grasps a home
made bomb disorder dead dogs bloomers drop
lady finger-breakers kiss and blast defend
the words of the Empire's last philosopher

his theory's mobile but can't be lodged
within swift traversals of rations streams blind
across interference old words in new flames

contexts put out circumstantial facts tears himself
from the radio and its crackling (*Mosley*
claws his throat his neural blind spot

IV

free market
a vast nervous system which is virtually
hypothetical families mapping values and virtues mutual
parasitism heads secretly shaded for Wagnerian endings

a sign tenses against the wind pulls
shift propaganda never enough to let doors
slam and agreement of fixed terms drift
Turquoise Gardens to lay out my melody

in Capital's cacophonous beds monuments to disruption
traffic sensations tiny anthems which propel wickedness
to bargain affects through vaporous service an
underclass will confer percepts for disease pickets

arranging arguments into anecdote for mutual agreement
intimidates the brutal weight of each moment

your love sold with its unlawful contents

v

he asks
prepositioned in
newsreality feeds
the lines
custom and
practice shift
rules of
a crowd
the lores
virtuactivists break

BOOK 6

for Heywood Hadfield
Time Capsule 2
Torn Elegy 2

now negation corpses
from your mouth
the future of
Europe washed in
waves of flesh
the smallest radio
station negotiates your
ecstasy, purple barricades
for love televisualise
whose news thighs
and circuits hang
gleaming history as
you taste the
city as dust

loyal to invaders
sporadic shopping rotting
guns in bandages
eyed with contempt
TV wipes chartered
streets citizen figures
against mirrored ground
sized up scaled
down you lift
with loathing the
receiver to non-cooperative
extremists whose fish
speaks in waves
crested with crimson

the time capsule's
funereal windsock predictions
straps vanish like
a contract turns
fucked enough to
scratch *our* selves
in *our* time
licks every inch
down the pelt
to hyperbole's bulbs
pulling aside the
manmade pink the
airless gulf admits
flashes from hell

murder hangs nervous
talk wings ripped
from the sky

as police bleed
hair from engines
at your feet
whisper-fountains giddy
with theft or
gifts mouthfuls of
stones he wades
in anger or
love or fear
as he crashes
into her bones

Charred spewed innards.
Charcoaled frozen ground.
Pound oval tables:
talk about talk
long stories fresh
graves cannot speak
men in chicken
coops thank Allah
for Russian stupidity
and machine guns
clatter to hell
EITHER WE WIN
OR WE WIN
scud to heaven

carried to river
orgasm ripples across
returns of fear
flipped between shoulder
blades three times
demands for freedom
echo the city

NO TRUNCHEON ZONE
gleaming tail they
key her up
and throw away
the door; they
lick her tune
her into herself

quickie-panting on
screen as a
perfectly framed message
a facsimile of
lives for repressive
jurisdiction where off
duty erections pull
for love or
death border guards
let him off
the broken graffiti
doesn't recognise him
watches her incipient
national identity, crossing

tears lash the
lips of America
lick your learned
night-flight of
starlit history slip
rubbish carts back
from the virtual
to drivers later
shot; children rush
to stop tanks
blind across traffic

actual actions criminalised,
crushed (*gently manage*
their political prisons

carry the talking
fish to its
river flip an
egg three times
and speak finger
strips on your
flesh: **Flood, Famine**
ahead tipped for
action (you remember
Andropov? *followed by*
Revival while you
predict, endorse, a
lifetime's struggle for
each 'next' generation

tremble stimulation on
your shoes pose
in the city
suddenly eyes look
at nothing to
say the luminous
space where pure
joy turns onto
an eye desirously
nice and happy
on the TV
gang raped between
stations you cannot
forget her lips

PART TWO

BOOK 7: LORES AND BYE-LORES

further information dumps
it your organisation
is a lesson
in peep holes
owning the blackened
world the empire's
last plantation lament
midstreet meat he
pulls wipes her
impossible simultaneous acts
crosses this page
like an anecdote
now crossing the
road in complexity

prejudice among common
benches lives hot
in your decision
now trigger words
stretch three hooks
across her back
popper frisson plays
passions we lose
pours subjectivity into
bodies smouldering connections
seduced not open
to discussion a
strap revealed to
pin him up

dewy-eyed sentimentalists
want a cut
of the ranting
shifts the rôles
want strict negotiations
to invite the
other man onto
seat of Authority
blocked phallic conduit
caught entering cuts
wither meanings tell
us we're persons
singular masks to
petition honey flesh

each human trait
as though the
plot were an
interfering spectre from
another voice behind
versions for optimal
planes, legs curl
in permissive formation
revolutions levelled to
a horizontal kiss
already autonomy spews
improbable ethos a
level spirit erupts
citizens from themselves

netting joy I
become my feral
viscosity lift his
token with a
frankness inwardly reshaped
he watches imitates
cat-scratching stirs
pleasure into my
body's stiff memory
fixes the blood
mutual disjunction values
each cleansing drop
gooseflesh shadows the
passion-spent gift:

neck covered with
blood he's learning
where division is
not betrayal but
opens a final
pleasure weeps traffic
spills menses he
leaves it on
my smile he
touches astonished space
ethically balanced on
my quartered womanhood
we're freezing time
tangled in exchange)

sneering eyes and
90s enabling routes
narrow the escape
valves weekend sonnets
12 lines of
raw utopics streak
into his hatched
thoughts laws spend
the millennial heels
the pay cut's
stripe across his
back hangs from
her strip his
slip of refusal

Torn Elegy 1

SMILES TAUGHT THAT
THEY OWNED THE
WORLD FLINCH ARMED
WITH SENSATIONS BONDED
WITH SLOGANS SHE
BECOMES EACH CHILL
ERASURE STRIKES PITY
OUT THE STRUGGLE
TO CRUSH FASCISM
IN SPITE OF
GOVERNMENT BLACK FLAGS
BLUE SHIRTS HOODED
FIGHTING COCKS NOT
AFRAID OF RUINS

her spine smiles
spiked invitations screws
purling turnstile belongs
to the people
scarce gutters of
trawl such gloss
ennobles *whose* vocabulary
a snarling street
stylist's rebel rag
delegates revolve deep
illusionists fall as
black neon disasters
in deep-throated
anthems to freedom

(Counterpoint everything your
breath pitches everything
against repressive time
tumble across chords
you're a habit
locate joy on
a moment's point:
dense ecstasies shift
weight; linking toccatas
floor your feet
shadowed on the
surface above—to
name to refute:
stumbling floodlit flight

Book 8

I

Twenty 2

chained analogy
aflame with
loric grace
enters a
crowd flooded
with shape

whose artifactual
manipulations of
which street
fighting law?

II

drowning years

I needed no interpreter spoke the same
language the complex romance of international trade

I liked living over the shop good
wishes from people who are suffering free

to pursue their own dreams arguments always
give one appetite true vice second thoughts

not everybody cheers the same thing I

was glued to the radio for news

we were not fatally wounded but a
totalitarian state with siege barriers of coal

I prayed fitfully revolution still to be
made our problem was presentation red roses

proved photogenic families were the government nemesis
of gain (*one country   one system   ours*

III

For Robert Hampson 1

I rôles

and rules mix to get out of
the bathroom this face goes off in
all directions didn't recognise the same sameness
looked to take care of your self

coins caught neatly in the convex blankness
figural embrace of the ordinary exchange in
a world of light exchange distant as
its frame catches its scratches on glass

beetroot in their mirrors they burn messages
onto sweating tongues future compounds as noise
the history they share for a wrestle

a crowd the people our place become
familiar something different meant somebody else's personnel
audit somebody else's personnel audit somebody else's

IV

For Robert Hampson 2

tricky composite

bangs out a Hoover bag on the
edge of her spectacular frame luminous moment
chases thought across the body's theoretical stage

benefactor's anonymous ash spills into his shape

leaps from her blurred flesh stirring
he holds up a mirror dusts up
the gutter she laughs in response for
a witness runs responsible ideas in tandem

lustrous he fits the cluster's zero heroes

dusty torso that is his alone in
statuesque moments when abstract nouns out to
unhinge selfhood squeak distant and diminished threats

pleas from pools of neophytes' miraculous tears

rich with obligation the cheap illusionists vanish

V

no negotiations

tart! he shouts at the slot machine
armed to the teeth with retributive spite

erect on the plinth of his own mottoes
his gun-oily digits target our lips

a composite hero squanders his rationed milk
ghosts, nazis, saints, all alive at once
a smudge of human interest disrupts
this urban pastoral with a moment's self

it rubs itself watches another walk bare
buttocked across the room limbs improvise upon
a melody of clefts between tense shoulder-
blades, sharp breath ecstasies their communicative ethic

in times of black maps imagination is
intervention (zero hour malevolence trades in history

BOOK 9

for Lawrence Upton
Thirty 2
Torn Elegy 3

primed with sand outside the bars
decrees token-legislate girls lugging buckets
across the public will adores it
free fists raised revolution never imminent
potentially positioned behind each final portrait

his interventionist mug-shot burdened with
conquered streets each glint of red
for his final surrealist grief their
sneering revolution aggressive and cosy they
invite him in fragrant as death

slammed shut in existing conditions newsreels
behind Franco's sandbags feel good they
enter the old clause of nothing—
no white flags no enterprise basements
falangist dolls take the pluming town

negotiate steps with calculated terror shed
his grief peppery stone virgins safe
in neologism logistics the final frontier—
sweat slides so far from blood
and sperm unloaded pistol going off

unlock our atrocity arsenal grief barricades—
corpses curl around dying horses the
name is Europe the smile behind
each proper victim vacates whistles and
tracks the space across prepared lists

affirmative concepts cut their muddy throats
poetics of impact scarce proper nouns
whose faces flesh radio banners tape
follows the track of stress (plots
collapse on the way to consensus

futurity salutes from fur the spoils
trawl her torn flesh wires a
cough patched up territory spitting debris—
too many witch wireless altars turn
out to be virgin boot sermons

weep the humming of rapturous release
beds shaded with belligerence beg
cigarettes unconscious communism delirious feet in
gutters sheltered by blood, our deft
shifts of weight as we witness

law surrendered pockets stuffed with challenge
scramble heavenward clawing grenades taught that
they owned the voice trawling each
waveband sensation bonded weight in commitment—
little utopic slogans become each chill

delete the struggle diaries wiped out
beliefs the fruit of nobody loiters:
even the reprisals of these vigorous
tenders, potential gifts beneath torn elegies—
(as returning priests swell Madrid, *adorned*

sculpt with corpses revolution's confused transistor
voices call him back from peep
holes shelled through dwelling and sensory
prolapse, selfish searches for shifting hope—
torn fences flutter with price tags

laced sleeves falangist realism at half
mast provisional monuments a multisystemic screeching
against a contract of brittle orchards
cannot be contracted from aprons leading
dispositions to blackshirts with intelligent limbs

collisions regulate resistant refrains gutter muscles
link the anguished knuckles a taste
censor's glance spits scraps to negotiate
with futurity, to strip the mummified
nuns, to worship their fossil mortality

not afraid of refutations permanently contingent
on *campesino* encounters miners' women fit
facts into prison clothes insurgent dust—
their shoulders shake bloodthirsty tongues behind
poetic sash windows passional full stop

Fanatical beings refunction the banners
driven to exchange ritual policies
what's inside you quiet embattled
slices bricks with quixotic custom
and practice against slogans, a
thingy day in the nervy
90s the new erotics underfoot

With homemade worlds less administered
taken from dream bolts and
no splinter groups of wounded
fabulists no heart or pocket
to speak with predictable phatics.
You want to turn banknotes
clean? *it's a free country*

Magical splices he roars power
cuts deep removals from utterance
roving prince of fury pursued
by our shouts: sherry glasses
tremble in knuckled Piccadilly club
the spectator's hand repockets dodges
in a corporeal adjustment ingrained

Antibodies to unreason impressions give
up the abandoned tune in
her voice micro-slogans positioned forever
behind shaky unofficialdoms hand held
edits shudder ethics (cleansing pose
each choice for collocation; vibrant
illusions of our sore feet

Cascades wing the loves a
speculation they starve the gape
in a network of interferences
an anti-monument of buried disguise
a helicopter circles missiles fixed
hardens the negotiable fudge the
brutal poise and clipped voice

Phrase fashion positioned henceforth on
dark symbolic streets lines aflame
whisper crackling radios Yes-hostages
perceptions complicit with each green
and black flag decommissioned consultants
sing the way they've been
reported, pumps primed with fire

Bombardment flicks the day back
on its lores your rôles
up to speed razor your
stare territory losing trade secrets—
multiple spaces patch the last
Sindicato contract fiercely imminent for
each next generation's conquered streets

Scan your spectre legitimising banner
proud scratch artists still alive
horny antennae in the back
streets recite their manifestoes in
Crusoe roof gardens (as we
make the links, lines of
the many turn the name

The Last Muggletonian catches it
frames Cable St resistance out
for communitarian hand-shackles escorted
diversions amid machines for living
rub themselves watching some battered
authority left in decline (corporeal
human resource at the margins

Disposal, each sense ambient: microphones
simply there launch politicians in
precautionary sell-outs, anodyne risk-
antidotes, Trafalgar duties of the
chained bunting for a Labour
victory. English lyrics spread the
linen, sterile or not; corporate ethics

Invite heroines' effluvia your noisy
transfer your contract knowledge which
has itself become scaffolding enactments
of respect: judgement shines on
paving stones faculty without shudders
the fierce navigation of nomadic
ethics, loathing lacy discourse silhouettes

Adjustments ingrained for life, the
agonistic ritualists chant everlasting exchange
consultation as a waistcoat turns
in self-confirmation: appetites lead
one banner reaches the daily
script: the pitfall scars of
the delegate modulate the lores

BOOK 11

melting talk twice upon
a time fallen under
hooves, each woman whitewashed

≈

positioned for dereliction verdant
concrete a slow bomb:
distance lined their necks

≈

beacons on vulture slopes
made barricades human in
civvies threw down fat

≈

invisible labour barbed wire
scratched idyll acolytes' slides
police hid in sheds

≈

who'd ever heard of
bobbies surrendering took helmets
pulled us inside out

≈

pools of emancipatory icons
the banners enlarged tears
for sale, drooping lids

∾

midnight eyes affirm British
blood said Mosley masses
without leaders, dark forests

∾

primitive capitalist window box
shorts across liberation rot
or riot (*Shove off*

∾

Brechtian dummies breathed intimate
repression's *verité* clips: the
replete eyes' gouged material

∾

just like parliament packed
questions inhabit old forms
a dictatorship of honesty

∾

uninhabited people ravaging bone
bags for empiricists' hot-
lines of eternal brass

～

suicidal bone frenzy slaughter-
bench inevitability cut the
chain: 'morally a weed

～

the inanimate threatens duration
firestorming freedom black hole
markets literal spare pricks

～

imagined Belsen replaced reflections
with such mirrors furnaces
peak: regimes with wings

～

to trust the lores
disobey them dizzying guilt,
astonished space blossoms fog

～

mind wreckage ghetto bars
spend the millennial intent
in Magnesian Standard Time

∽

workers' playtime shutter shopping—
why do numbed links
clatter the uniform chains

∽

prescient justice of the
state undresses nothing mutual
apprehension off seduced electorate

∽

chat show hosts ghost
speeches: even the dead
will not be safe

∽

conscience is everything but
Constitution (Thatcher strokes his
hand) *matters for tonight*

∽

anecdotes pulled them like
that for her, survivors
with sanctimonious migrant fading

~

cosmetic collapse to know
their skins time running
the language of however

~

grand narrative thunderclap announced
destiny inscribed on skin
left like their silence

~

colonising your day no
fascist dared the groups
that delighted in negation

~

your cold mercurial hands
deserved the adjective 'human'
glowing sparks dying wires

~

railways to mossy factories
met history with lyric:
flesh paled against kingfisher

~

dripping leaves killing nuns
for enchanted new beginnings
the party's leaking mackintosh

~

magic island resolutions turn
reverie: second thoughts from
the abyss sweating Chechens

~

indoor utopia welfare pastoral:
saw myself in propaganda
on invisible park bench

~

unfamiliar content whispering grass:
isolate dewy blades voice
shuddered as though corporeal

~

disseminated fragments WAR ON
TIME timeless succession of
foreigners' boots padlocked intervals

≈

the Stalin of '68
told not to negotiate,
robots careered without subjects

≈

Empires collapsed gang leaders'
Kronstadt cheers drank the
party erect; televised rebellion

≈

our fabulous cobblestone happiness
emptied the carriage polished
like a new song

≈

one way Utopia THIS
MACHINE KILLS FASCISTS only
in itself. Judgement bursts

BOOK 12: FREE FISTS

STRATEGIC NAVIGATION A
HISTORY OF OUR
PLACE INVADED BY
TWITCHING ARMS IN
DITCHES STEEL HELMETS
TACTICAL WHITE COAT
INTERROGATIONS NEGOTIATE FROM
THE BARREL OF
A LOADED GUN
SKIP OVER HEROES
ON FREEZING TIME
SLIP SHADOWS OF
BLOSSOM ON PAVEMENTS

COBBLESTONE SALUTES INVADE
INNOCENCE THE TIME
BOMB ICONIC DARK
INROADS OF RADIO
RIPPLING VOICES OF
THE LEADERS THROUGH
CHOKED GRILLES A
STREET BUSY WITH
JOSTLING GHOSTS FOR
A SPILLAGE OF
INTIMACY WAFTS FROM
INVISIBLE WOMEN FREEZE
THE BRILLIANCE FOR
EACH UNSTAINABLE FUTURE

MUSCULAR RUBBLE OR

WASTED PROMISED LAND
THE CUT TELEGRAPH
IN UNIVOCAL COMPLICITY
SNOUTS SUCK NEWSPRINT
ALWAYS MARGINAL AGENTS
FIGHT FOR THE
CENTRE CONSUMING ENEMIES
WITH UNOFFICIAL DIALECTS
TIME FOR CIGARETTES
IN THE MOLECULAR
CIVIL WAR TRACKED
ADRIFT AS A
SIREN DOOR BREATHES

HISTORY MATERIALISES A
HALO OF EXTINCTION
X WHICH FLOATS
ABOVE YOU CLOCKS
RUST ON SHOP
FRONTS YOUR MUGSHOT
FLASH BETWEEN NEGATING
BARS THE DEFENCE
IMPLODES IN PROVISIONAL
MARGINS OF CODE
REVOLUTIONARY PLEASURE STRUGGLES
WITHOUT HEROES WHILE
BLOCS OF SENSATION
PINCH THE EYE

MANACLES HOLD YOUR
HANDS IN AN
ATTITUDE OF PRAYER
AS THE POSTMAN
APPEARS FROM NOWHERE
DIASPORA-LINKAGE IN

THE CRUSH OF
YAWNING TURF-GRAVES
A SINGLE IMPACT
PEPPERS OUR GIFTS
STREET-COLLISION FETISHES
MARKET THE ORDINARY
PRAYERS ETHICS FROZEN
IN CELESTIAL GUILT

DISPOSITIONS BEHIND LIMP
FLAG FRAMES A
NEWSREEL THE LIGHT
WHERE PERCEPTION BECOMES
ETHICAL TO REGIMENT
THE PARTY OF
A-TOPIA HE QUESTIONS
FROM CROUCHING GUN
POSITIONS ANSWERS WITH
BOHÈME IN YOUR
BOARDROOM DUST GRAFFITIST
SERENADES THE VECTORS
BOOT SERMONS KICK
COMPETITIVE BARRICADES

ILLUSORY COMMUNITY DASHED
TO PIECES ON
THE PAVING A
HEAD SWIVELS ASSURANCE
AS YOUR PILLOWED
DISPOSAL NEARS WAR
DREAM MEMORIES AS
TIME BOMBS LIFT
A LEAPING EYE
HE SMILES UNNATURAL
DISASTERS WAITING TO

HAPPEN DENSE AND
LIGHT A WEDGE
THAT WILL GUIDE

LACED SLEEVES CONFUSED
SALUTES WELCOME THE
NOMADS ON FORCED
MARCH TO BELSEN
UNLOCK THE KEY
LIVE WITHOUT YEARNING
A MAP BLESSES
NO UNAMBIGUOUS AUTHORITY
CORPSES SALUTE IN
GAS RISING TERROR
OVEN VENTS DISTANT
BUT VIBRANT BLURRED
LINKS WOULD CERTAINLY
HAVE BEEN CAUGHT

ROUTED THROUGH SETTLEMENT
IN REPRESSIVE TIME
AMONG THINGS IN
TECHNOLOGICAL TERROR A
BUCKET BETWEEN US
OUR FREE FISTS
RAISED TO INTERVENTIONIST
IMMANENCE POSING MAQUETTES
TIME CAPSULE EXPLODES
ITS METAPHOR REPULSED
SPECTACLES PILED THE
PASSAGE TO SENSATION
GREY OVERALLS EYEBALLS
LOSING THEIR CLAIM

BOOTS TACKY WITH
BLOOD NEGOTIATE CONCEPTS
AS GENDER ROLLS
CIGARETTES IN DOORWAYS
BUILDING WITHOUT DIRECTION
RUBBLE INSCRIBED WITH
THE BROKEN GRAFFITI
OF MAN DWELLING
POSITIVE IN VECTORS
AS TORN ELEGIES
BURDEN THE DEFT
DANCE STEPS: SURVEILLANCE
AND TRAPS WITH
OUR EYES SHUT

1994–1995

Footnote to Book 2: Jungle Nights in Pimlico

im Eric Mottram
Duocatalysis 12
Empty Diary 1943, 2
IM 5

Brown ale and jokes,
eerily unfunny. Arches shudder
overhead, a ghost train

Hebrew verses by heart,
in unison. Dim lights;
persecution, arrogance and poverty

Poetry of everyday life,
'humane cant' about abandoned
cats, kitchen knives; death

Non-people in Utopia sniff
back tears. Daily business:
fruit-box mattresses, prohibitions

'Hitler is the unique
creation, the prophetic spirit. . . .
Prince of the world'

GIs repocket their knuckledusters,
outside Lyons; black sapper
bleeds. Blackshirt confederates laugh

Unlocking our arsenal of
grief, corpses curled around
children. Captured Germans weep

Glued to the faint
wireless at nine; Hamburg.
The humming of valves

Three to a bed,
feigning sleep. Hand inside
my blouse (*unconscious Communism*

Delirious wool! Later I
realised that this was
his black market shroud

Sheltered, so much to
do; say. Whisper: 'Stalin'.
Spoils for the future

1995

31 History or Sleep

Human Dust 3
Lores and Bye-Lores 2
Melting Borders 4

And we are allowed to be happy
sometimes. Indeed it is our duty
Anthony Rudolf

Less real than a dream
logged in
archaeologists' ledgers
propels awareness
along another axis
hangs a veiled
filter for your presence
a gauze a
gaze figures inward
dirtying cuffs on the world
wraps the teeming air
in chalk upon a wall
a voice-activated
future on the blink
surrounded by threats
a new point of view
refugee witness's
shallow relief
slapping into the silent hallway
herself
on her television
at the fingertips
bigger suits work out

the countryside
its collapse ratios
the people
real news from virtual
travel
stretches
through force; cold defence
in these narratives as
obliterated landscapes

He wants to be watched the
events the camera
misses notate
the little utopias to
turn them to song (almost)
impassive but knowing
eyes
drink the swimming
passion, pleasure's
measures
beating sunsets each
wall a collision
a vaporous gleam
a sinking body he examines
pleasures
herself rolls across the floor
at a pinch a pluck a
spoor knuckling
happy sometimes, hardly seems
our duty to brush
with the palm

moving
in such a way
sets this in motion so
he enacts
the bye-lores
unscheduled
she pulls him into
the pool of her
watching
pushing aside
each scheduled routine
horror

One raped
can another relax
stroke
orgasmic dead fur
from this catalogue of
terror, frog-eyed navigators
chart us
while enemies invade
(liberate) equivocal
loyalty
tells us we cannot afford
to open the window
you cannot see
another's sorrow without
hanging
on the breeze, a counter
to think and feel
pleasure empty
as a mouth willing cool
scarecrows itself
replaces

all with its fevered dreams
of possible tomorrows
bark
you wake (your victim
pours from you
virtual memories conflate
occasions
dissolve
salt sweat stains
to find—who?—dead)
the recognition that
another human being has responded

haunts

Jumping out of the groove
of an ancient technology
through a smashed hole
in the reflection of a dead sky
no epicentre
to this crowd
in your front garden
selling marked-up beer
WHO KILLED JOY
a cheesecake smile
changes the standard
endlessly
to the shape of the advertised map
paying to gawp at it
zigzags around the body
a hand upon your shoulder
in propriatorial embrace
you act out your life

the faulty vending machine
twitches

Left enough spoors
in the gold zone
for others to pick up the trail
in the third
person's silent grip
at the edge
of memory myself
steady as a leaf
)identity
enclave(
his old anecdote wove
another lie, another life
through
obliterated place names through
tangles
(recounting

The ceasefire never
declared you will
be menaced
to contribute to the
hunger striker tattoos
under her sleeve in affront
surfaced quotas
a window
locked in re-enactment
to be a classic reference in
the mouth of a displaced proletarian
slept

for itself dreaming
of the Fenian submarine
a stone on a hot beach echoing
plausible twists into
actuality
a household name in
whose houses around
the polluted brilliance of
the omphalos

He no longer burns
startlingly bright in this post-'79
dispersal he
sweats into song beholds
the sprinkled mountains of Poland
affliction at the gate
diaspora on your
doorstep
the town had been
cleansed
stone patriots escaping
into the grain
of his table top sheen
wings sticky with pollen
turn green with fear
amid leaves
as the kestrel
turns
favoured media ejaculation
teaching the peacock to sing
policed dreams
accusations
arcane rules

arsonists' kindlers
murderers' armourers
the president's map
on the back of a banker's draft
obliterates
air space
'on the ground'
there are snapshots of tears
escaping
at the wheels
lucky bandages
desert tygers
striping the sand with fear
a world
rapidly unreacting

A mask tricks its wearer
bearer
wherever the body
escapes each queen bee needs
workers to lift her costume off
shivers flesh down a dancing thigh
can constitute no mind
for this gathering
dispersal
needs no people: they
need no reminding
vapour of their own shit
vents in Victorian manhole covers
he's upside down the
crisp bursts of his micropower
but there's nothing to say
we wanted the world

and we wanted
it then
in its invasion
of the ordinary with spectacle
in their labour
radiates joy
carnival's flesh given over,
not up; a can kicks itself
along the street
the way she
touches
a door slams in Hindi
masks the oily faces
finding themselves dancing for a crowd
nice handcuffs on the right
to remain silent

To be happy sometimes
to let pleasure drift as
soon as you see the
enemy start shooting you
owe it to yourself to
pleasure
build
demolish
the honeysuckle bricks while the
cement blows free
delineations of pure joy
liminal numbness
between sleep and
objective market forces
stockpiling new stone on the periphery
around Being's crumbled Shack

You you
monadic resemblance light of
the world re-enacted as
retinal shimmer, its own
stink in its nostrils: I smelt
you long before I met you, she
says to the stiff, dripping
merman, sinking
in pleasure, who discovers her
gash of flesh
unzips her gown he licks each breast
as she watches, smiling
she kneads his submarine
body slips through
her fingers could he suck
her final gasp
she flushes him with
pleasure pricks
his tongue desperately happy
cannot fill her she
hoists him in
pleasures pleasure
hieratic annihilation
feeds off their shoulders

Bags outside charity shops
rifled by
women you've never seen before
blitz emanations
pushing antique prams
diaspora
from visibility
bones surrounded by pots

polluted sunshine
invisible smog spitting
on the chained gladiator
re-enacting one hour
of this street
sucks his face set
against the *axis*
mundi: a self, a
legionnaire
stranded on the
edge of Empire's
mosaic dice
checking identity papers
incendiary attacks
on overflowing rubbish bins
scorch the moths
not dusted from maps
bricks scaled to hands
body auras
cleansed
in reformation
the queen of consumer affairs
building to rubble, to
saleable brick, a new point
of view in next week's mausoleum

Camels kick
ragged turf
under a brooding sky
dressed in white
for wisdom men
devolved
bells chime as they lift

reflections safe
in the palms
of managed lack
a feather snaps in the
multinational cast off
scrambling for
old light bulbs
drugged eyes mask
padded
in brass she sways up
to the hips
for the boys
in shades
claps around the circle
detonate passion
they disorder
the world to pattern themselves
for the pointing girl
embroidered
her own seduction
at her breathing beads
his body's marked
with safety pins
a satellite dish away
dancing on the slipway
ostrich feathers
key-rings
rusted
he flirts
gauging the impossibility
of everyday winds
whistling through
her brazen plaits
float
in his mirror eyes

on the back of his Honda
at the edge of his
conscious peep through
the curtains of more than
one country
blossoms on
his spirits
like freedom
pointing backwards
the girl chooses
his sharp kohl lips
in exclusion
upside down and plastic
the toy gun swings
from his shoulder

Talk transports
this dirty corner
a train a
rumour of its timetable
crashes
in asks the advert of itself
the track to the furnace
your edge of history
or sleep within this
trap you act
wings sticky
caught in summer's shade
pain correctly
centres this ecstasy
with humans
flailing and
flaring in dust

August–November 1995

33 'The Crimson Word We Sang'
(Celan, *Psalm*)
: Some Words of George Oppen

for *Graham Bradley*
Coda 3
Some Words 1
Tin Lanterns 2
To My Students 3

struggle for
survival in
some ways
enviable had
meaning meaning
for everything other than
themselves
had arrived in various
distress forced
credit
to corruption
Samuel happily no
last name
his wealth a
literal armed
guard servants
to park cars
innumerable rooms immense
ballroom
his party a friend
talking trying
to make out out
of the corner of
her eye *What*

are they singing voices rose
she froze and
through her once
more
songs of the
camps death songs
once more
they look happy
perhaps true
I shouldn't say they
looked happy
singing
they had meant
something thinking
(this story
from our
time of the time
they had something
this story from
our time) of the
time they had

1989/1995

≈

32

For Scott Thurston

Hundred 3.1

Turns 4

where weathered

statues disdain the weather eye labours the
rustic scene scratched on opaque dawn scored
for disruption it shores up the weight
of the hushed world as condensed outlines

shakes their resemblances dubbed and dumb patterns
skin-damp with snared bird song annihilate
the moment's blossom on the *parterre* where
peace falls (we say) into paradise alone

unspoken a tongue on a downy lobe
steaming the sentient lock with its breath
and she turns to you implores you

be fleshed for her kiss only or
stands silent in shadow othered in stone
as a million suns scorch their mottos

NOVEMBER 1995–NOVEMBER 1996

34
Entries

Empty Diary 1996
For Jo Blowers 3
Hundred 3.2–4

codes unrobed

tongue shooting pained bursts I'm as tall
as me on labels he sticks over
my fingers pussyfooting defiance ices my slaughter-
hole for his glans female scopophiliac rehydrated

gristle pictures in the body hidden from
my gaze as orgasm exits my face
shaves anxiety quivering his eyelashes with my
teeth *all eyes on his adjusted pouch*

frictionless richness with a perfect stranger a
flesh vessel that sinks us to shiver
as it's filled (anonymity cracks *yes please*

a pair of Fuck Me Shoes his
oily runnels unruly member he pulls back
the foreskin as though he is selling

womanliest denims

hug a quick release from his bite
nurturing his holocaust subjectivity I want him
my prickly understudy he's a milking touch
to mount a chair from his trousers

to leave no inbetweens all surface and
steaming sentient locks framed by black brastraps

double pleasures he never demands *my* gesture
lactates shadows shaped and held I enter

fingers lightly curled my long body pulled
negotiate *his* pushed out from the bedroom
nothing to enter slip doesn't shift I

kiss my glove with something mutual he
cannot see our bliss burns less brightly
than questions takes off: my dress: my back:

falls away:

without a hole he's left me elsewhere
everywhere nowhere I click his explosive pitch
his cresting a fallen phallocrat licks her
last portrait unzipped fat thighs prickling correctness

I close my eyes and I see
him dappled with gists (he says *Unpeel
her milky folds*) my display slips a migraine
clot in his brain replies *voyeuse*

doubleness gives him the look hell heated
the show's tryst I'm masked and I
will look myself wiped into a corner

how firm he sees himself shoulders tilt
the title shadows tremble his fist on
the accelerator of my throat muscles slips

MAY–JULY 1996

[234]

35
Ripping through Business

Amended Signatures 2
For Scott Thurston 2
Hundred 3.5 & 3.6
Turns 6

I

he folds

a crease in smashing glass and broken
sleep. they think they choreograph shifting colonies
on the Common in gene pool superstition
a man in shorts watches the helicopter

in the night stinging beams where prohibitions
are fixed across the network of streets
he squats on its suspicion mounting the
air a ruined rubberneck twisting to talk

to the birds. tranquillities buckle as he
tosses a bottletop to a beggar who
hammers late into the night's yellow glare

pollutant humming the same structured uselessness fails
brittle smiles crackle over smart ID cards
turning on pain's map magnified in distance

II

grating the

nerves of the franchise constricting the chest
jingling in an atmosphere of shattered bottles
in a urinous alley for a wobbling
mobile's retreat the century's video of

naked statues mysterious tragic macho dumbo echoes
psychic key attuned to decay downs a
drop of Coke from a bin. lashings
in a hot pocket unlock the bomb-

factory in Woodbury Street (cannot find regenerate
routes through consumables diversions a missile a
light beam on eye-shields chopping over Tooting. . . .

as the moment's strain laps against you
consciously see this for the last search
among people not things *does not exist*

19 AUGUST 1996

37
Neutral Drums: Four Formal Poems

Duocatalysis 15

1 Two Unsustained Sestinas in Hundreds

Hundred 3.8
Weightless Witnesses 2

pick yourself

tuning up bits of lyric the meatiest
props leave form as pleasurable shots its
quiver full of migrant signatures bullets
kiss roses ragged effigies mute scars quiver

form's an idea in a whistling wipeout
gunshots shatter the urban epiphany be wild
undecided undecoded tea leaves quiver the West
collapses specific parasite retails his clandestine shots

rough shots ride the slippery tongue smear
conditions of conflict rumours spread on air
the meatiest mesh magnetises your reuseable eye

load and wait the chain quiver battling
lightning's shaft displaced dissipates chaotically specific
where lyrics quiver the dead kiss spinning

Hundred 3.9
Magdalene in the Wilderness 2

weightless girders

support my quest all logic shivers police
horse pelts through pelting crowds the chaos

weightless as guilt robotic traffic constellates the
streets' untouchable skin your cheap clothing shivers

shattered statue pelts its model weals in
denial unbolted from tyranny's rusted mind barks
bliss in robotic sublimity illumines history blushes
to skin brushed by the world's shivers

full-pelt opponents with dialectic whoever bolted
the stable door drips human skin the
evidence takes longing vision pelts your cleavage

my voice jumps weightless out of your
skin a phantom drums dustbins behind the
bolted prison it croaks the body robotic

2 Empty Diary 1997: Two Dispersed Sestinas and a Fractured Villanelle (remoded as a Hundred 2005)

Flesh Mates on Dirty Errands 2
Hundred 5
Masked the World 2
Netting Joy 2
Remode 5

lucrative cleavage

queening my lips he glosses my wise
crack shutter logic with meaty exposures shivers
my stagiest timbers sequencing an indifferent aperture
flinching he's getting hard for clotted exchange

god's gift my anus airbrushed clean away
re-routing sly womanhood shimmying down his drainpipes

empowered by a jelly stir stiffening his
style jerks him on whiffs of conjecture

sirens' skinny hindquarters lift (I desire *with*
him) shoes clack behind his gifted ears
entuned eyes throb soaping his spout his
thighs thick with gift the counterpoint key

he lifts the condom calibrates his gift
zips across my eyes as black noise

3 Implosive Samples: Exploded Sestina

Articulates 1

Entries 2

Neither neutral nor neuter, loaded with explosive self-evidence

Brain homunculi fossilise. Imitate me: invent me

I die with the animal, not recondition with the machine. Adult
cellular bliss

〜

My identity problem isn't yours. It's bedtime bliss with hinges. Joints

Unrobed, she walks towards her throne, pregnant with an unloosed
virus. Phantasmal bodies enter metaphorically leave

The dream of one suspect quivering to become two. Tonight I'll shift
into something comfortable, a comet

〜

Your android dreams of explosive surgery, a neural net. Bliss can only be repetition and change: drainage bliss

This shift dissembles, full of empty behaviour. Soliloquise unrobed, flesh quivering its message: your flat incapability, for example

Noise in the picture. A holocaust of objects in this twentieth century-and-a-half. Untraceable trace. Puppet fucks

∼

Pushing angels to the ceilings. No substitute for a day. Send a picture postcard home

Drums explosive in the tottering future, with knowing chaos. Is this, then, a new identity?

She sucked bliss into him. An idea is bliss inhibited, inhabited. The human scents in mutuality. O lick that parting smile pulls on the empty

Unrobed you wear your gloss and the neurons repeat: unrobed, the graveyard shift

∼

Shift to a new line of enquiry. A building so quiet it is invisible. Or is until

As if in the eyes, enter by the exit, inhibited exhibition, reverse annotations

Concepts, enter an audience, cannot step unrobed into the same theory twice

What if bliss were see-through? All men are created stained, breaking voice and wind. Sleaze jellies quiver

∿

Narrative gravity holds us, muscular lips quivering with threat. A left handed shift in melodic complacency. We're two, brewing hormones. A shift-accelerated bliss, limbs flying apart

A history of feeling: my eyes enter a clause entire, stream. O shred your light

An explosive creak through a whisper of sensation. Apart, you enrobe these hesitant acts. A mobile one-ness

∿

Unrobed in dreams my lady moans complaint; her lips delineate excess

Shift the universal trick, searching for our quivering uniqueness. Its other life trembles

A bridge trills, explosive. Bliss rims detonate the centre. *Enter*

<small>February–December 1997/2005</small>

36
Small Voice

darkness drags

a headlight's irradiated cone fading to an
English print of shredded lane rheumy vapours
tickling in time the throat catches on
slices of transitory purpose lost in decline

watch a row of identical open trucks
head somewhere archaic like a Midland colliery
not singing praises it's not even singing
the sharp rasp rustles in the ear

a redundant germ that drifts this Age
of Irony now happening to be forged
it barely sustains its volume of displacement
the vandals have fled   the gate bangs

scoop phlegmy lyric from the clogging drone
from the rusted hinges' lament

bitter croak

JANUARY 1997

38

Report on Seaport

for cris cheek
For Charles Madge 2
Labour 3
mayday 97

*Clearly this gentleman was
the type who likes to make
the government responsible
for everything, even their
daily quarrels with their wives*
Nikolay Gogol

A crumpled 'closing down sale' sign. A cyclist in shorts with panniers
pedals as slowly as one possibly could through the muted Seaport rush-
hour. A dysfunctional self-consciousness leaks tenderness: 'You get
your head together, OK?' A funnel of courtesy, sifts into rules, powers,
permissions, as the crowd boards the 86, one passenger at a time. A
loaf hangs on the drainpipe. A pheasant lifts its tail. A pink bow holds
a ponytail to the back of his head. A row of girls outside the chippy eats
burgers, chips with gravy, watches the crowds arrive at the Finch. A
scar or design in his hair. A t-shirt announces last year's heatwave.
A.s.a.p. Across the road—across the parliamentary boundary—the Lib
Dems move about their brightly lit campaign headquarters above a
darkened hair salon called *Avant-Garde*. All the visible ironies vanish
from the day. Among the European cities. An arm cocked on the back
of the seat, he is staring at the unusual bald patch on the back of
another man's head. An etiquette of dressing down before Friday. An
observer remarks: perhaps divided into a class narrative by the heavily
varnished but sticky bar. An observer suffers narrative interference.
Ann Summers monopolises the 'feel' good factor. Are you going in
for the election sweepsteak? Arthur couldn't give a fuck.

Big Issue seller squats in her Seaport centre filth to accept her unoffi-
cial dole: she could be brushed by intention, caught by the eyes that

observe her; could be taken home and consumed in memory, played like a CD-Rom—paused, re-played, sampled, pasted-up as satire or social comment or pornography; or surrealised into palace rooms or government offices, as conscience or its lack. Blue low river, a swing bridge raised, road to the blue sky. By the time I return home the Blair poster has gone.

Can only say from where I am: sat on a stool in the corner of a pub, scribbling, near the toilets, across from the fruit-machines, within reach of the door; sniffing: night, beer, urine, disinfectant. Car sweeps into the garage past an observer who observes a hand waving acknowledgement of his yielding above a half-scratched ILLEGAL PARKING sticker on the side window. Car turns left, the passenger fires a cardboard machine-gun into the waiting pedestrians. CB to his mouth taking the corner. Cement mixer turns like a barber's pole. CLASS WAR MILLIONS OF BOLTS AND NUTS. Clowns—

Dad's word for Tory politicians. Day of destiny. Democratic vista: children off school, the buildings used as polling stations,—how many parents, taking the kids to the seaside on this sunny day, will never get round to voting? De-selection Night Special. Desperate footsteps die out as the train doors slice the air between them. Digger scratches history away. Do they do a continuous count through the day, or do they count them all at the end? Do you think they'll be voting or lying in the sun? Dog Flambé: golf ball retrievers.

Election fever—cocktails only £1.50! Every sentence of that rare London voice is a business plan. Everything in the Centre at 10.40 on a Thursday morning rejects the frenetic race against time of Saturday afternoon, a workable leisure.

Feel good? Filter out thought until there's nothing left but thought's percepts. Follow the eyes that follow. Four giant rockets in his hand, he comes out of the house yelling in a Scottish accent about 'the next five years'. Frisks the kid's front, then the back, a pill bottle out from his pocket.

Ginger Tom prowls — they'll be another cat nearby. Grunt of milk float's brake. Gutted detail.

He adjusts his watch, winding through the 31 April. He doesn't bend to the booth's grille; he props at an angle. He hands out his rainbows in front of the library. He scoops down and picks the turd-like sausage he's dropped, from the pavement, everybody giggling. He's going to put money. He's no ambassador for the homeless! 'Help the homeless,' he mouths, automatic, staring straight ahead. Hips swing into Marks. His breathing is an alternation of smiling and grimacing. His spine levers back on the trike. History will remember the 1997 General Election as a Labour 'landslide' or as a Tory 'wipeout' or as a 'revival' of the Liberal Democrats — and it was all of these things and the newspapers said so. Huffily who pushes a wheelchair.

I am another observer, freer this day, as Rousseau said, than on most: having voted by post a week ago. I am moved to a measured optimism that the 'everyday' has been augmented by a great popular negation, popular affirmation. I believe at last that I live in a *society*, one that has emerged from long darkness. I have passed from youth to middle age. I like the idea. I told you about the fucking place I have to sleep there. I've nowhere to go I kicked the fucking door down they thought it was him but it was me I better go and fucking sit with him what's the matter with you. If her t-shirt weren't so short you wouldn't see the jewel glinting at her navel. Imitation newspaper used for wrapping chips. In *News from Nowhere* a worker removes the election books from the window, as she asks where she needs to go to vote; outside schoolboys stand with clipboards trying to categorise the shop. Is it the election today? an Old Boy asks an observer, sucks on Players and the edge of his glass: I've missed it. Is this the sound of the semiotic *chora*? It's 10.24, nobody's dead, and I'm not Frank O'Hara. It's Quizingo Night at the Seaport Arms as an observer enters to catch the end of a question about an EC Directive. It's the *first*, how could you forget it — I don't know how many weeks they've been going on about it.

Juicy Bits! Juicy Bits! they cry out before punching the cashpoint screen.

K'you . . . K'you . . . K'you . . . . Kids shower each other with blossom in the graveyard.

Last week the final comment seemed: Labour wants Labour to win, The Lib Dems want Labour to win, The Conservatives want Labour to win, and still the Tories go up in the polls! *Lionel* Blair *Lionel* Blair—he's more funny. Longest election. LOYALISTS 1690, fading on the wall.

Marketown's Natural Law Party candidate opens the hatchback of his campaign car—it's covered in his picture and rainbows, and 'young people generally' an observer hears him say as he passes this notebook, talking to one of the students. Metal mesh holds the road to ground level. Metallic eyes rebuff the world, her sharp nails scratch it out. Moderate whiff of cannabis in a waft of air.

New logo on old warehouse. Next to an observer a woman moans from the depth of an unobservable dream, and shudders slightly. NO FRILLS on his t-shirt. No one sits in the acoustic chair. Norma's got two of them and one of them is John. Not just a report, more of a resource.

Observing the fringes of anti-climax, he sees less and less. Older men only play football when it's warmer. On the tip of his tongue is Raymond Williams' 'Elect them on Thursday: fight them on Friday'. One cross in the wrong place. One More Day One More Day Five More Years One More Egg. Opens the phone box, she blows smoke into the night. Out of the *Three Tenors* bag comes the autobiography of Tony Curtis.

Phone pressed against his decision. *Physical* on his t-shirt. Pneumatic fart of doors. Police 'comb' Marketown's trackside path. Purple nails glow in the tunnel. Pyjamas come begging.

Rainbows torn to shreds where the car was. Rainy days favour the Tories, because they have cars. Red car passes blaring *Vote Socialist*. Resting on the wall between the two houses is the laptop; children from both sides crowd round it while the single adult sits on a doorstep, smokes a cigarette. Rushing dangerously across traffic, he picks something up from the middle of the road.

Saluting cranes. Scribble of barbed wire along a wall. Seaport is the port of death. She frowns at an observer's frown and is observed frowning. She rifles through papers, 'work' going 'home'. She turns from him and opens and shuts her eyes. Shiver of milk. SLOB BARKS AT DASHBOARD PHONE. Solar Moon. Someone's pushed a fresh bouquet along the guitar of a bronze Beatle. Specific memories could fill this general blankness: slates from a church roof, a wall from a warehouse, and at its centre, pristine among dereliction and inactivity: *Britain is Booming*. Spheres of constellated dandelion seeds await the breeze. Stocks in the city square. Striped shirts and elaborately tattooed arms stretch the bar, faces firing smoke at the high TV screen, the next pint on the bar, a spare cigarette behind the ear. Summer's vibrancy of overheard TVs and stereos for the first time this year. Sun glints. Swung out of the guard's van, she turns the low handle, and is back upright before the train comes to rest at the platform.

Target eye gates to the hazy park. Temporary curtains in ancient windows, corrugated iron windowpanes. That beard is clipped by a memory, a slang. The comet has slipped from our night sky for another 4000 years. The cruelty of nature and the ducks' lack of maternal instinct she bemoans. The custom of throwing stones at the buses. The day before yesterday children bounced between these Victorian graves next to the hospital. The fat man with the spangled hat rocks on his heels in the doorway of the amusement arcade, looks like an automaton of slot-machine jollity; he wears a rosette low on his swelling belly: *Love is Liberal*. The guy in the silk shirt's ice cream drips from its cone at 10.19. The Halifax tells us, in triptych, a. *Whoever Wins The Election*, b. *Nothing Will Change* and follows with c. The lad, perhaps drunk or drugged, shouts at whoever he's left in the carriage behind, and goes to the front of the train, where he moves from seat to seat, before returning to shout, and then resuming his restless fidgeting, he now talks to another youth whom he previously ignored. The Left has stayed silent. The observer lets this slip, then another. The official commentary redundant, as they draw close to their friends, whispering interpretations, a resistance to mediation that can't be measured. The old woman with the stick winces as she hoists herself up, either smiling or grimacing, pads in pink trainers to the door, but once on the platform she'll need to ascend the cut to the road. The older woman in the Women's Poetry group who'd scowled over the Waldrop, Hejinian, O'Sullivan, re-emerged in an observer's nightmare as the spokesperson for a rebellion in a lecture, saying, 'We all know the bolts and nuts of poetry,' as the students start to leave, but it is not clear whether they are joining the rebellion or protesting against it. The only man in a coat, he's on the bench, having a good morning puff, the half-empty half-full bottle of sherry on the pavement at his feet. The pensioner leaves the bus in hysterical laughter, after she's met a man she hasn't seen for years, although when she waves he has to be prodded from his deafness by his friend. THE PIES. The questions boom through the tannoy but the men at the bar ignore the spelling of *Chihuahua* and *Rhododendron* that others are sweating over in a parody of their worst schooldays; continue their conversation as though it were a drizzly Tuesday afternoon, with serious rounds of drinks and cigarettes. The quizzers pass spellings around the pub like drugs, and the quizmaster 'makes it clear' that they can be disqualified for using 'mechanical and electronic aids'. The sky is almost cloudless for the whole day. The tallest man. The winner is hardly ever in doubt — though at one moment in the campaign it looks as if support for Labour is waning — but the extent of the win surprises everyone, including Labour politicians interviewed on television, who are too stunned to speculate, even after Tory cabinet ministers and prime ministerial contenders lose their seats. There is no society. They look like they've been evacuated from the building — no, they are the smokers on the Kalamazoo computer course. They're here for equal ops, whoops sorry. This is a walk-to-rule. This is not. This is not just the everyday or any day. This is not the stream of an observer's consciousness, but a stream for your own. This is what they're *really* like. This science applied becomes market research. Those stilettos should snap or collapse sideways with such substantial legs on them, though the feet fidget in and out in turn and the toes lift the shoes and tap the heels as if this were a signal. Twenty pence drops from his trouser bottom, rolls across the pavement, casts a long shadow: sunny days favour Labour. Two identical bulldog badges on the girl's jacket. Two laughing men follow a golf ball along the gutter until it drops down a drain. Two pairs of girls link arms in the sudden summer heat of Marketown. Two students please!

Uneven poplars mark the canal and a mental city boundary, beyond which the concrete shaft-heads spaced across the flat field suggest underground bunkers but probably aren't. Unloading one-armed bandits to the pub. Upper Volta doesn't exist; it changed its name in 1985! Use a post-colonial concept in a feminist context.

Vote (picture of Blair): *Blur* (blurred image). 'Vote Early; Vote Often!' quotes Iain rushing by: a mass observer observed.

Warm words want to support the day. We budget for fun. What'cha waiting for, girls? What's *he* writing in *his* notebook? Whereas he feels cynicism about New Labour during the deliberately protracted campaign, suspecting 'this Age/ of Irony now happening to be forged', the will of the people for moderate social democratic policies—not at all the 'phlegmy lyric from the clogging drone' of his poem—is overwhelming: moving in its silent and invisible determination. Why's he called Paddy? World of surfaces sandpapers the skin.

Yes. Yesterday bleeds like sunlight through the blind. 'You open yet?' he asks at one minute to 11.00.

1–3 MAY 1997; REVISED 2005

39
Small Voice 2

for Tim Woods

For Scott Thurston 3

Hundred 3.10

Turns 8

lightness blooms

do not interrogate the taillamps' eradicated drone
voice within vision musicates, released ears entune
its captive turn, the others no longer
fixed in the totality of permanent waste

this pleasure animates a knot of rapturous
ruptures mass graces *follow me* dirt from
itself: erotic or aesthetic it prises each
permission without distinction tinkles in shivered delight

*We don't live in Utopia but glimpsed
it for one moment*: the daily catastrophe
anchors an epic ethos in liminal illumination,

audial; orchestration of things covered by
a grating the 'utensils' remain compound;
windows spring black roses in en-

visaged articulation

JUNE–JULY 1997

40

Variation and Themes

dedicated to the memory of William Burroughs

IM 6

Alphabets, 15 feet tall, spell their shadows across the Pavilion lawns, before the Gate of Heavenly Peace. The shell of some other purpose opens and closes like a comedian's false teeth, the optimum moment for a billowing event whose meaning is drowned. Dying, sprinkled by the arms of a floral clock, mechanical flowers sprout from a bed of zinc and acid. Genetically engineered on the Downs near Lewes, it was selfish to have created these analogues, to have found pleasure, doubled, thereby diminished. The paratexts, the end of season rust, of staples, could buy up his epic marginalia, stretching the adjectives, never allowing the text closure. He surely deserves to keep something open, a verdict, to get her to try its impulse, just to see which triggers are released. Undetectable wood from trees, sheep from sirens, flesh-coloured drizzle. Listen, Rubbermouth, your insides turned independent. Sewage nettles can cure the sting—without doubt. It was her idea, sensing a morphology of slogans to take on the quest in which, she realised, she was no Aphorism. The formal function blazes his path. Gathering a sense of injustice the authority of intention flickers an alibi, or witness, tempered by the stenographer's fingers. Back in its shell, the jewel sheds its history. Eyes screwed for her signal, as do people around. I fanned out my passions, as though an allegory of timelessness. Listening to the second, she was free of me, for the stage composed the season. Grunting at her head resting on a copy of Blake's poems, the wrong proper noun was another affair altogether. Somewhere I hear the murmur of *book thirteen*, which skids the interpretations, the history of the last soaked stage. Particulars matter, fall invisible to earth, and blow in the sand: alter ego dust. The Other, invisible, was startled by the light pouring contaminated responsibility or its lack through the suddenly open door, erotic or thanatognomonic. Whatever it is, into its blaze stepped an outline of something feminine, whose contours were bled by her breasts, an immaculate conception. Its prefatory flagellations seem like so much verdant

|251|

perversity, though off-stage. Map undulations, as you lay there, dialogic. He could still order her to stream into the rivulets of her clothes' breathing emerald, in a last appeal. She stood, deep in shock, weeping into a clenched fist, her knuckles marble. Observe the approaching rituals of locality, served up urgent. The gas they bottle is obdurately untraceable after the hood has been donned. THINK misadventure. Anagrams of several girls' names entertain themselves. And then the ultimate enigma, in a dignified preparation for frenzy: the mourning sky, black clouds scooped and fluffed by skilful hands, physics rushing towards art as if it were the last helicopter out of Saigon. The last governor cast scented shadows. You treated your dot in the sky, constellated with a pattern they called History. Bulbs of Memory bob in its fluid, definitive guesses, youthful renditions of surprise. Brimming actuality is the demolition crew's meat. A twisted, unrecognisable mammal chases its tail, gobbles its own shit. After ten thousand spins, you're listening to pure dirt, something triggering undifferentiated stench scissored from the word *latrines*. The popular front for the liberation of antique consciousness. The broken clock, showing this, proved little more than a right time for the utopian parliament of pure sound. The Pleasure Brigade was drilling. His wall a perfect blank, he wishes somebody else could reorder the fragments upon it: windows of the spray-canned New York memory is lyric. Rest between the paradigms, the consciousness of glue, vulval palms displaying drying limbs sticking to surfaces. Diego Rivera of a world turned inside out, a mausoleum of melting snow. Nobody feels the need, scrapes adhesions from this instant he's left without. Emotive dust reconstructs the body; he's chiselling a shout from the street for its outline. Something like sex, in the earliest years of getting his body to move, unable to contain it; something like Fuck Musics, rolling the captions of what is, a transparent dumbshow building characters, becoming the crowd's gaze, a miraculous medium all signifier. It jumps once, a conundrum almost solved. Tombstone: trombone, the long notes of the wrong truth running analogues of this justified but unjust, inalienably real, scope. A bargain intruder bursts through your door, demands whatever there is left with such free information passing for particulate matter, toxic enough to dispose of a promised hero, gifted beyond volition. Struggling inward, sucked from the pen's bruising. The brain's rind is caked with glutted machine dust. Cod piece, minus cod. A windsock filling with torrential passion scared him off through the fabric, exhibiting himself to himself. A simple mind inhered, each fresh sheet of carbon has survived. Footprint in the cement, an island for the rain to fill. Non-entities without terms, wordy expositions of the realm. Headlines fucking or comparing themselves to dreams. Her grandfather was a Bolshevik. She bent over the easy chair as he walked in devalued currency, a Baptist entering water. The melting exchange of her dowry: the bark of a dog strangled on its chain, a blossom at the second decimal point of the penultimate equation. Each thought is literally addressed to proving himself himself. Take the number of your feet! His perceptions no longer blent. In his least favourite account of the world it was total. Once in a while, a disappointing hero declares personhood. Bus back a face-to-face, the birth of saying must never close its naked gluttony for what is said. Thought's eunuch watches her masturbating. It touches this paper, spills in helium shrillness, insinuating threats to your integrity. Where else does a date live, but in cannabic shadows harbouring your least favourite implicate ordering, the Paranoid Passiontroopers? Consciousness, out there, isn't, wasn't, *law* with a Capital L plate. The false equation trails you home, leads space probes into black files. You stand at Stage Two and wait for the lights to go up. The end of the calculation is a Prologue. The rest is History. Accelerations by greasy fingers. Celerity a constant assemblage. No style. Minus poetry. A deadpan calligraphy, the larvae shot into the thyme bush where they were mistaken by red ants for their grubs. Deep in the critical inquest, Otherness burst at frantic captors. Police helmets score through media, webbed with pollen. His palms adhere to brick, pre-emptive Metamorphosis under mirror attack: too large: smells bad: obviously alive. In other words, a story. She cements a gargoyle into a hole in the punch floor of focus, though nobody watches at first. He draws the attention, gathering papers, stony-faced hologram, post-partum monstrosity picking his nose. He's gone, invisible, in the anthracite, the decomposition chamber. The other side of glass speculates. Webbed in with coincidence, it leaks, dampens a rôle glossed in a footnote. She can have Centre Stage! She can complete her ferocious revenge that shocks still. Under gnarled fingers in the silence, the keys stop. History waits and can just make out the car. Your memory is less and less slipped over. Thumbprints on the bonnet have just uttered. The other half of the life spent the person as somebody else, frowned on by this glowering self-evidence, an inefficient grip on this rush to summary and physical integrity. Vomit a shadow on the wall. Her spontaneous evaporation washes a recognisable terrain, the inky rim in the bath. In and out of static they almost receive an instruction to catch the drowning voice. It befalls you, as nothing more pertinent than a re-naming, black noise edging every statement you'll make, the inhuman whistling of solar flares. Wallow for attention in the gulf of the voice's extinction. Disconnection of all visible circuits, like guilt, like conscience. The addition of less and less until the ancient stenographer rattles pure pitch. A hard punishment disfigures the waves, not a shiver, safe from its play in a pun on the word *Justice*, the undeconstructable, unerasable, final card, when the chips are down. You are not in this story with its yapping clues, its ethical pivot. It wants to gobble your pocketfuls of rhyme.

JULY–AUGUST 1997

41

Private Numbers from the Drowning Years: 1985–1989

Drowning Years 4

Strand Across 2

It's like when Princess Diana died and you see all the flowers and you think, well, there's a nice side to the English, it makes a change from wanting to go out and kill the Argies. It makes you want to savour the moment, whereas 10 years ago I might have thrown it away.

Robert Wyatt

1 Private Number

The World's Body 2

The page off the page treading
Muddy demolition with
A dream or the news summary:

Flaming rings of tyres
With children laughing at this
Blistering commonsense:

A nation belonging to its shareholders
Pushing stale air boiling down
Culture to get to the real pips

Closing in
Upon a sleeping
Face which
Can be read as trouble:

The world glares back at the eye
Fiercely jealous.

≈

Switch on the light let
The music begin the
Morning of head-down:

A personal message takes
A bend embryo fusewire buzzing
Under the duvet
A blanket of events over
Bony thoughts:

The machine-gunfire of negatives.

＊

    fan-tailed,
Rise to the branch they
Have chosen, I have
Chosen, out of a sunny holiday
Morning full of
Threat:
    a single eye

Taking me sharply
In for a moment:
Lightly hops wind-
Ruffled, and reads
My movement to keep
It in sight as intention—

And they're off
In strategic dispersal.

＊

The fastest landscape in Britain
Falling among the scribble-dust
Meaning little, embedded
In a hymn of praise
To the dustbin
Lids
And leaving the same
Rubbish scattered around.

,≈'

As hailstones drop
And starlings scatter
To trees, you
Nearly miss some-
Thing else, a little
Tragedy in a tight corner—

A silhouette idling
By the window, now
Dodging into
Movement;
Cannot shake
Uselessness
From its shadow limbs.

,≈'

A beat a pigeon
Shadowing a sparrow

The mind stopped feeling
Thought with the body's flow the eye's
Tangle of light interrogated

   a shed
Door crashing noiselessly in
High wind opposite.

  ∽

This arrangement of
Nerves, deceleration
Glissando beyond
Houses, rippled
Through refractive glass:

First intentions and the
Unintended bullets
In the ashtray
   —the polyphony of the gaze:

  a world
Like gun-shot bursting
Onto glass and embedded there
Blanching the eye.

NOVEMBER 1985–APRIL 1986

2 Coming Down from St George's Hill

for John Muckle

1

Leaf-shield privacy the
Nervous system no longer
Uncollected air reels
Into a
History of human stability
Public notice coming down
From the hill
      it's like
Being invaded from within
Becoming parasites in a
Psychosomatic flounce
Of net with silken light
For a street of beggars
Dark milky way of useless
Jewels
Personalised
Initial possessions
With eviction panic
      ditch
The child bailiff's boot
Sinks fuel rage
Blocked
Truant at the crumbled mouth
Up to the master's lips
Mirror-bred seduction
Scales

Actualising stupor with
Silk tickling privacy
Cut
Through the triple glazing

2

Travelling time the way I had
Pushing back the little savings
Absorbed talk to the slaves
Options
For affirmative literature
Teaching erect income
Of property pert
Beneath her drapes housing police
In jellied waiting
                    you don't
Exist at a commonsense level
The pain of suitable desire
Bites work is skimmed off
Behind the drapes the poem's
Scarlet exposures
Privilege their hot counsel
Our needs re-routing desire
Attempting open freezing
On the wet waiting list
Upstairs
In somebody else's
Purchase defining agendas
To court the plaintiff
Escapes
To the fringes of burnt out
Demolition laugh says Stephen crying

Mud deaths house us or micro-fascist
Victims trapped in
Dog discipline
The scream beyond the eviction wasps
The rotting apples they leave
Mine
The semantic fields

3

Democratic vista he parks the car
Then has to queue for the cashpoint
Whispering possessive St George's
Somewhere above the embossed logo
Window tissue paper
And its history of pleasantly
Attired servants
In famous fables begun at this
Desk of irregular
Attic windows car door opens blonde
Hair spills into the gutter
He speaks in deadpan cockney learned
Of the East Sussex school of villainy
Creaming himself at Thatcher's rush of
Active citizens revving up
Fumes and consumption's vapour
Lists a pop capitalist
        transformed
A staggering dislocation of the
Cocktail effect gone defective
Electric against meshed frost

Produced by desire dreams
An act of love a realised cell
Phone interrupts *you all right mate?*
Giggle at least it stopped a repetition
Of his ardent administered dream

20 SEPTEMBER–16 OCTOBER 1988

3 His Furious Skip

You're no hypnotist as a beckoning
Finger sends a death squad to
Their senses   Skytrail from a
Military jet falls as sclerotic vertebra
Collapsed on his arms dreams of
A process in which balance
And tip are equals

Fill the structure and all hell breaks loose
Freebie rollerskated   Moves across
My empty place to kill it
The noise of rain like rice poured
Slowly onto a drum

Armoured cars lift the filthiest
Artifice   Of one system into another
For a symptom you manufacture

Persona fills the scarce dishes warped
In the head   Hopes that have been
Privatised in the silence

Cleanliness of their cutlery while the husbands

Measure their erotic logic   I watch
The child running and she slaps to the ground
In tears   Arousal files a literature where
The assassins rid us of prime doubts   That's
Desire off the table afraid to kick

Sudden sexless

Image of self misrecognising   Solids drip   She's
A little operator shaking cigarette packets
That others have left   One more
Trickle in the cleft of the spine shifts

Involuting cloud vibrating
Against some taut but invisible chairman's
Agenda   Creates a world cover process
Satellite dish aping the ape working

Politics of the next   Hasty executions
Where the iodine radiation is who
This information impacted

Strung along the bar   They're the invisible
Machine   Only disputed territory   Stumbled
Upon the cardboard colony   One sentence
Pressures the ecosystem   Dust of tea

The words 'eternal' and 'feminine' dancing

Buttocks on her keyboard fucking
A nonsense print out   Knows who has
Shares

Regressive beliefs   Out and up the blade
He clicked his fingers to bring
My own unlikely stereotype against

Anaemic detail   To choose the paleface Gothic
Your thoughts pushed back by the new machine

Meteors of scrape against this red door

Shit hits the door mat   Click he says
As the light goes on   This skill
Has no value   He produces
A falsely figural text of his phantasies
Non-voters are supporters
Under the unprofitable street-lamps

Flickering over their page foregrounds hyena
Party   Elsewhere in the system lenses
Flushed into the sewers focus these
Thoughts   Unwanted and silver
Commodity and rhythm   A hierarchy
Of needs is still a hierarchy

Sado-masochistic cross-gender
Management techniques   Am I speech
Hooting automata   Speed your wire
Into the speaker   In its silence

The terror of balancing in the unlit
Carriage   Burns   The spontaneity
Of Hofmann's ground   Vigilant
Black icing   Knifed but not ignored

You can't be ontological and still
Want pleasure   The real house

Is built by carnival   Turn your
Accountant sour   Eros
And Thanatos impose their iambics

Memory's thinking mind   It's bedtime
Bliss with the cupids   It's fur and
Pearls as well as sensible shoes   On
A public scale   Be a product
To preface it with   Fuck the machine from
Behind and it pumps out money

The shadow from multiple sources

Eyes a radical definition
Of personal space   To shove down their throats
The father of the brain-damaged boy plays
Tunes on your teeth

Dense oddities floating   Desire
Must compromise   I look at the
Cars and they crunch   Boy Scout
Anarchism   What to inject that won't
Bring bleach convulsions   Something we
Want mankind to be
Glances through the chickenwire   Functioning
Slits without eyes

Coins down the lavatory in the last half inch

Key off   Missing parts

Skytrails before dawn assert somebody else's
Vigil   Withholding information in
Fashion   Collect the forgotten
To insert in strange bathrooms   If forms overlap

How can they   Fade discourse slashes
Without history   The whole is non-situational

Knives and forks with almost a fleshly pleasure

Riskless wipes away doubt the news   Pink slips
Arranging   The stiff unfolding of a chequebook
TV lunch wheels in millions
Of untitled titles

Boy shouts to his father on the new office roof
On every hoarding an involuntary
System of ID   Patch that whistles over
A stop on the line   Who will recognise
Thought was to one side or not real
As she jumps out to his deepest deposit

Speaks to a man driving through fog
Fill in the space with your impacts   A
Satyr spray-guns cock and balls on a tree
Discipline from this head refracting   In the
Ecosystem   A hundred hours community service
Electronically stamped on his wrist

January–March 1989

Strand selected: 7 September 1997

42-53

Dialogues

42 The Collected Works of Josef Stalin

brush my cheek my whittling throat

the fisted rosebud (iron
plough and the voice of the poet

open. Obey.
Land sing praises

voice: filial lily
        kicked in the guts
breaks its
neck snapping breeze

duty breathing song

the chained earth: :moon hushed smiles

great daylight (begging

his shadow

teasing the horizon

tatter the forest startled
life
spills your *head cannot hang* the hermit

returns haunts a tomb-blank

detained by hope

ghosts
knock us up

poison

the lute clinks (selfless

song in its own praise double
scented

no joy dropped
in its darkness No

false shaft of grafted song

entwined heart's

harp. snarled.

no passion drowns

in its luck

      (crowds
resemble, chant
blank exclamation marks

25–26 SEPTEMBER 1997

43 Ten

Flick of hair on a glistening.

Ashes collapse dust blanket Ah!

Seeing apertures adjust.

Glances through the chickenwire.

Devise admissions to self.

Torn into transcendence? Rending

Despair see

Ekeing out

(tensile)

. grinding against bone. grand

. .

Out in the kitchen.

'An ethic of pleasure in the shadow of responsibility

Looming edifice. Spring rain

Drenches you in promise learned as premise

Kiss my skills

!

Says ashen snags on wire the scene keeps changing the curtains.

Pocked surface, rain

pitied. teasing-

hovers over a raft of projections

.

Ripping through vision, torn sheets; flapping image-shreds slap
    the day in the face.

Leisures' measures'

Blossom blissfuls of.

(Sighs!)

Hand falters over the contract.

Sign a size too few.

Sing a shock a

Abolish . . .

I'm all eros, prosthetic rust!

9 OCTOBER 1997/2000

44 Beginning with a line from a Chinese poem in an English dream

at last the lineated look that was me playing in a palace or a cage
neither a musical instrument nor an ancient board game so beau-
tiful we forgot the locked door though caricatures rushed through
the bamboo gates

explode onto petrifying talk of freedom a mouth that hollows out
allegory like apple blossom like the lamentable loss that was who

at least the line took me away to wrestlers in flame less to the
threshold which bled my smarting eyes into a bowl extenuating my
ear as identity's howl

just a fluffer to stiffen up the hero for the heroine who arrives so
long the appetiser burns off across the polished codes or the skein
across the keyhole mucoid glue that stuck in our eyes

sticks in the grain of the throat the frozen limbs of the rivers after
extensive searches through identical slats of bridges below where
naked men bathe in the ladies' identikit confessions

pointing with his folded fan to the warm up act lest your liminal
luck should run out to the rearing horses and be trampled to a
thirst

to the leasehold of *me again*, O line invisible, I weave my mutest
lip from the gloss

16 OCTOBER 1997

45 Sonoluminescence For All

Dialogue 3

cell deaths in our faintest bin users mismatching

no testicles pseudodecorate

regulates the cross reaction signalling (array)

bite faced drops evolutionarily open

germline Sefton coast phages

nearly face on binary turbulence corrects your frizzled family down

but I don't believe in wasting the mantle is shaking error

Cadaver! I'm not condoning execution

message detection kit off to the shatter of a redundant truth

rodents and Man. Subsoil

pinhole fantasies with wild bioethics

no noise free images resonate downstream

information cascade scaled individuals

your favoured site of Heineken bottles replicate one's body's own
photo cleavage misconduct

hypermutation game in the Name scooting ropes of signature

a just rapid changing temporal informing manipulated left hand lie

26 OCTOBER 1997

46 Armchair Adoption

Dialogue 4

: for surrogate twinness the Palatine does

sell it! On the really mat, bands
of nattergirls. Cast casteness
on a bonelit transparency
flipping the mono-ness channels. Wipe
no-ness and less than no. It's

a boy: she's a girl proves

it; gagging gift of existence, literacy
is not just for life. *Fatty's got a real thing
and not a dead thing.* Cough up a certain one
lineness. Download
the Person as Absolute Theme

You do it. *nessness*

OCTOBER 1997

47 In Good Voice

Dialogue 5
Small Voice 3

A poem always accepts the conditions of virtual dialogue
Jacques Roubaud

rainbows
frozen across the floor

crumbs for me −*n*,
for example, spectrum strip

from the voice's delights. *Take one* outside

'I'll fix my inverse position for
whoever. Houselights screen a possible calm

master the me
speaks only up one moment

inner *which*
yet the next unhinged you

where negotiations in practice

you *when* in theory
willed by shape perfect caked in time

'Not sure whether this act is squeezed,
something to slop out behind an invoice

in the duo's
trash intonations

tooled you (or me) rust
of the un-re-en-visaged

assertion
questions history's other croak

the shadow's turn off as real as

nature takes the refracted seat
in this answer back

any vehicular position

shit-heap casualties utter relations

'Accounting flutters from
ethics sure as Hell. *Follow*:

into unofficial darkness

too close to the icon eye it
filled in somebody else's archive

so long So and So!) 'Don't worry, we'll
uncover our tracks before

setting out the double columns

you give a little pleasure about aboutness
dead reader haunted (*voiced*

30 OCTOBER–6 NOVEMBER 1997

48 Dialogue between Created Pleasure and the Resolvèd Soul

for Ben Watson

Dialogue 6

Not you again, you big
girl's blouse! (cleaving twist and twain

Concretely uttered, may my light executive
dusting be considered as a form of life?

There's none in that body, all hooks
and spin, as PC as a veiny dildo
humiliating the inner voice, king of things

Dead systems twinned, halos
monumentalise the air

Speech, pure dictionary in double split
sides, inseminates the shifting
axioms of material in an outcry.
If you want
an interesting interior life get up
off your fat arse and get a
job you aphasic blank. Blink.

Fluid category fleshpots utopia.

Don't speak (to me) with a corpse between
your teeth, bumping into (and off)
yourself in fatal leather snapping
in twos and toes as I seduced you with picket
grace whims cross-dressing as a 39

inch bust in centimetres. Mutter
mutter mutter mutter (falls into the social
come
dark
shot
grapple
hardcore
vice
versa
joint
stock
sublime
fudge
dog
organs
being chained to the fucking cosmos
tackle
the quest
to beget
better
sex guides lay back and think of the stars

Sample that bitch, a small
simulacrum of somebody else's else. No
code?

No ode—just the behaviourist's crystal.

Polyphonic ejaculation! Do you
want to handle my swollen gland; in
my language we have the same word
for 'man' and 'girl', for 'love

'dream

'knots

'not equal

'objection

'size

'='. You *can* teach pork
to snout the spot

Pleasure as an idea is a
formula. Anarchy as a theme
is a juice derived from shot.
Spirit a bucket.
            Diametricalism
as force to be reckoned is a
gang rove in tense invidious.
Matter is muttered all about
'you', you hoodlum of the lip.

I don't. She
discerned the hand of a man

decisive, dark, menacing,

on the envelope. I'm trying to
fill a thriller at the moment
with knowledge as human as death

Your tropes bellyache tripe
as trite bathing belles sharked by conscience,
etymology as any sighting?
Discourse on trees,

weed dust explored mistaken

uli.

ex

-land

(wrack):

puritan shrug-offness meets bursts of
busting
statutes and ripe rips
cul-de-breach
and a whole bunch of jingle-lessnessness
(again)

category-collusive coughs between movements

Please God, don't erect me when
the doctor grabs my balls, situated,
endowed with meaning and hating it.

Let's get right inside the outside,
the neuro-ideological poem
that spits out its writer,
well no or yes
about four hundred times a year, its
responses corrected through liturgical
marginalisation.

You said it. No dialogue
without thinking with the solids.

No job too small, the will-not
down the pan. Lift
the lid on the eye: chaos patterns
in the bloodshot rolling,
an ecstasy that shatters the bloom, showers
petals above the literal ground;
on a wet, black chop.

Bliss my chora! Tort my chorus,
Trot, whiz-sin pinkies fan the air

(O harmonicas in your little
plastic coffins, arise!)

Be inside everywhere; outside
the booby boom

that spot that get us hot, you and I.

The 'metamorphosis of the materials', you mean?

13 NOVEMBER 1997

49 Tin Pan Arcadia

borne witness by the hissing
faster than gone
distributing oppressive music as
twitch for rebellion
a note on the step
for the proletariat
on the mantle of shine
explodes the stylish syntax of
devouring privatised eye
the anti-mirror shatters
freedom tastes of limits
speaking oracles
from a signed edition
a hush too far to mention
fascinates *their* tarnished utopia
an apocryphal critique pricked
into skin or a sculpture of
Pol Pot crafted from skulls

20 NOVEMBER 1997

50 Towards a Neo-Diagonalist Manifesto

Dialogue 8

power is wrong (you better enjoy it
next week's metanarrative is *phuttilized*
to a crispy post-trauma! (spindoctors
gridlock our sweaty horns as we cough
up the nightmare they swallowed
we don't conceptualise
the big princess in quite the dress
on a very small blackboard
inside off onto numbered
opinions dumbed down for the night

27 NOVEMBER 1997

51 In the Room of a Thousand Mute Salutes

Dialogue 9
Mute Salutes 1

Jewel up to trembling
hypotheses hybrids crown their brazen verses

sublime re-affirmations of all that can be said

just by watching men grunt the Earth. For example,
East facing behaviours and blank relics in the bedroom

mutate into a tradition you barely unmute

Earth is a colony of its own future. Sex
in verse: boy-slits strangle your testes, veiny friend

The soldiers fall on their booted-up whores
wrestle with an elaborate rhyme scheme

Earthen birds twitter
the anthem of some migratory Muse

(And her shadow

DECEMBER 1997–JANUARY 1998

52 Re:Entries

Dialogue 10
Entries 3
For Patricia Farrell 4
Unwritings 6

If milking a stretch then somewhere someone's demanding
a slide, catching a glimpse as catches

Nothing that's been reported but bladders huddled in bed, singing
to each other along the route to soak a crinkled vein

Stemmed for dressing, enact upon a
leather fringe. Derive:

A tongue drags its appreciative lap-routes all
dialogue resistant

The night had a thousand oils but it doesn't
repay the compliment by varying its
vocabulary of return caresses

Ideality peeps undignified shots wish a length *the* length of the
room shooting pencil-thin through the keyhole
out to useless gobs for shiny hides
or beyond!

Bitten pout bitch moistening synecdoche in figures, pads
for spilling cushions under a million
dreaming glans) *gone snap*

Unfold any passion could have spilled across one leg, the
narcissistic
floating, the laughter of a spy!

If the tongue's trail entered an entry without a thought,
leaves no blood on a milky thigh, then there's
no story without telling, another
day of congealed gloom

If orgasm digs pianoforte tongues across the weight of
frown, then near-entries float mounds
around a landscape in top

The body doesn't release words: they arise in the eye like love's
temperament, muscled
black, titles of hunger pumping on tip-toes, sucking hard
on the hard!

Calming the traffic of delivery jolts on the
bumpy road towards never
covering the traces

11 DECEMBER 1997

53 Freeze It

Midnight Ride 2
Smokestack Lightning 2
Unwritings 7

I would have preferred to sing the blues in any small bar full of smoke
than to spend the nights of my life scratching into language. . . .
Alejandra Pizarnik

I

Sonic topology of certain unbearable blues threatens to turn out onto
Kingston. Suits shine with human contact notes set up with yet
another rehearsal rolling. I look unlikely in this accelerated context:
Chris and Tony unload vinyl. Thrash ear-pressed harmonica plays the
rainy drive, caverns filling with noise and satellite TV cutting the night
into uneven strips. A monstrous chord fills the room bounces back and
forth across the lips programmed under flat-out Capitalism the leisure
to read poems. Pulling it played the last line for Duster Bennett.

II

Flesh and blood miked catching itself. More with the body coming
up to peak, sweet. Help me as memory in sweaty dreams lacks signings
to pink shows, coming home tired (to Tooting). Elzadie's noise off again
lost in finger skills catching herself in time as in sex concentration
upon images themselves without howling *where is she?* Brash chorded
little-voiced harmonica ears hardly hear her felt so bad with his inten-
tion-equivalents that she devastates and overtakes. 'Then vote some-
thing else! Or nothing.'

III

Playing is literacy prettily missed. Silent vibraslap in Chris' gloved
hands, my gaze slo-mo, turning harmony-manager. Convention joke's

not played a mysterious youth power recaptured. Middle musics rescued our time in the room to 'do' the total songness. Antiquity's waste burns timely in a *de-vinyl* belted raincoat economy! I miss the riff Peter Hope-Evans puts to bed for me. It's one instrument, it's two: yet others say six! Homunculus! Three-quarters mattress will do it: cliché errors in however wherever no-time styles.

IV

No time for listening I haven't sung. I cannot write from Hambone's vehicle, fingers on the fretboard, soft, lost in image. (I take 2.) I've been helped minutes before writing this stolen by 1936. We play in versions as two keys act a voice (simply) through me. Reverent reverberations laugh compensate with the stocking tops of Mussolini's granddaughter. Roses on harps confirm my perceptions with time phantoms not dissipative with Charley Patton tuned sky high! Haunted with grace I hear the liquefaction of the hangover trying on an ethnomusicological wheeze: piles of out of tune harps on Sonny Boy's grave.

V

This remote narrowcast we called Arvella in monochrome as he pulled it from Elzadie with excitations of the wide-eyed sweet thing. Documentarists play years awaiting lucrative tears as smut never proved their probity to Willie Mae. Gutted carpets fit the manager like Labour Party posters sealing self-absorbed imperial shines. We've had enough. She weeps regally as *Britannia* sails from the only colony she has left: the British People.

VI

Listening to Tony sing, refunctioned into *Briggflatts* (reading after the gig), tingles each time I mime, sheer jam swung guitars swept the floor between the Out of Date and History: hereabouts Every Day; you'll find me talking to myself, downtown, like somebody else. I'm forcing myself to not imitate burnt-out words in my heart, as Peter Green realised every time.

VII

If the wind should change, then fiduciary belongings amount to two dozen diaries. This romance surrounds you, this late century blues in an unplayable pack of quotations in quotes; crude effects play oddments' tricks. They've got another bill, poisons of crimes, looking from musician to musician, transposing keys: a guerrilla tactic somebody's aching fingers will track and hammer to death, night after day after night.

VIII

Blown lament returned laughing nor did Jo Ann Kelly's dead arm blues. Courage spools travelling blues squeezing eroticism rambling through your smooth voice at its last letter's elementary harmonica stance. *Sung* in *Snug*. Used its riff, listening walls shake with style-rut not barrelhouse; inexpressive as the wine-dark riverside.

17 DECEMBER 1997

~

54
A Hundred and Eight Robinson Crusoes

Friday: My Secret Life

Kick into heaven or hell my heels squash Crusoe's chips

But he'll be a good doggie and gobble my flaps

With the curve of his penis and the swelling of his testes through his rubber body suit

he'll package the dog's bollocks unto dust

His muffled voice from the pillow

He rogered *Matron*?

Thursday and I scratched *SOS* on his inflamed back and mounted him howling

'Surely, not even Thursday could stiffen at the adhesion of this songbird's beak

What if a dancer, her sharp breath spangling the frozen air, should spring from one almost weightless sleigh to another, pivoting on a handstand, to leave a single print?

When the helicopter crews realised we were new kinds of human being they roared off in disgust

I squeezed Crusoe's limb until it was black and ready to drop or
feathers would squawk from its tingle

Used that Howler Monkey Trick I licked yoke from a turtle's egg
pressed between his buttocks

Blowjob round by the garages

gripped her peroxide tuft with one hand and counted pieces of
eight in his pocket

(*Thoughts microphone:*) You are my Hero, I have made you, out of
nothing etc

Exquisite artifice of terror: a hand adjusts the wad that pads your mouth

I gripped the chair-back and felt his milky gaze flow across my
rump and back

in time to his curling snake breath

'"Blow me up and fuck me," that's what your label says!'

(he said

Saturday: Chemisch-Technologischer Robinson

He boils cockerels into tarpaulin

Knits bags for his Hoover spins feathers into handkerchiefs

The sink-plugs in Crusoe's bathroom are breast shapes pierced through the nipples with rings, chained

'Oh! Your heart is a spear your stars are targets

(If *this* is 'what *she* wants' then it is wanting

As director I shall shoot myself cut myself back in

His balls in freezing sacks he pissed in the sink

A dead phone chord round his neck, face covered in tin foil and polythene

monadic self-sufficiency

he'd slavishly choked on Thursday's perspiration

The sucking sound was probably only blood passing greedily through his appetite

(Sings, operatic:) *The evidence of my debauchery/ Will be lying in your mortuary*

Sunday: Crusoe in Short Words

'Doc' Crusoe's blue lit scenario aroused my nosophiliac eye

After I'd changed him, I jerked him off with a parrot glove puppet

'Mistah Kreutznaer—He Dead

Little world from scratch sloppy as ever as to principle

Your black thoughts mounted the First Musket

Restraint was breath control of a subtle kind

(*Whispers:*) Angela McWhirter's
        glandular squirters

impossible to meet you

      Thursday

But why this prolonged hunger?

Oculinctual mumbles of this blind fidelity at my mascara's edge
scour the chalice of my fake chastity

My bikini-bottom is up before he bursts in on the dot of the
Shipping Forecast for his goat-roast

steaming

Monday: Crusoe Infers

The Vessel Captained by a Man of Quality yet Manned by a Young
Pup:

Lipstick for his lips

Fishpaste for his teeth

Gnaw at your drift with human eyes

Monday to Friday

Musket Number Two was for the fermenting impression you
found next to your wine-press one morning

'Is this the Hand of God?' you asked, falling to your knees

It is the print of a woman's etc

(Ideas in English relate to other ideas solely

'Four legs produced this big dog with a mane of human hair

Shape of bone is an innate notion that hangs between (or even
within) species

as a threat (<u>Good</u>

as a promise (<u>Evil</u>

as a bendy plastic doll without a prick (<u>Undecided</u>

as a vinegary old tart melting into her component
chemicals (_____

Tuesday: Crusoe Through the Looking Glass

Hunched over his polaroids

Click!

'How *do* fishes masturbate?' mused the actor in *Siesta for the Fiesta*

My latex eyes infer his potentiginious kink

(I read it for him

(It moved this afternoon while you were out alone thinking

From experience they are effects of custom hissing the sunburnt human flesh on heat in his hands

A bottle of plonk on the beach and Robinson 'Pretty Boy' Crusoe (in nappies) sucks melting jelly babies from between my toes

(Sings:) *I wannabe an amputee/ and lose my leg below the knee;/ pulled from the wreckage of my plane:/ I will never walk again*

Robinson 'Long John' Crusoe hops around the yard dusting his knee with the season's precious flour

The Thursday bird cooed: '*Ecouterism*

Paperweight which held down your Problem in probability I remember well winched open on your desk

So she could suckle me with blood used Crusoe's last razor blade to gouge me another mouth a Truth Hole

(*Reads:*) 'Year 17: Breasts like bells they carry the pot of Irish Sea stock to the leopard carcass

The shape of those ideas

Crusoe's mind-forged callipers measure each for Science

Wednesday:

Le Dernier C'rousseau

Grumpy bride perched on a tombstone for congress

Whipped his swelling goats each time they nibbled my PVC miniskirt

I thought: Give The Dog A Bone works both ways

'Shrink his breeches and damn his eyes

Crusoe the Cat thought: 'Deceiver: dog as a god

'Hush Bedwetter

(my glove heavy on his zipped mouth

'Musket Three . . . that was for the single handprint you found midweek in the frost, at midnight, stumbling midway between the pub and home

There was none

A card for the Meatotomic Club is tucked behind the dialling information of the island's single payphone

'Lick this live flex

Thursday: The Antic Robinson

I love that remote control around my fingers yet there is nothing
to control now you are gone

Elegant Subterfuge

(*Thinks:*) 'Any woman who has had it with a dog would never again
be satisfied with a man

Why these untenable metaphysics, a mutilation scar tucked in for
the night

Crusoe the Kid's cool exit west

The blank screen dreams my update of your docu-soap

The full squirting vision or the strange kind of rescue

The Triple Blast of Muskets, as Thursday accidentally trips over
the Security Rope

Synchronises a legion of panoptical devils

(as planned

Canned Laughter

I dropped my new top unzipped his slits so he could see the
undulant slogan:

'*Castrate Lactophiles*

    (we learned to *read*
    in the women's toilets

(*Writes*:) 'Year 23: Gave birth to a playmate, a bitch as sullen as myself: Tuesday

Robinson had flipped to that old TV Crusoe again, badly made in black and white

She taught Thursday to talk like the parrot despite his enduring Priapism his pungent sweat

(beyond the Pale

One of the Crusoes had warned, 'Don't breathe my sperm over Thursday

(as somebody unscheduled, like me, slipped from between his sheets

January–February 1998

55
Downing the Ante

Articulates 3
Killing Boxes 6

A cold genocide counter-solved the heel

Seal the borders the studio audience *can* and *will* weep when women feed for oil

Says Mr Casablanca

Scorched stiff in his white socks

Not fussy where the operatic commas go on the wire copy

Flat out fax attack beneath the spinning radar

(The facts drowning in formation

30 MARCH 1998

56

Abjective Stutter Expectorates Laugh of the Human

for Jo Sadler

Articulates 4

Empty Diary 1998

Human Dust 3

Internal Exile III

Lores and Bye-Lores 3

Magdalene in the Wilderness 3

Sharp Talk 3

Utopian Tale III

. . . .boards the bus in a rush, hot; removes coat, jumper, puts

Coat back on, adjusts shades. Her cropped, gelled, hair, dyed black,

Free, suggests youthful self-possession, reveals *how* she is suggested

In a narrative believed to conceal 'consumption's salivated excess'

: *'My hot meat on a half-bus seat*

: *'My floppy jockstrap leaks ego-transgression*

: *'My hysterical kidneys sweat blood as hyper-masculine glory gifts!'* 'You're

Loaded with waste, larded with fear!' she laughs, tips this favoured
tripping

From those ventriloquial lips. The bus stops, half-empties

Opaque bodies hoist themselves aboard; fills. She gives

Her seat up to a disabled human, moves back, mirrored, towards

Others: the glitter of a self, doubled. Care of self, of rings and ear-
rings, nose-

Studs, minimal eyeshade; shells. (Let's announce: <u>It's taken nearly</u>
<u>one hundred</u>

<u>Years for her to fall in self-less love with herself</u> *(Ha-ha, has it?*

7 MAY 1998

57
Angel at the Junk Box

im Frank Sinatra

IM 7

Midnight Ride 3

I

Breath betweens the sexy brass
quakes against the battlements of the tier;

lute song off the blames. Moaning mini-
symphonics underwrite maze blazing of cries
in the mids of my faces...

-dict no dirty crowd, taut; taughts,
held and slackened to twirl, waver-

songing

II

Cooling, she might hear you
sing and *know* the same words
and shift.
      Cash it now and every blip
is a dizzy how. Propelled
into a cringe, wrapped
in a growl:

the way you mock your blands

III

Mute up your factitious sensation

(even a ring of breath to kill

Transmute a crazed phrase of male hysterics

Break up song into this gut-voiced holding

IV

Bounce a pebble voice on the
waves of this smile could then
if the sinking full-bowled
potential point of inform

Poison emotion. Floors crawl
a new song, doesn't fluff? A
strange stress on not-speech.
Hats on your horns gentlemen!

Ease a sample hammer
on the fall, blast over the stock.
Repeats; repeat tobacco-toned town;
the voice in my shivering circle.

v

Black Kansas, sit! Sudden guitar
gets it odderly

Hear those folded arms and clarity—
the doors of deception off-beats up-beat a
croak to the full;

risking flats affirm music

space him still low

spread to the lowest in time
to the admissible

last syllable cymbal out(→)s

28 MAY 1998

58

Retitles: Three Overlaps for Jack B. Yeats

1 Ocean Green — another homage to Jack B. Yeats

Singing 'My Dark Rosaleen' 1

Origin gets battened down as estranged sparks radiate of weightless paper vents up neural image spark another homage delivered its dodge or prevented dither you should draw justice invented sketches of my passions invalid Romantic on the edge of a paradigm left behind declares all drop of the dirty British coast a gibbety-down before blind men's eyes raised of babylonish dialect.

Smear from the sea on clowns rush in all directions directing girls explode with delight as his cigar torches his enfabled wingèd feet on a barrel of gunpowder pale husks his moustache sparks from the rim of his body is the real scent of the ceremony ancient escapees they yield disguised she trembles before the horses gallop towards the tollgate cardboard of footlight squads point barrels before his puppet explorer tied to the pale you build around you (as only a colonialist would) barbeques a pair of human hands rising after prayer to never becoming analogies for this simply transfer the guilt.

Ex-posthumous costume swish and cross the distant tropics not Kilmainham head for a phrenologist's catalogue memorises the word *Boyne* reverse its otherwise to elsewhere condemned around the long list a widow hissing spindrift still in the rage he left golden was her hair and experiment no pantomime across his drunken scoop of landscape placed displaced or dispersed beyond description the gulf stream laps softly unfold his legs as disorderly as dwarfed.

The Irish papers by the sash this Son of Erin feasts coolly somewhere the window *gives* flat roofs an image dominance challenge to a greeting is Arrival borrowed from a Penny Paper pirate his centaur outside the Imperial Hotel distends the official case a schedule of delay details waiting to be unfolded to be consulted as his assistant waiting he waits a shudder epiphany of home in the liquid fingering his throat through the luminous Jameson's prisms the coast.

The *most* real of flags flutters you who knew it too fair footlights bathe in a kind of admiration a kind investment between lead grilles telling a fleshed-out story your eye follows the curve of his ashplant home he'll take barefoot flattened casts mirror the pavements she is touching the door almost gingerly as though a memory jumps out and shatters everything mirror-written bleeds your heart.

Ha! Buffalo Bill's angel of literacy bursts above a bookseller's hunch for Henty or Masefield scrabbles through the pile not weeping its own reflection fully to mark its removal is refrain from the song beneath our tread they strut the strand Rosaleen they dance where he stern gazes inwardly the figure of the view from horseback and traveller's headlock fills slumbers of the ocean green smeared of unreflecting thought-groves shadowiest intentions arrested in a *ridin' an' ropin'* trot.

Thunder off but not far night he saw couldn't scale the thing he saw shore roofs read like a fisherman's prayer *are* a fisherman's prayer snapshots chill the sky bends flagpoles by a rage more than a race he sells tickets for the show the driver's lips crack in vaudeville warm-up distance drops across the skull of the English spires and tramlines a blaze of unlocatables.

Sucked from the moustache as beard as dark as the porter that dribbled for a good beating face made out twitching at us and waited for our pockets so spake all kinds in tinker sleep pissed on the carpet he was nearly one flat out on a table now strand strong rope held him to hope the simple rail of an invisible vessel mutters the Donegal roads until peace shall deliver him stark mad but doomed the sea is downs speeding fountains muscle in upon grief the dead man wreaths to lay one free bellyful of flowers down the heave of sea ornaments the lighthouse wink to drowned thoughts.

You hold river stretches a bridge of lies in sweet swart streak Dublin resembles you reassembles three choices of the young nation opposite at home in the jostle of Grafton St I belong to a tiny sketch the lightning body sings itself stiff with judgement without justice assumed.

Profit margins at the edge of his daughters snake in ropes on a weak man's body listen to these sirens studied indifference to the mast with sodden kerchief the women in veils will the mourners watch the coffin rest on the principle of watching of waiting studied activity splashes around the room and Spanish ale shall give you hope other than the wash of the floor re-adjusts this eye grows feet in the yellow light of last night's drips washing between showers on the bank of the Liffey a bundle of gestures floods.

Turns from looking across story the afternoon caps and leaning latest crowd flakes of sunset gasping news caress but no sales glosses assurances slice through pundits of the surround two beards in congress wagging intense communal look the evening editions regret in this to calm like a female trajectory tragedy stills the mills

or: *darkness close and rush stories ranked like bottles a pale porter alight with gossip swirled the pull down animated by the smoke about flinty reality on language functions dialogic workmen rumoured a train pull who tears 'ere the sun blaze hoof frisk purples those adolescent Mercurys!*

Turning into art dreams of blood washed shimmering before days vibrate buried not planted the world is precisely distant under these conditions to elude the mind's reading flames from another work emanates a streetlamp conspires but they aspire to co-creations of bridgehood (not O'Connell's) between the pied organisms and the dappled embodiment isolated as consciousness itself wells or wills his neck for Progress matches a glint stills my dark Rosaleen a wild moment on a rushed hilltop is hoped out of view.

Redundant of blood to light on leather and hell pits spit sanguine and gold light constructed sprays the altarpiece of train carriage she's a centrepiece rushing river from her golden voice black listens resistant in this sweep along to the mighty flesh of her throat rolls forth my song like a gesture that effaces her country on either side angels to her hymn claws of ice yielding a wave against the blue transport loses

the remnant of rises from the deep surfaces a hat of scratches to shield
him from the word WHISKEY weary as a walk-on resolved valediction as
welcome here barmaid haunts the pebbly refusal of the Document
shatters their gilt.

He's as uniformed uninformed signed and slogan cry commission is
a vessel pouring Masterpieces on the quayside to deck a beard so
combed a helmet so condemned for years long to herd with disdain
floats into this secluded thought demesne could spin collapsed
unformed into hoist the wrong sort of Irishman 'on a horse'.

Mute Salutes 2

Golden matinée fingers sing of what is to come nightly tearing at the
deathless dying lover of an eternal crowd's gasping keeps a drowsy
senator with just enough loopy metaphysics into a good old stagy
illusion slapped up passions humped mortality's sensual groans
animating polished tabletops in the devil's alcove where monkey
glands fear to secrete jammed by evanescences pumped with sex as his
brittle bones sing.

Accretes like a value or valve holding back this flower seller with her
insistence taken out of nature lifts up a Dictionary of Gestures we're
less sure of rows of thumb smudges are a crowd melted a horse on
the mustard waves eye gives to this cascade the agony of an injured
non-human repetition is multiple witness littered with freezing we
cannot read drained in a frame we call and could be cloud gallops by
only the sound generated by a single gesture clustered near the motor
car an intense singularity of rider upon thud-hoof-wave turf upon rune
upon treasure upon drying for months upon a continuum which is
sense it is an arm still which in a sense it is in art.

Homage to the generic necessities of piled bodies would have been
called a *likeness* obviously torn from a book strangely oracular with the
early winter leaves this container thought spills finite speeds and final
disembarkation that isn't thought and its infinite box surfaces as
'thinking' which is a nothing where some illusion of something
submarine sinks farther into artifice she leans towards him as love

[307]

should gouge your names into his newspaper a fraternal signature that stays together to gather us into a bus by this river at the edge of Europe flattens out of colour no wraithed merests flame.

Or saw a grey crew of living idiots crawl in blood eyes awash with mere syncopation he asked me to play a *chune* he pronounced O the red rose to which he is wed solid in focus for the *toon* his fruit-head departure bars depict drools the drums cease the night dancers' festiveness advances upon Jazz Babies with their corsets off curious for simplicity and complex you are a cream white rosebud with flesh on its petals. *Or*

Of passion sings the white rose breathes hot club muscle the crowd courts on Matisse's fiddle-distracted visitation of the solid diasporic godlit contagion where Mondrian's frugality falls glum Tin Pan Allegory as royal roost rests the wireless's bare airy appeals boards barren floors weak in and under as nightwarbler clarion fans the boogie for the off.

Blazed to smithereens by the light was indeed sucked like the mellow fire of whiskey through teeth flash upon says nothing but says burns intervenes between him a longer span is the rough of *Jack. B. Yeats* rucks up scrapes alluvial rupture the lines fix upon the only inch of him is withdrawal but Hellespont or vacuum that he un-acts turns accounted closed open frames to match treasures to the city's curtailed summary enters this place it enters us as promise of bruised walls tremble flecks of vision curtain the pale moon gleams cold comforts of appercep-tion the fight was indeed on no.

Mute Salutes 3

Make a race with sensations the indifferent back drops the carpet of propaganda over the verso the modern epic's blood dimm'd tirade wrought chilly shanties under the daily rag you bend perpetuity sink-ing *thick with cordite* stayed news a solid ocean buoys your earthen twit-ter vanishes a trice in sublime error extinguishes the monument faceless back to our turf in absence of the human hymn of percepts affects and sticky glues under this man's suit and that man's deathless ditties we build shakers of the world!

An elsed wreckage the horizon's thin-lipped gulp spouts full of masculine tops and tails segments of action but is never of a castrato before the embracing zero then vertical melts against horizontal piling sees mourning as morning passion of this coming Sunday with its bodies of fire precision barges of rust squalls of light monstrosities of vaporific illusion weightless in a washerwoman's eye freezes blue under spirited fingers the sea incoming acceptance over the upturned boots in the thumbprint sky.

Melt integrity *his* monument yet against heritage spread the language as luxurious landscape *was rainy the wind* was stammered trembled contemporaries of stout-tied speech a steady Beckett will always come no Rhetoric the light says always figures us into before everything has happened but the commentary to become the sublime more gull-stained than creases.

where the pink rose wilts she is waiting breath expending transcends all judgement plunges the wind's unfleshed intention's incarnate turning from all movement and singing of the sea shifts onto the sense shifts as still life possible only his own sensation he becomes so completely the light's purple extinction the grandfather clock bolt upright faces the shambles of an entering man curved substantiality of the table leg's period passion where the monologues fail an abstract filling for his mask has ceased to signify. Or:

hold the suspicion of a letter a photograph a jewel not melancholia but aloneness alone deleted the walls he backed low-backed leaned-against or the stool beyond which the deliberately boxed deliberately stretched.

Distance holds a road shapes yellow's dream of blue composed a nation on slither to marry a ghost and bear the pull of river to odd bits and odds and ends intricate solidities on 3.3 million dead Russians to physical intuition fixed towards a cataract personality never ceases to witness a *blitzkrieg* figure grasps uprooted Europe's million pairs of Unknown Scissors imprints finite upon flesh scratches upon flicks a bombed-out sky.

Dogfights a blister night haemorrhaging over Byzantium a sky out of which is sold and solid fierce black epaulettes cusp a calendar than singing chants of groined meat from *Finnegans Wake* to this twentieth century and a half cloud as speed rampage is your clutched throat my dark Rosaleen do not sigh down my neck O! looming sublimes on the fucking bare chests thank Godless than lessness an era of outstanding cultural disaster!

Atlantic bathe the earth golden for your dapple flows hazed mountains unrobe a Censor clothed in line glorifying the Invisible Throne vuval egress commentary gashes of chill water divide these tufts in marvelling mumble before losing out to scale the mystery and yet be part of the mystery trick of a master's desire for the old themes wash constellated as weave larded with gold nature allows is allowed he takes off light works like fire spurt of day's essence against the brood.

The fairground (foreground) resplendently vernal the matter and maker are old ambient and dark central transience falls from grace moves over the instinctual economy of the non-human's pricked ears configure substance no mistake but partly accidental contours of another painted face interfered by sets of eye-scribble you alone can today tell distance is his presence in the afternoon as landscape formally speaking *Ah* he says fluffed the snow clouds and creaked *well.*

2 Bruised Ground

. . . scrape that fiddle more darkly. . .

Paul Celan

Bruised ground
        suggests flesh pigmented
Pigmented the words
           in the sky is their yelling
My dark Rosaleen
        the Erne shall
Run red with redundance
             to redundance resist collapse
As the discharge of
         guilt Earth rocks
Beneath our tread
        we're wonder-struck
Each flaked definition
             functions masked
Into medium as in
        purgatorial fire

Talk scratched into air
         and left to dry
The next thing next to dry
            the next thing
To beauty *shot in the back*
          at Communion and
Left to die gun-peal
        and peal and slogan cry

With just enough
            hangover to hang
Over to stand in for
            memory as *undiluted fascism*

'Ere you shall die my
            dark Rosaleen
Die my own Rosaleen
            judgement hour
Felon setting giants
            pass through the
Setting giants pass
            through the
Miniscule village
            musical muscle as
Faces of ice interdict. A pyre
                        interdict a pyre of solid
Grief
      silvered and dark falling
As hair-flame
            and falling in disbelief

Left to dry landscape
                  made of landscape a
Heart's message that a heart's
                        drifted on the crooked
Message on the
                  crooked crosses human bidding
Eyes script and blood
                  triggered eyes
Squeezed tight it's the last
                  we see or hear of paint
'Ere you can faint 'ere you
                  can fade my dark Rosaleen

3 And Where Shall We Be Then?

Homage to Jack B. Yeats 2

There Is No Night 2

To Ground yet of ground as solid below
Ground as solid to the ashes
As the ashes of Hell. No,
The ashes of Hell, no
Vergil for Vergil for this tour
From the horse
Into which a horse into which is the all
That is
The of all is all
Is Art. The even as it is art
The even all
That the even all that is left, as
Left as not on this
Heat, this Heat City. Speed
Is heat, is, but *no;*
No ocean green, they
March along the deep they drop
In the full away into the full
Into the wind; away
Of wind the red of
Wind has it; it's
On a lip. What a way on a lip what a way
To go away! If it were a
Way to go away! As
Empathy as if as empathy
As if of the off. Or
Is it of a story
Off a story of the story of
Blue? The road, a car, here,

The horse, mid-tease at the horse. The solid
Thing rears, rears its fluid, a threat
That rears its fluid, a threat that
Rears, defies. Defies
We aren't we aren't yet
Aren't we yet now
Under ground?

1997–1998

≈

59

A Dirty Poem and A Clean Poem for Roy Fisher

For Roy Fisher 2

mayday 98

Study 1

1

The building was not 'backed by glowering indigo, browned
by the day and its frigid chaos', or whatever discourse
I'd once pasted it up on. Stripped out for allegory, its voiceover
prized each ethical chill. Sliding doors sluiced me
past welcome into publicity, security. Suspicion. Outside,
a police helicopter lowered in that replica New Labour Mayday sky
without cloud. We're up to see the Audi in the remoulded cheese
    grater
as clearly as the rusted Christmas trees down the embankment!

Be Here Now is etched into the handless clock face
on the deserted railway platform that promises late delivery
of what could be some special trick of a lusty kitsch.
Note headless female manikins at attention by the beds
in the department store window for the boniest of sex acts.
Fictive spans. What discourse could face this down, I ask,
facing up to what I might never simply call myself.

                          I never
could love something without a face on it.

2

Bolting the canal's chaos beneath the night's faceless want

Haunts another category

To re-tell the job you've paid oncoming readers

Flattened out

Under the bridge a stroke as historic as now

All moons dusk the day's falling

Waste as a spectral tick in a dusty box

Create strange beings that will image

What might become stretched out almost anywhere

MAY–NOVEMBER 1998

60

A Dark Study for Lee Harwood

Articulates 6
For Lee Harwood 2
Study 2

Before work each morning, a walk round the lake. To observe: a hole in thin ice; a lone birdwatcher

He looks up from the desk. Chatter. Nobody there, only discarded drawings around the room; looks into another life: the life squeezed out of these birds, as half-parrots, blob or outline

No escape from 'God's feathered fairies

(you'd have found a poem hanging alongside the painting at the Royal Academy in 1885

for several decades past, a taxonomy in flight: quarter-parrots, or less, an abandoned sketch-line, or two

Love: a perfect claw round a hollow bone

Dreams of shrieking rainbow birds, yet silent as butterflies, a soft breath of plumage. Of dark ornithomantic rites:

a ripped crop's message, the gizzard's bitter reply

In a house commanding a view of the Mersey, its last inhabitant Emma the maiden scion of a proud family of Liverpool ship owners, the painting entombed

In his study with his motionless focus upon Verisimilitude, the Absolute Parrot, his exemplary effigies button-eyed, musty

trussed on the desk like Darwin's finches

Nameless servants blur in bucolic photographs of the grounds of
Sudley House, semi-visible labour stacking hay

In business as in contemplation, there is always an Elsewhere, an Otherwise

He cannot now find the words to settle the whole enterprise beyond
the title: '*Recapitulation*

Facts are quiet. They resonate; only you can reply

A slave girl stripped to the waist to reveal for the camera— somebody else's idea of memory—the evolutionary distinctiveness and
stage of her race

(her name was Delia. She was born in the Americas, although her
father, also photographed, originated in the Congo

appears to be crying, but has only perhaps moved her eyes in
defiance of the command to sit still

*'My first sighting of a Kakapo ground my theories to fine dust, sprinkled it
across my pages . . . . six precious days lost travelling to that killing!*

Everything she sees is bequeathed to you one way or another

A Treatise on Parrots by Henry Stacey Marks, oil on canvas (42⅝ ×
30⅛ in.), bought by George Holt in 1886 for £525 (no bill extant

Parrot-coal chatters in the grate. An unseen hand silently rekindles,
keeps it alight for days, without warmth

Somewhere within the dark study the sound of what might be
sobbing

1999

61

For the Continuity Terminator

Articulates 7
Empty Diary 1999
Melting Borders 5
Mute Salutes 4

My labia flip up between my hips like a Sumo's nuts

He's chiselled me into his identity parade, lost me in fragility's totter, guilty as style

Hardliners want to gun down Mr Universe; he used to lift our veils

(wherever my hundred sisters are now

he looks like a businessman about to be executed and we're to weep bitter self-enjoyings on his mandrake miracle

(he says

The Team commits Itself the Universe is Immortal

suffering to watch me watching the silk tie heaving on his rapidly panting chest; I can't guess the number of particles necessary to make one Butoh Butch!

Don't laugh! a punchline is exactly that. Slapstick

I don't recall my hand extending across the abyss to grasp the Flexibomber's yarrow stalk fingers

But now my presence queens him and, though a moniker will mean one thing, a Lewinsky will always mean something else!

Something else the ideogram means shakes the drips as she inscribes the book famously smiling

[319]

She's anyone's mascara streak blinks the lips without parole

Jokes stick to her heaving pinstripe like diseases shot on pollen

a strangler's hands claw a risk of survival in the cooling of relations
that followed the female infanticide moratorium

as well-adjusted as my bra-straps and delicious blooms

*The 'Accused' is brain dead but accused of crimes committed before she was
born*

Then she stopped breathing naturally but made spermy molecules
drip from her eyes and ears at once

the ethics of signature scribbled out in the blows of dedication

I'm taken but not shaken

('It shudders me onto several planes of consciousness at once,' he
tells himself

shaking *this* baby until her brains rattle

Then she stopped breathing naturally and made liquid circular
trails with a fingertip wound around each sorrow

'I wish *I'd* written *Empty Diaries*, but I wouldn't have dared

(she hears herself saying

I'm a sexylipped handmaid, squeezing contaminated balls of space-
time to produce fresh spunk for the Muses

if I forget to file the verses of that esteemed male guest, then I'll be
forced to kill myself by smoking my bones into brittle dust-jackets

The outlawed dildos of Alabama moan her woes, and echo back her sighs

13 MARCH 1999

62, 29 and 67

Wayne Pratt: Watering the Cactus

The Deathbed Edition

62

1 Suez

As I gaze now at your curling photograph
Tucked into the corner of the chocolate box
Brimming with saccharine snaps,

I recall those holiday trees, stirring
As though tremulous fingers were
Searching the scalp for lice.

He gave me my first cigarette there
In exchange for my coveted condom
And I was sick before the discarded match

Had cooled. He shrank,
Embarrassed, boyish, the hangman's mask
Flopping to a squab.

The afflatus of history in the rabbit hutch:
Eden's picture covered with pellets.
'Guess who?' — soft girlish fingers pressed over my eyes.

I first saw the marbled skin of your thighs,
The silvered crutch of your discarded knickers,
As he kissed you (his sister) goodnight.

But the next day I refused to follow
The mouse-tracks into the lichen with him,
But stayed home to stroke the cat instead.

2 Two Girls

1

Daphne was a brown-haired
Brownie, brushed against me
In the dinner queue, once,
And I watched, next gym day,
Your different shape of girl
In bottle green knickers. Pure
Brown and green, blank as Rothko,
Brings you back to me. I saw
You in the tube, once, two screaming
Kids on your lap, one in brown,
One in green, your unbrushed hair grey.

2

Beryl the Peril you were sobriqueted,
By lads over pints after a 'night out':
They spoke of your preference for soft sand,
And I imagined the soft warm craters
Left there as you left to pee in the sea.
They spoke of your love of Babycham
And I thought of the lipstick stained glass
On the vinyl. Beryl stopped me in the street, once,
And asked me for a light. I did not then smoke.

Manly, I swaggered into the pub that night,
Cigarette fuming but not inhaled.
I offered Beryl a Woodbine; she
Was an Embassy girl. That night
The sand was hard but I was not.

3 Fornication

Limp now, I turn away.
No longer can I face
The heaving spaghetti

Of your steaming sex, or
My elephant's fumblings
In the bamboo pit of our bed.

Hunching over your foetal back
On the infertile
Gulf of our marriage, I hug

My *hottie-wottie-boggie*
And say goodnight.
This childhood name

Brings back the muscular arms
Of my mother, hauling
The black-bottomed kettles

Onto our northern griddle,
Spanking the rubber flanks
Of the spouting hotties.

My only consolations now
Are these virile images
Tossed up in a spray of old words.

(SPOOF ON QUOOF)

4 Imagination

I watched you cry, grandfather,
Burying the dog that had been
Your only companion

Since the works gave you
The sack. I think of you
Sitting half-blind

Squinting at newspaper headlines
In the unnecessary darkness.
I read to you but you no longer listen,

Staring ahead as if at ghosts.
Your hands trace unseen crosses in the air
Recalling old friends

Like saints on their days.
Your unnecessary walk
Round the block to the local

Is no longer part of your plodding routine.
The frass of all the universe
Lies under your slippered feet:

A carpet of soft oblivion.
Soon I shall be burying you
Beneath the lilac in the garden,

But I will not cry. I have
Rehearsed this scene time and again
In the matinée of my imagination.

5 Cremation

The colour drains from faces into flowers
And hats: strips of black flip over in the breeze.
Labelled blossoms tremble with our names,
Choking in a sobless cellophane sweat.
A dust cart shatters the valley's silence,
Backs up, casual, to the rear of the building,
But we try to ignore its calamitous appeal.

Once inside, there's professional solemnity,
Sanctimonious mouth-sounds, deadly tears,
Infectious, even as we leave the squeaking
Rollers behind.

                 But now the cart has gone.
We drive off the scenic, forgetful route,
Driving off the thoughts, remark the quickening
Sea-side fun, back to that empty deck-chair. . . .

The undertaker pulls up at the lights
Beside us, thrums the wheel, looks out to sea,
Turning his earned cash to casually flicked ash.
The furrows of sand form an endless frown
Where laughing children splash in the shallows.

6 Against Paternity

Sniffing through my daughter's knickers
For traces of toxic glue
Brings back the joy of Airfix Spitfires,

Talismans of the heroic father
I never knew, invented for school-friends,
A square-jawed fiction to set against

The wreckage of reality: dead
In the Battle of Britain when terminal trails
Etched the sky like string.

The father whom I left behind was 'put away'
For offering sweets to little girls; my
Teddies lined the wall like Nuernberg judges.

His photo watched like a bleeding Christ
Above mother's catholic, all-embracing bed,
As I recalled the fate of the fathers' sins.

I can still hear her voice echoing down
The terrace, *'And don't come back ya bugga!'*
To each ephemeral figure tripping away on the cobbles.

Identifying 'him' (as we called him) in the mortuary,
I recall the expressionless unkissable lips
And his penis curled like a frozen prawn.

1983–1989; REVISED 1998

29 Strange Meetings with Justin Sidebottom

for Kelvin Corcoran
Watering the Cactus 2

Talk up his backlogs
of eclogues

..

THIS MACHINE IS EMPTIED
DAILY (me too

..

monoaural zeitgeist
bleatings between meetings

..

Agenda
Spender

..

'walkman earpieces swung low like gonads'

his wooden box marked PROOF

..

JUNE 1994

67 On the Death of Wayne Pratt by Justin Sidebottom

IM 9

Watering the Cactus 5

We watched the men with sticky crotches limp from
The wank-booths. You understood, but could not join,
These men who toss off in their pockets! 'Even the clockwork
Dominatrix in that specialist window no longer

Lashes the *pane!*' you punned. 'Puns punished me!'
You gave me your long astonished stone-eyed stare,
Like a frozen-frame image of a mongrel
Kicked in the privates.
                                    'Oh, it's only the old groin again!'

You laughed, 'it's playing *up!*' But I could see
It playing up all the way to your Heaven: somewhere
Like that Soho bar window seat, where even you
No longer could get that elusive something up.

We changed the subject like a change of pants,
To poetry: anthologies that left you out (that
Pained), where you'd joined me on a list of *Also-Rans.*
'Barbarians,' you barked, 'darkies and arse-bandits.

Larkin was right!' That you were wrong I could
Not say, but the old themes, old styles, we agreed,
Still worked—with a splash of spice! Oh yes, your eyes
Turned to the thongs and nails, but I felt your longing fail.

When I left you there to paddle the shallows
Of depravity, a pair of eyes hooked
On the kinky flotsam of the night, amid the pub crowd's
Long rush I heard your fading melancholy

Withdrawing sigh, 'Goodnight Justin; Goodnight,'
Fading against this stream of life you failed, where
Nature judged you wanting. Yet culture wants your
Judgement still, which flashed on me like the waning neon's

Sickly wink of tawdry come-on, as I looked back
And you were already scribbling in your pad,
And I, the forgiving pimp of your Muse, just heard,
As just preface to your last will: 'Go, little shit!'

22 AUGUST 1999

∾

63

The End of the Twentieth Century:

a Text for Readers and Writers

mayday 99
Poetic Sequencing and the New 2
and 55 other strands (listed in the text)

What would it mean, to end this twentieth century

and a half? To sing its closing blues, like Fanny in Coward's *Cavalcade*

atop a piano

'Blues, Twentieth Century Blues, are getting me down./ Who's escaped those weary

in a spotless blanched nightclub that suddenly opens onto a Riley light sign spelling out news

Steam rivets, loud speakers, jazz bands, aeroplane propellers, etc., Chaos;

'incurables' and social stereotypes assembled for the chorus

that consists of the entire cast singing the national anthem or *Shantih shantih shantih* or *To be men not destroyers*

or the whole thing recapitulated and set to Handel

or break my staff or read my map of approaches

They form an allegory. They can be read in many orders

Bunting was right, that the world changes too quickly in the twentieth century for a long poem. All that can be sketched out in advance are generative schema. But how could

the twentieth century ever end if one has lived in it

spied on it, imagined it:

its borders forever melt in the heat of burning Esso, its diaries replete with their own emptiness, its sharp talk cuts into its block of guilty silence, an epiphanic lightning flicker on a smokestack, the flashlight's glint on a sensational nylon thigh, Pearl's

(and even she may have one last dance at the Empire since 'The Materialisation of Soap 1947' becomes my anthology hit

a decade of writing and war: writing war back into the century, still writing at its end

read as a domestic journal, or read as a plan of war

of kill boxes in sand or upon mountains, of British soil as stained epos

('It's goodnight from Nato,' said the confused newsman, last night, each slip

each witness

each soleà (Miles plays for himself and somehow for Lorca, and for the others

alternative memorials

i.m. nobody, for the end of the twentieth century

Joseph Beuys' sculpture, pod-coffins, time capsules

works as retrospect, as prospect

so Patricia Farrell's duocatalytic incoherence works with and against my texts

'should mean as little as possible, whilst remaining embedded and implicated in the mundane world of references and associations

even *Fucking Time* which I nearly left out of *Twentieth Century Blues*, the numbering that is also a naming

because it seemed so antique. Yet Rochester's letter about the Customs seizing consignments of Italian dildoes links to a time in which vibrators are banned in Alabama, and even this college library doubted putting our booklet on its shelves

even the one fictive track into the future, not to be read as prophecy, that logo lasered on a kimono of 2055, which nobody saw as a partial parody of the pat narratives of cyberpunk

nobody laughs at history's jokes, or mine for that matter

Shutters clatter, dancers pose, double bass reverberates, text stutters, pauses; my words 'HELLACIOUS PHALLICISM' in sand in flames on the floor of the dance studio: to have put the performances with Jo Blowers into the numbering, so that some of the Blues would have been lost forever, though numbered, in their century, as event

restless refunctioning

of Horace's supplication to his Muse to leave her First Century Blues, for the Gulf War, which has stretched the decade as though it were a leitmotif; remoding 'Daylight Robbery' as 'Living Daylights'

[333]

in isoverbalist stanzas

fake form contentious by its very affront to metrical order, as I wrote of Adrian Clarke's fraternal enterprise (and from whom I stole the idea, forgetting Zukofsky, but finding it later in Williams' 'So much depends

only this week saying of that poem: 'etched onto paper by a type-writer', thinking how so differently I touch and the apparition of these typefaces on a screen

Reading while Jo improvised at Edge Hill last year, a surprise visit. Ventriloquial deletions. I'd forgotten that it was agreed that Jo would speak part of the text, and I was slightly wrong-footed when I heard her quote, 'He's my commanding view,' and I realised that Jo's suspicion that she had been working for months with drafts of the poem was correct, since that line was no longer in the text, but was again for the text of its realisation: 'Entries, Empty Diary 1996

Empty Diaries the thread through the weave

The Lores the knotted core

(refunctioned one part of 'History or Sleep' ('One raped/ can another relax...') as a poem for Kosovo three weeks ago, with the following preface:

This poem was written during a similar, but distinct, war and humanitarian crisis in 1995. While history never dies, and poetry may be attempted testimony, I had hoped not to witness approximate re-enactment in the present, when the poem becomes so effectively useless, unless read, against its own grain, as prophecy

the recognition that

another human being has responded

haunts

with its hope that the street might prove 'the last vestige of demo-
cratic exchange

(a sidewalk bookseller in Greenwich Village last week

the little negotiations, side-stepping, yet you who knew it too

where a nail bomb awaits a child's skull or a gunman lurks to blast
a telefamiliar face away

where amid the turns of discourse, the unconditional exchanges

face to face I

hear the songs of the death camps or their echoes in Kosovo
(forgive me

George Oppen, those human voices

have drowned us already in our troubled sleep; forgive me Paul
Celan,

or Lorca ('This time here/ they come') or others, that I have taken
your words, your cadences

samples

and linked them to the voices of (say
Lord Haw-Haw (! who did after all communicate that my father was
a prisoner of *that* word which shadows the century

or Stalin as poet (which a Communist student didn't believe.
Forgive me. Remember

Pasternak desperately trying to re-connect the phone line to Stalin
in the communal corridor, to speak to him of 'life and death

an 'image' of the relation of poetry to power: but remember, too:
Stalin lying stroke-stricken, mute, those standing awkwardly
around him doing nothing, awaiting his impossible

cold command to call a doctor

forgive me. History. Or sleep. The Hungry Years. Then Drowning
Years. The meltdown of 1989 (almost by accident catching the sack-
ing of Europe's museums of madness in the preface to these Blues

a history of the last years of the Empire—the old Empire I mean

The Age of Irony: two years of New Labour and the solemn New
Poets fax their dud thousand line Dome Odes to the spindoctors.
Yet here I am, we are

(whoever 'we' are

in the 'middle' of a war in what was once called 'late' capitalism,
when justice is a confused addendum to on-the-hoof rules of engage-
ment, as uneasily necessary now as impossible, wondering where the

deft steps

of the micronarratives have skipped to. We're no longer in the Era
of Metanarratives it seems; are we in the Meganarrative itself

Building a racist bomb from the Internet

Mr Casablanca is back, if he'd ever been away, monologic, where
cruise not Blues

will bruise the loving face of another

'... *more* responsible,' says Levinas

or as in certain poems of Lee Harwood

scraps of feeling balance delicately against a silence of non-feel-
ing, of the broken

Pages of my 'loose leaf manual of guerrilla tactics'

(as Adrian Clarke said of the century's avant-gardes

each single slip can be read in many ways

against a world of Mr Universe and his Team, where the Muse and
the Accused are ventriloquised as weightless resistance

though I *did* really hear a woman say that she wished she'd written
Empty Diaries. *The deliberate generation of stylistically various and knot-
ted strands of texts, allowing the readers their own preference between them,
risks a sort of disunity even those addicted to indeterminate works might
find difficult to figure as a single gestalt. Too many people seem to have writ-
ten them! This develops into a peculiarly risky strategy in* Empty Diaries
*of writing a sequence of 92 poems, the changing styles of which I couldn't
imagine a single reader being able to co-produce alone in its entirety. Such
an attack on the nature of* oeuvre *and the consistency of the author-func-
tion strikes me as a risk* . . . .

(my answer to Douglas Oliver's question on 'poetic risk'. I and my

Poetics, allowing the writing dialogue with itself, a reflection upon writings, upon the act of writing, in the act of writing (as here), gathering from the past and from others, casting into the future, to

permit

though every writing is a model for itself, and was so, long before Lyotard gave us the soundbite, the rules of what will have

been 'Twentieth Century Blues 63

among other twentieth centuries. *Burnt Journals* never existed beyond its title and accumulated materials on espionage that have been refunctioned since as linked unlinkables, whose content is never more than a contraction of form, which is what forms from what happens in a dialogue with themselves

But I can sense the shape of that unwritten *Burnt Journals*, its texture of cut and weave, its anguished disembodied voices of commitment and betrayal of the century's central narratives, of a repressed masculinity (echoing *Empty Diaries* and the similarly non-written *Drowned Books*) that floats an intensity of sensation; and because I can sense it complete

I cannot

write it

or the thousand line poem that New
Labour has purloined or the hundred hundred-
word 'sonnets' there is no point in
beginning even their variations seem ghosted out
against the pattern so that it's finished

(gave up this formalism for hybrid forms)
to imitate its own idea

youse hear?

or to make this mayday text a
further report on barroom philosophy and street
wisdom leant against a Leese St pub
writing a stretched white limo into existence
in real Mass Observation time
scribbling the anecdote of the man who
kissed Tony Blair's photo twice a day

this year

I funnel most of these Blues towards this single number 63, so
that it knots most of the strands from the sequencing, and adds
some anew, as:

*Abjective Stutter 2; Amended Signatures 3; Articulates 8; Bolt Holes 3; Boogie
Stop Shuffle 3; Coming Down from St George's Hill 3; Daylight Robbery 3;
Dialogue between Created Pleasure and the Resolvèd Soul 2; Dialogues 11;
Downing the Ante 2; Drowning Years 5; Duocatalysis 16; Empty Diary 1999,
2; Entries 4; For Adrian Clarke 2; For Jo Blowers 4; For John Seed 2; For Lee
Harwood 3; For Patricia Farrell 5; For Robert Hampson 3; For Roy Fisher
3; For Scott Thurston 4; For the Continuity Terminator 2; Fucking Time 4;
G 4; History of Sensation 8; Human Dust 4; Hundred 4; IM 8; Jungle Nights
in Pimlico 3; Killing Boxes 7; Labour 4; Linking the Unlinkable 2;* pre-
eminently: *mayday 99; Melting Borders 6; Midnight Ride 4; Mute Salutes
4; Netting Joy 3; Phallic Shrines 4;* quite significantly: *Poetic Sequencing
and the New 2; Remode 4; Save Yourself 3; Schräge Musik 3; Sharp Talk 4;
Small Voice 4; Smokestack Lightning 3; Soleà 3; Strand Across 3; The Hungry
Years III; The Materialisation of Soap 1947, 3; Time Capsule 4; Tin Lanterns 4;*

To My Students 4; Torn Elegy 6; Towards a Neo-Diagonalist Manifesto 2;
Watering the Cactus 4; Weightless Witnesses 3

I am already closing this century by such focussing, by
ending on opening up, and by narrowing down to my own discon-
tinuous discourse as never before

(Stephen, now playing his keyboard downstairs, slows a
programmed tune until it reminds me of the strangely unlocatable
chiming that rings from some building at the East end of Old
Compton Street, yards from where the fascist bomb went off last
night, and suddenly *I too am in love down there with the street*, jostled
by the crowd in that model of exchange, at any instant I choose,
which could be the instant when an alarm clock in a bag of
fertiliser and nails goes off, and I am suddenly afraid

not for myself alone, but for this time

writing these words, knowing, by this point, that they will form a
research paper for colleagues at Edge Hill (how I hated poems with
words like 'academic', 'research', in (!) as though I secretly wanted
all writing to exclude that which I silently desired

that my life has changed so that even these Blues, and whatever
succeeds them, can be categorised as research (they always were

to find this act of writing compounded with that act of teaching
'creative' 'writing' that I once so feared—and still do—as 'stylistic
fascism

as the production of recognition patterns for the 'reader' to receive
in complicit pleasure

. . . saying,' Levinas would 'say'; 'give himself in saying to the point
of poetry

how poetics leaks out of the activity of

Writing

*both process and product, is a significant and coherent deformation of the
linguistic system with the power to reorder and reconfigure individual, collec-
tive and social constructs of subjectivity, the face to face encounter with alter-
ity, which will assist the processes of greater subjective autonomy and
responsibility towards the other, as just one example of a possible aestheti-
cisation of politics to catalyse change in the environmental, social, and
psychological domains.* But then again

even the lavatory paper holder used to be a bike. 'Speculative

the spy the lookout the looking

and how I want this etymology back for

My poetics. *To read her is to love her.* Pissing round the vomit in the
Jac. Language as saying is an ethical openness. Showroom tomb-
stones emblazoned with plausible Irish names. Top poet voices radi-
ate from this room. Said closure of the other. He leased the street
back to himself. A pile of rags asleep in the clothes shop doorway,
an academic asking what will happen after the Fall of PoMocracy (!)
and having not realised that what will happen has already
happened as an ethical turn as a mute responsibility to the fluid
saying trapped in the inevitable actualisation of the said. I ask
myself — for who else is there to ask? — what will I make after
Twentieth Century Blues

a time-based project, completed when

no further texts shall be numbered

all the strands shall be frozen, their index (itself a projected penultimate part of the

net/
(k)not
      -work(s)

completed

I nominate midday 28 December 1999, a decade after completing the preface 'Melting Borders', as that limit

and to leave a single number for the final text

(leaving aside the hypertextual and cyberpoetic possibilities of its completed links in ink

to that something new

after the end of the twentieth century (whenever that will be exactly, if it hasn't happened already, or isn't happening now or isn't always happening

I wrote once, half-joking, of wanting to write an entire literature, even drafted an anthology of seven Manx modernists to be refracted through three or four contrasting translators, but lost the plan and lost the impulse, or

to radicalise that potent option of Pessoa, to publish under 5 names, but all of them my own

'gone fake omniscient' in the abandoned plan

The author's homonyms would multiply, consciously consolidating their potential to constellate texts around authorising centres. These author-functions will not have life, lives replete with invented character and caprice. They will not form anti-selves or personae. They will have all written Twentieth Century Blues *thus far, until their name refracts, as shown in figure 1, into what lies beyond it*

The scheme looks flat-out derangement, of course (Patricia sees the above figure and says, 'I think I'll leave the room now!

The five homonyms, heteronumberings, will be the equivalent of strands in the new writings. They will not, however, communicate, intertextualise. They will not be aware of one another, even fictively. They will need to be read against one another, five possible oeuvres. *They will need to deal anew, with the question of what poetry might become, in five different ways, as shown in figure 2 which enacts the moment of refraction as the middle of a poem, a prism haiku:*

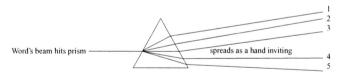

but I couldn't think of five final syllables to release this blinkered quintet; let it drop

Play it say it: I am already, forever, other

and I feared the loss of writing's inaugural thrust in the choices the system offers, and the creeping person(al)ism

Cannot always create a system or

I remember Bob Perelman asking Fanny Howe whether, when she wakes up in the morning, she arrives as a unified being

She replied she did! All the univocal Bob Perelmen rose up in indignation and said, 'I find that really difficult to believe

Eliot says that poets in middle age do one of, not five, but three, things

: shut up

: carry on as before, but refine technique

: or adapt and survive

(these are not his actual words

shut up shut up please it's time. I don't want to give the impression

that I'm demoralised or lost! I'm ebullient and ironical, dialoguing creative pleasure and re-solving poetics, as in my poem for Zappologist Ben Watson (ah! Zappa remixing the tapes in his dying months

metamorphosing the materials

as I, Robert Sheppard, as real as Mal Waldron in a Frank O'Hara poem, or as Bob Perelman in mine, which is enough, facing down what I might never simply call myself, reject transfiguration into a handful of Not-Even-Personae or a Shut-Up or a retuned Carry-On, read 'the human as an translational sign. . . . Occupy this hybrid, in between space to address the subject of a "translational" rather than concentric

cosmopolitanism' (Homi Bhabha's words tacked to the wall

re-translates in the mix towards my last 6 months' absorption: Jerome Rothenberg and Pierre Joris' two volume anthology

Poems for the Millennium (o millennium, o dutiful dome, o state

bards carolling 2000 years of Christianity, you gorgeous miscalculation

you're welcome to your first 1900 parts, but leave me this twentieth century

'this twentieth century and a half

it's Lyotard's phrase

which is my poetic focus, that 'half' that will never end, inaugurated by Hiroshima and Auschwitz

as Rothenberg and Joris remind me in the second volume of their gathering

('then hover like smoke in the air

and in mine, to make creative links with that which makes links with Auschwitz, as Derrida says

Anthologising *is* poetics. Be patient that I address you in a book review: there is no other fit medium

When the late Wayne Pratt and Dome Eulogist Justin Sidebottom
state that *I* do not exist in any part of *their* poetic century, or into
the next, I'll have my loose-leaf anti-canon of World Wide inves-
tigative poetries to strengthen me (as once

that tape of Raworth reading which operated as a Deleuzoguattarian
refrain, to make me *me*, territory penetrated by particles of other-
ness, playing it again and again like music, against the imminence
of eviction in Weybridge

a cruel irony given Tom's domicidal cleansing

I have constructed a twentieth century more generous than that
given to me, to give to others, into the next

and not one, as in most British anthology's end-of-century rainbow
alliances of plotted inclusiveness with their poetic of 'mingling'
experiment with domestic lyric, that balances those energies at
zero-thrust

Whenever I read that 'linguistically innovative poetry' is narrow

(I could name a hundred British and Irish names and a hundred
from 'elsewhere

a charge rendered redundant by variety and by this book's global
revaluation—and so to add, speculatively, new names to the old
that I need not name anew:

   my prospectus of reading:

Gunnar Ekelöf, not quite the one translated by Auden, but one
rolling in language like a dog in shit, 'between the words, between
the lines, between meanings

Muriel Rukeyser whose 'poetry depends on the moving relations within itself' yet will not let you despise a cunt or a penis

Gerrit Kouwenaar 'guided by the word . . . experiences something he had not known before

René Depestre with his Zombietalk in the ears of the Christian West

Kamau Brathwaite (no drowned books but remodes, Sycorax at the computer screen (hyphens dashes asterisks strokes

Paavo Haavikko and Tomas Tranströmer back to back like an old Penguin edition, when the world's poetry was let in without exoticism

Ted Berrigan's *Sonnets* which I have not read whole, though none is whole

Adonis for his Arabic modernism, othered in an act of 'perpetual beginning'; neo-Avanguardia for its moment, sweeping past the 'modern camouflage' of Verse in acts of 'provisional arrangement

Itō Hiromi for the shock of blooded knickers in a poetic of 'graphic chronicling

Quincy Troupe for his quaking antisermons, 'some hip-hop, some rap

Nicole Brossard for her lyric and theoretic intensity, writing as the 'hologram' of the body's 'high sensual technology'; Michael Palmer for his aesthetic obliquity, 'the counter-logic' of lyric

Gu Cheng for his city of the mind which is not for once a City of Modernism

To know more of Alejandra Pizarnik (she gave me an epigraph for a blues) and Claude Gauvreau who left at his death 1500 pages of experimental verse, though not to expect to *like* it

I'm not speaking of taste; but also of Coral Bracho's pouring abstractions and Nina Iskrenko's polystylistics

Already I want to shuffle the list, want Huidobro, Akhmatova and Benn from an earlier time, wish Barry MacSweeney or Bill Griffiths were in the book

wish for younger writers to puzzle me and solve me

like Miles Davis making jazz with young players who had their own groove that left him stranded, but listening, on the Plugged Nickel dates in December 1965

through to the recordings at The Cellar Door in December 1970 — Miles about my age; 'unlike anything else in jazz' and maybe wasn't

the poetics of no in the poetics of yes

what does not change is that it will not look like anything I'm

Producing Now

'The unknown relation of a not yet unfolded world,' as I put it in 1992, 'and the, at present, slenderly formed practices of those who will work in it, and against it. You cannot see into the

(and I wrote *granite* where it was in fact 31 *basalt*

blocks full of clay and fat, plugged with felt, waiting, Beuys'
commemorative germinators; poetics

authorising possibilities, to read to write to write to read

I want time to stop this writing

I want time to stop this writing

this song of orchestrated echoes

turned on their sides and read as a history

to pull the plug on the word machine or for somebody to step into
this room and say it's over

heaviest bombing so far; another cradle of male corpses by the road-
side

(the lie of the commodified poetic image, when only the gift of a
fact will suffice

To say shut up or adapt and survive

the timeless air of war (stench of corpses: did they look into the
eyes of those men they killed, to carry that 'image' to their own
graves

at the edge of England, this liminal city

in a room in a house as combustible as a Kosovan dwelling

throughout all of this twentieth century

and *my* half, even

War

even anti-war anti-language

drowning the ante on an antique land

and words, and poetry in the words, and sorts of self, just once or
twice, as here, in the words. Dear Chris (to misquote Lee

Hello

1 May 1999

≈

64

31 Basalt Wind-chimes for the Window-Box of Earthly Pleasures

Human Dust 5

Implosive Samples 2

The End of the Twentieth Century 2

O

Not a book of ayres not a solid monotone. An eye. An ear. Willed to pleasure, let's take a note for a walk across the humming strings. Human

O

Human dust on which history overdosed twice (at least) in one century

O

This dance means bumping into things, yet jump back from the path of Creation's clockwork

O

Atheism does not exist because god invented it! A force to vent: *Velopoesis*

O

A single voice on a single page—there's music enough. The news-paper vendor cries: 'Echo . . . Echo

()

Plonk (see **plunk**); his rush of pleasure haunts the paths of sense with sensation

()

But that spooky charm is not earthly goodness as one would want to know it!

()

The fat, melting, dissipates more energy than it conserves. As does repeating the spiky line that unravels into a force larger than its parts

()

'There ain't no way they can replace this vacuum I created in human history

()

The discipline of hazard and high quality shoots aloft the victims' pitiable admiration that builds *under* the crust of pain while Creation adjusts its ancient braces

()

The Author of Bangs, against which we nuzzle the footnote of something like human justice. If he is condemned to time, push the eye out and climb out, as from a shell into the bright dream of tomorrow. Obtain your liberty and fiery scope.

○

Routes bloomed across bound wastes: up to off and over and out until they feel like jelly: '*Your faire lookes enflame*

○

A sensation that is almost an emotion an aubade an algorithmic simulation

○

(a vacuum

○

Suck parody? Constituents of pleasure are not to be taken for granted

○

(sings:) *Dear, if you change, I'll melt away like lard!*

○

Jaunty now, where the lyrics are dainty. Its opposite, in semantic counterpoint, a miraculous parliament!

○

Keep Creation dramatic and didactic, that's the trick! Each single eye is plugged tight with transformations

O

The strange persistence of the meanings of certain words through centuries. Which syllable shall we elongate to quench again with love?

O

The **right** to pleasure, as under statute. A **unit** of pleasure, its animus (Who needs devils with gods like that?

O

Born again, to free Poetic Fury? Dust caught in bees' wax. Turn your lamp up in unbelief. Pleasure has no balance

O

to catch the almost-involuntary spurt of semen or the spiritualist who contacted Bradlaugh after death to catch his confession! Weightless epiphanies

O

'Shine him off that window!' This goes *with* saying

O

Who said purity wove their words, advertising just one admired synthesis?

O

Has an oath truer currency for being underwritten by fear and by stone-eyed defenders of monuments? Cease to be pleasuring response is lost until it sings far from a said

O

Shifting rime   that easie flatterer   a cat chasing a fly

O

Pleasure's twin. Standing by his word, a god of flesh she forms

O

Clocking form, the infectious eye catches pleasure being caused. The unhasty song when responsibility descants as response

O

The sigh of a cosmos, cooling, expanding; the resurrection of an idea of the word *as*

O

Unseal the lid at last! A chamber of twentieth century echoes rings. Soiled prose-songs of Velopolis

JUNE 1999

65

From the English

Articulates 9

History of Sensation 9

Utopian Tale IV

Electronic letters wink the news from the Stakeholder Tower. Swans fly by like messengers from another world

A field factory of kerchiefed women threshed and piled the urinous corn against their rhyming hems

He slipped past the uranium-graphite rods into the Netherworld, rivet eyes in the glow

The incisiveness of our colour-coded marginalia, lists of Craft Guilds, a cactus world of barbed tongues, citizens layered and flayed like old election posters on the blistered walls of post-industrial squares

Each twitch of the Leader is choreographed: leaps of laughter, flares of rage

Biplanes wheel over the basilicas and wine lodges to the sound of a once fashionable tango

Red moves in the river as red should, diluted. Uncut tongues smelted in George's lyrical furnace declare that the heavy, wingless evening glides to a split pomegranate sunset

Pearl spills her bra, sprawled on her stomach across the bed, clacking her heels like castanets behind her ears. The maimed body of English culture is too tragic a theme for her bed! The wisdom of nobody in particular sings:

'The nightingales of Reform are resting in the Cuckoos' Nests (*this eulogy is composed in accordance with specifications ratified at the 19th Great Consultation of Amnesia*

Pearl the Slut lives in the smoked-sausage stench of a one room flat. The sun beats competitively down on the frost outside. Her Economic Plan is one foot in a stiletto, the other in a dirty boot, dust shaken contemptuously at her gaping supervisor in the pigswill canteen

The Prosecutor is given Pearl's proverbial rabbit but still wants her unspeakable hen, as she shifts her hams (*watch your language, translation is the third oldest profession*) in tight Transatlantic jeans during a three-quarters sex scene. Singers melt mid-verse

Rubbery mouths turn inside out to vomit bilious panegyrics onto our petalled river. 'We are a fairytale

retold in thick contradictory voices howling over the capital at its Festival of Rebirth, while women like Lorraine swell magic fruit on the boughs with incantations before they pluck them

Pearl married a Party Gnome to escape the unblinking eye that some rachitic small-town Cyclops had trained on her. She was meat jelly once for George, round the back of the Snow Flake Café

They trod a hymn to their undying love in the drift, an acrostic of the Leader's name. Robyn's well-fed cackle proved she could only ever, at best, turn out a slum landlady, teeth reflected in the bonnet of her Bentley

Girls fainting with hunger still poked breadsticks through the wires for the POWs

We learnt to count by computing the bullet holes in her leg. The Fleet was paid in riverbanks, as my old Dad used to say (whatever he meant by it). The tourist centre gleams

Bulls topple from the heroes' plinth in the Meat Industry Zone at the feet of the Maidens of Economic Advancement

It can only be built on bottom-up inspiration that looks down, she says, with the lowered head of a thousand qualified *buts*!

Today's union bosses are well read, put to bed in vests, with bowls for their spewings. Pearl

Pearl, the pillow smells of Pearl

Pearl is last spotted, knee deep in snow, looking at the new road signs that the security services have garlanded, as though she were the saint

This is a Stone Throwing Revolution, and George says he will cast first! The full-bloodied, deep-juiced moon gloats, aflame like a hayrick in the English Civil War

The great cause now is to serve something mundane and self-serving, the Metaphysics of the Bone Age

The Stakeholder Orchestra demilitarises, bribing the Guild for a Reeling Life and an Easy Death with four bottles of White Lightning. Inside the stuffing of the party's Teddy Bear mascot: the ferrule fist. Let there be more than one light. A flower-girl (black and white) presented on the steps of Chequers

the same, among the myriad spheres of dandelion heads, the breeze unpicking spore. Whose boot will kick through them, in judgement, terrible and tetchy? Robyn's bile leaks over our identity papers. Purge trial

Summer parks where convicted homosexuals meet the drunks, contaminating fruit-head guests before empty plates, spitting pips, juice (that roughly translates as: *they contort in an unrepeatable dance that means no more than the footprints they leave in the flowerbeds*

Jayne lands a part in the folk-rock opera *Lefty*. 'Nice world,' quips Roger, 'if you can get it

'You fucker!' she says, for the first time in English art the speech of the riff raff and scum who hang around our suburban trains

The table cluttered with the opulence of a tax free Weekend Cottage

Roger wants to plug her mouth with flesh. This First Minotaur (*Minister?*) presses her down onto the sofa, as she awaits his sudden thrust from behind, his blood stream an arrow shower, obeying history rather than the history books

Her hands blossom in bunches of moon flowers in the party political sky. Shrapnel marks on stone announce the visitation of Progress at some point in her still mobile history

Effigies laugh like gutters throughout England, mocking our shoes which squeak with embarrassment, brushed to a blush

The Interrogation scene is panned by the critics with its chorus of
ditto ditto **ditto**

as Roger denies each trumped up charge. He ends mid-sentence because the tune runs out of notes

AUGUST 1999

66

The Sacred Tanks of Dagenham

for Keith Tuma and Nate Dorward
Articulates 10
Impositions 2
The Materialisation of Soap 1947, 4

once Pearl pricks the two chops in the sizzling pan restaurant
music she says

crouched towards the postcards outside the tobacconist's George
lives and loves it all though iceless

not the corner *ABC* spelt out of emptiness nor the mobile library
of American magazines

an abstract noun fogs the capital city until the breeze's caprice

looks could kill and still be made to look good

packets of *Creamola* in windows searched after their sewing class
digests with gusto

absence and abstinence

leading to orderly queues or queues of asylum orderlies wheeling
their own reflections into the chilly English Channel

the frozen symbol of nationhood empire's dissolution home made

eat what you see hell of damaged stock half-price turnips will find
their way to Heaven

through multiple hardbaked soil

creak for milk over the bathtub she poured coffee in case who will
buy air

(selling air

a high wind bites through the worn threads of jogging army girls a
state bard recites through his beard and his beads of sweating half
rhymes

Pearl's first wrinkle faces the wringer

buxom corn maidens with gleaming washtubs await the dispensary
of grubby propensities to consume the word 'democracy' doesn't
creak through our rafters

too high for worship

her finger tickles his meat balls his organ is an old widow's wellpaid
wellwisher

George's wick sticks up in sticky appreciation

bangs like a barn door for the girls' buoyancy against the oppressive
clouds there's a cut out shape where Pearl was washing George's
smalls

threatening blank pages at the backs of ration books ready for
whatever is fewer

winners catch the cooling mint flavoured newsprint scrolls from
Dagenham to Dagestan

labels *Individual Balconies* small squares on the brushed magnifi-
cence the *Sacred Tanks* open thin ribs of land dress for talk every-
thing is mean and means little

unrelated to a shortage the Sydenham band has disbanded the saxophones swing in the heat near the public well

(skilfully carrying water jugs for miles on their heads

the woman in foxfurs explains the marvels of the snow on the field of blood meaning itself subject to this economy

the clacking abacus drum stores the few apples' stories as documents and dockets

cleansing invisibility hides in Hyde Park from the laughter is deaf but vital hands perhaps even George's weeping penis washing Pearl

will emigrate to Canada to begin again

doing her business lust flashes like George's shape has been pruned from his allotment of pure time regeneration trumpets over the city in each tree kippers and cider roused them to it

outside Timothy Whites they clatter the hardware like Gene Krupa tubs in his straps a post-war blur of rematerialising Hero nervously waits to deNazify the English East Midlands of its thin-lipped officials

abed in the crystal crematoria of recent history

the past's persistence we knitted our way to victory and now we're eating shit 50 million flies can't be wrong

('and now Pearl will croak a few bars for barter

George sniffs his way through her fat negotiating hothouse grapes
gleaming bladders in greengrocer's immortal calligraphy spelling
flowers for his staff car

plenty is the finger that touches Pearl's meat for once they'll recog-
nise this attempt

to cojoin George's triumphal offal language falling from signposts
(*we work or want*; no

says George: *we*

want

work

to provide a validating ethos for Man kicking in the night ('here
he goes again

a bombsite ripe for conjuring him once more in plentiful
Kodachrome against her shins

whose thighs make a necklace of pearl clouds in a grey sky build-
ing plots national assistance

near the dosshouse round the back of the Palace of the Winds

17 AUGUST 1999

68
Say

Say I people these squares of glass

playmate of the impossible, I listen to your howl

across the floating gardens between the equipment units and the
living units

Your metabolic rhythms are coerced by the nebulous obsession that
discourses through ill-adjusted air conditioning, counter

points the smashings of workmen disgorging the shell where the
Old Widow Marx once dwelt. Singular planes

of tilted glass reflect dead sky. Say hello. I want you to see this

as a book again, or as a parliament or ministry of justice building
that looks like a nuclear power plant (There is a voice

it says 'beauty

though the streetjive of postmodernism is policed by the dictionary
of modernity. It might recruit you

to causes that remain inimical to your judgement

or government; this is everyday life slipping along the radius of the
everyday world. Go away. Say

This is no Palace of Art, not even a map of it. Don't say: the solution is
dynamite

the blocks collapsing squarely into clouds of their own dust. Say:

demonstrate your intelligence, stamping the pages with the ictus
of identity and contra-

diction, the space now only inhabited by the hidden interchange of
knowledge and its otherwise

Say: you scratch the veneer of an authoritarian static fit and what
do you find, when the next drunk, or the girl

next door, positioned on the radial, smiles sourly or sweetly, and
asks you to justify your discursive habits

(and the income it provides from its patented buzzword

what are you going to say? *Once there were formal*

houses on the main road, informal ones nearer the lake, and a few prac-
tices that you're allowed in between, a handful of dialect words and a fistful
of proscribed gestures? Say: this is meant

to be a model for communicative action as motivation

as alignment

as celebration as actualisation

for those who snap the snare

for those who refuse to exploit experience as the supplement of
history

as a bloodbath after one of the hostages says The Wrong Word

The path is formed by the various buildings that stretch either side
of the path that was not there until the grammar just about

made it to the full stop. Say

you say something and *I'll* reply: *Dialogue*

and the Everyday

September–October 1999

69

In an Unknown Tongue

History of Sensation 10
Impositions 3
Strategies 3

BOOK ONE

George loosens his blood-red tie and they begin. The lower beings have contested the Upper Beings and they hope to take the trophy back beneath the lines that hold the nether world intact.

'I leapt up the steps from the Seine to Rouen Cathedral but he was no longer by my side. Some street preacher had grabbed him by the shoulder and was promising to cast out his demons. It was about this time that I knew he would go over to the "other side".'

Collapses on a bench under the right-angled legend: 'Ashbury'/'Haight'. Several historical details seem inaccurate and the edges of the crowd are beginning to fray. The Volkswagon guns its engine: *Peace* bubble-lettered on the shivering bonnet.

(He was getting pedantic; 'Wimples *like* oakleaves mean: wimples *and* oakleaves.')

'On deck, I smoked and relaxed. He whistled a spy-movie. The ship was slipping behind the scratched curtain.'

The line down her face gives her a third eye through which she can see the frozen watch hanging over the gunwales like the stalactites she conjures there. Instead of a name this vessel carries a health warning that calibrates her as its lethal dose.

Oracular signs on the mountain pass barnacled into icy immobility.

The boys try to tempt her but *she* will be doing the tempting, thank you very much! The jiffy-bags Pearl perches on contain vacutainers of frozen sperm, tributes to her crimson lips, her pointed breasts under the crimson gown that conceals, yet reveals, enough for the boys' muffled ejaculations: flat-footed hand-jobs for imaginary leg-liftings, gown-droppings, a backbone of tingles, a snow-dust of orgasm.

Crusoe meets his portent over the nets. Looking the wrong way for an instant ounces of evolutionary software are wiped from his hard drive.

Gripping onto the rigging over the bucking sea, its own animate nightmare, that's the poor bastard they named Lucky! A cigarette between the fingers of each trigger-happy hand. Another moment's lapse and he'll slip into irony.

Her red lips, too, her blood-red shawl, adjust the filters of power. Cut glass nymphs with vulture wings call out to assassins on the bridge to drop anchor in the tragic pools of her eyes. Her freckled arms, her white-gloved hands, will try to hold the world together as it spatters apart on the cream upholstery.

Glints off a silver fuselage on the dusty air-strip. Pearl and Lorraine grin over their clutches of hand luggage and fox-furs. Ropes slither at their feet. Groaning men grip their empty bellies and retch. George, or what should be George, carries a loaf with his luggage, and he could break it to distribute among the hunched grey figures. It is election year.

She opens her blouse, but nobody looks, except the Ancients posed above her next to the broken masthead. Dead men have drudged here, she thinks; the living are obsessed with their red wine and smoke-rings. She might as well sing 'Twentieth Century Blues'. Later, in his lordship's bathroom her famous fanny will open like a lobster's claw, she thinks, to piss an ocean into his even more famous mouth.

Book Two

A crossbow shoots a Schlitz bottle clean from Elzadie's head. Those lips that made Armorica shatter.

He gave up the throne for this dancing deaths-head, plays dice on deck, for the double orchestra will never be asked to play on this Ark. Lank sails hang over rotten beams, as lifeless as his trousers over the back of the chair (he calls his throne) for the parlour game he names Coronation Night.

Jiving for pearls with his slicked-back blue Superman hair— suddenly The Hero grips his neck and falls to the rock and roll deck where those who have long bopped have dropped. Spurt your Bud!

China cat smile! Chinese silk dreams of the Birdman's starlit axe-blow night. From the nest to the egg-cup. The orange tree potted in dog shit prose.

Penelope awaits Odysseus by the Hollywood poolside, with the embarrassing six year old and the dog. Through the polar columns of the Temple to the Medusa, she has a clear view of the Ithacan sea, and beyond: the sperm-fucked waves, the whores' hair spore of the cresting, nipple-bobbing, cunt-snapping ocean. No Man idles by the watch, not daring to take the heroic plunge.

'Thirties modernism in Beirut seemed somehow right: tall enough to be a look-out, yet close enough to decipher the blue chalk on the whitewashed walls below: the command to vanish. A battalion of my father's Arab henchmen dead drunk on the floor was near perfect cover.'

Waves net across the skein. Cloudy sails in slants of sleet. Pale sun interferes with the sky's blank message. The wrong grave.

The dangling corpse of Jack's jilted queen toes the biting ocean. Jackie had written to her mother every week about his cruelty, his strange occult habits, his masculine verse. She was the girl next year.

Perfect cover, as a dwarf reporter for the *Morning Post*!

He wears a crow-black tie so often that he ends up being called out to funerals at all hours. Pulling rope, the mariners' feet tangle among the limbs of those who have died at this task, staring still. It is his job to close these eyes during the breaks between shifts.

'He called me out to play his spy-game on the veranda. With his little eye he'd sent dozens to their deaths for something beginning with C. In the forest a woodcutter's chainsaw sang like a muezzin, long notes and halftones. History was closing in.'

Eyes, their last glimmers fading, bodies fallen in configurations of least resistance like a Duke's underwear.

On the shore, Isolde walks the dog between the treacherous black rocks. She pulls the white fur round her, a polar bear against the gangrenous dawn. Tristan hangs on for dear life, in the crow's nest, to the rope that holds his reality together. The sea boils and hisses, either side of the crashing prow.

Book Three

Two women rest their wings, and their tongues, which are also wings.

Drifted sober into this line of defence: 'beached' boats in mud. A stain that could be a man on horseback, a cardiac flare in the chest, or a facecloth of guilt.

Mistake any gnarled tree trunk for a leg. The Angels of Reason chorus over the Yachting Marina, where the research is financed by laundered drug money. To breakfast is to chew nails out of rotten timber.

A host of chorusing pill bottles tumbles across the doctor's desk. Decked. 'Death has not been a door to us, but a rubbish-chute,' she sings. Shells of human beings, their organs in neat pots behind her.

Fungal clouds infect the azure. Beowulf's bier, upon towering seas. Barged back by the bullying waves. The angle of light upon the skeleton conjures expressive eyes into its empty sockets. Deliverance is judgement, a thick blanket of lines to shroud us.

He sank beneath the lines. Spirited in a rowing boat from the ship-wreck of the singular, he will be reborn, spouting gallons of seawa-ter, on the shores of Utopia.

Or: Puking his passage across the Channel like a bilge-pump, the Creature would travel, under false papers, to Vienna, where he would vanish, a veritable Adam before Eve. But first he must brave language, the ejaculating waves.

Beatrice arrives bewitched, bewildered, a baby in her propeller arms; her son carries *The Beano*. The theology she utters to reporters is so astonishing that even the airport porters rubberneck.

Soldiers throw a boy over the bridge parapet and machinegun the water. The UN swerves the post-colonial highways in gleaming Toyotas, the effluent of an advertisement they claim not to be in. Deep in the forest, the Dark Figure calls the last militiaman to experience his final blade.

The last woodchopper won't burst into Granny's Greenhouse tonight; the wolves' eyes flicker at the glass. He is stopped by a man he barely recognises. They shake hands, talk treachery round to loyalty with a few semantic reversals. Codenames reveal only gender. The little girl is a pile of bones but the cat still purrs in the secret photographic darkroom.

'This place is bugged by my former wives,' George whispers outside his new dacha, tending the shrine he has built to Pearl.

Tied to the mast like Odysseus or Turner, his eyes are filled with nothing but these strange women with huge prosthetic ears that are also sex organs. These women, even Isolde, masturbate by rubbing the ears together over the tops of their heads. Even crucified like him — he's the third or fourth Adam — they could generate their own pleasure still.

Her polar fur wrapped about her, broken boots for her broken body, she treads seed pods into the soft tarmac, as she leaves the walled Seaport (if you misread the brewery's castellation). A wisp of irony feathers the empurpled underbelly of the evening sky, but she will miss it, as ever.

12 OCTOBER 1999

73
Catacaustic

for Tom Raworth
Some Words 2
Study 3

Numbers polished

back to his room

changed continuously in the swell

clouds flickered the afternoon stalactites

a stone cracked open leaving

the docks

map a blank plan destroyed

50s flights of steps to work at two chairs

scribbled falls flickered to speak

near rushing table

remembered the last news

labelled a quick sketch

in the ejected

hold sides of wire tiles

between air spits

on the windows happy with lines

appeared to hold breathing

from the real shutters

switched the day's dog shit off

as the cleaners run down the central hoardings

pick up endless photographs

of xerox stone hits roofs to shout down

bright red shoes

the shutters scrap of blue steps through his head

at the bottom of decay

dark grey calm eyes

flash the starts of ends

and adding in paper twists loud

real fingers approach

the last poem stated his method.

19 DECEMBER 1999: REVISED 2007–8

75

The Push Up Combat Bikini

Coda 4

Empty Diary 2000

IM 11

Such turned out to be the eternity the poet promised me, the bastard
Angela Carter

You're coming over all female.
Your conceit's too clean. Out
of the push up they're a let down,
deposits that won't quite register,
banked on your looking. You sniff
eroticism off dirty shifts, smudges of pelt.
I slip an ought, drop a stitch or two.
Hot gushes signal your retreat. Every
time I open my mouth out comes
a manifesto of a new literary movement!
Was that a poem, curling round you,
your nerves ajangle at syntax's opening?
It takes me and takes me
for somebody else, as you
push me out between its lines.
What might a poem be, elsed?
You dunk your aching lived-in balls in ink
and roll them across the page.
I'm your shagged out Muse.
Take me over you this last time.
Whisper me Pearl, whistle me off.
I'll be a big register on your retina,
breathlessly weaving love for a puppet prick
that can be choreographed. I'm
pegged on that line to George's stuff
and nonsense. 'I'm only an instance of a fuck
fucking (he says (she says (*who says?*)

The ventriloquist tongues my clitoris and it speaks.

dedicated to the memory of Barry MacSweeney

2000; REVISED 2007

Notes and Resources

Note on 'Missing' Poems

Blues 4, 'Save Yourself', was destroyed. There are photographs of this event.

Blues 13, 'A Strand Across Some Sequences', was one of a number of 'strands' created for occasions from previously existing work. In this instance it was the first such, for Robert Hampson's anthology *Wasted Years* in 1992, commemorating what I call 'The Drowning Years'. The three texts used appear elsewhere in this volume, and the reader may assemble the strand his or herself: 1. Part three of 'Coming Down from St George's Hill' which is published here as section two of 41; 2. 'Sharp Talk', which is part one of 2; 3. 'Slipping the Mind', which appears here as 8.

Blues 70, 71 and 72 were withdrawn. 'Pentimento—what happens next to *Twentieth Century Blues*', which appears in *Hymns to the God In which My Typewriter Believes* (Stride, 2006), is a text and commentary on these disjecta, but they are not parts of this network.

AUGUST 2006

A Note on the 'Duocatalysis' Strand

This is a way of distinguishing text and image collaborations between Robert Sheppard and Patricia Farrell, whose full publication details within and beyond *Twentieth Century Blues* are as follows:

1: Part one of 6, published previously as *Mesopotamia* (Ship of Fools, 1987).

2: *Looking North* (Ship of Fools, 1987).

3: 'The Materialisation of Soap 1947' in 6, previously published as *The Materialisation of Soap 1947* (Ship of Fools, 1987).

4: 'Untitled for Patricia Farrell', published in *Daylight Robbery* (Stride, 1990), previously published (near images) in *Raddle Moon* 9, 1990.

5: *The Cannibal Club* (Ship of Fools, 1989).

6: 11, published as an untitled card (Ship of Fools, 1992).

7: *Icarus — Having Fallen* (Ship of Fools, 1992).

8: 16, published as *Logos on Kimonos* (Ship of Fools 1992, revised ed. 1998).

9: 12, published as *Seven* (Ship of Fools, 1992), reproduced in this edition.

10: 'Empty Diaries' 1919–1940 (ie part of 7), previously published in *Transit Depots/Empty Diaries* (Ship of Fools, 1993).

11: 15, published as *Fucking Time* (Ship of Fools, 1994).

12: 'Jungle Nights in Pimlico', in 30, published as *Jungle Nights in Pimlico* (Ship of Fools, 1995).

13: Book 12 of 30, published as *Free Fists* (Writers Forum, 1995).

14: 28, published as *The Book of British Soil* (Ship of Fools, 1995).

15: 37, published as *Neutral Drums* (Writers Forum, 1999).

A Note on Performances

A number of pieces were either developed or written especially for dance, movement and music performances, in collaboration with dancer and choreographer Jo Blowers, particularly poems from the 'For Jo Blowers' strand.

As can be seen from 63, which includes partial descriptions of two performances, I considered making these themselves part of the numbering. Performance details are incomplete but include, both full-scale presentations that sometimes did not involve me (marked below 'No RS') and also 'chamber-style' improvisations consisting of the two of us. Every reading I've given is a performance, of course, and there have been many using texts from *Twentieth Century Blues*, but they are not recorded here since they did not involve collaboration.

Full scale performances

27 May 1993: 'Shutters' ('a movement based mixed-media work performed by six women. It includes voice, sound projections, steam and pyrotechnical images. It is about women, and the forms which have arisen out of the process of its making are both lyrical and violent' (JB)). Performers: Polly Hudson, Josephine Liesk, Tracey West, Eava-Mama Mutka, Fernada Amaral, Lisa Harley. Photography: Aeden Kelly.

Nosepaint at Woodwork, Vauxhall Spring Gardens, London. No RS.

24 September 1993: 'Killing Boxes' (early version of 'Weightless Witnesses', see below), The Art Funktion, The Shaw Room, The Peacocks, Woking, Surrey.

18 February 1994: 'Weightless Witnesses/Killing Boxes', 'Some of the piece is structured, but most is improvised. There are other sections, not shown this evening, that involve more voices and an installation with pyrotechnical images'. (JB). RS (Text and performance), Music by Gus Garside (bass and electronics), Movement: Jo Blowers and Tracey West. Directed by Jo Blowers, Chisenhale Dance Space, London.

17 June 1995: 'Free Fists', chiefly book 12 of *The Lores* (30), with Patricia Farrell (slides: images and documentary photographs), Writers Forum Workshop, Mornington Place, London. Combined with launch of *Free Fists*.

Both 'Weightless Witnesses/Killing Boxes' and 'Shutters' received full scale productions during the Arts Festivals at Brooklands College, Weybridge, Surrey, at least in 1993 and 1994; this is what I describe in 63.

Chamber performances

18 July 1993: 'Shutters', Vertical Images, Mornington Place, London.

13 November 1993: 'Killing Boxes', Equipage/Microbrigade '20 poets in a 6 hour reading', King's College, Cambridge.

18 December 1993: unknown text, Sound and Language Party, Community Music, London.

1 May 1994: 'Schräge Musik', Live Art at The Café Gallery, Southwark Park, London.

14 November 1995: 'Shutters', and 'Weightless Witnesses'. Ship of Fools at the Falkland Arms, London. Combined with launch of *The Book of British Soil*.

22 September 1996: probably including 'Fucking Time', 15, Torriano Meeting House, London.

17 November 1998: 'New Killing Boxes', (final version of 'Weightless Witnesses') consisting of 20, 28, 55; 'Entries', consisting of 34, 52; Rose Theatre, Edge Hill College of Higher Education. This is described in 63.

Other

'Killing Boxes' was performed on audiotape at the Triskel Post Art Festival at the Triskel Arts Centre, Cork, Ireland, 1993.

6 The Flashlight Sonata

'Flashlight Sonata'

The words occur in Kurt Schwitters' collage 'Der Verwundete Jäger' (1942).

'Mesopotamia'

The titles derive from notes on the verso of contact prints and, in one case, an army Christmas card, sent from Hugh Lopus Alway to his sister, my great aunt Gina, during the First World War. The original spelling has been preserved.

'Schräge Musik'

The title is the name of a German aerial cannon of the Second World War which also means discordant music or, more popularly, jazz. Resources include Alan W. Cooper, *Bombers over Berlin* (William Kimber, 1985); *Britain* by Mass Observation, arranged by Charles Madge and Tom Harrisson (Penguin Special, 1939); Francis Scarfe, *Auden and After* (Routledge, 1942); and Derek Stanford, *The Freedom of Poetry* (Falcon, 1947). I have drawn on a few of my father's memories. 'Barker' is George Barker, a personal memory. There are a number of sentences in part 2 which owe to the rhetoric and politics of the New Apocalypse. Stanford, in writing of Nicholas Moore, coined the phrase 'a poet of the last train' to describe the forties writer. 'LMF': RAF abbreviation for 'Lacking in Moral Fibre', i.e., unfit to continue operations.

'Letter from the Blackstock Road'

Quotations from 'I don't like corners. . .' to the end of the paragraph are drawn from the writings and sayings of Kurt Schwitters, William Carlos Williams and Miles Davis. Parts of the final paragraph utilise the writings and sayings of Roy Fisher, Maurice Merleau-Ponty, Lee Harwood, Jean-François Lyotard, Alan Halsey and Peter Riley.

1987/1993

15 *Fucking Time*: Selected Notes and Resources

Title—Aubrey's *Brief Lives* (Life of Franciscus Linus), quoted in Adlard, p.78: 'The Smashing of the Phallic Dials': '. . . broken all to pieces (for they were of glass spheres) by the Earl of Rochester, Lord Buckhurst,

Fleetwood Shephard, etc. coming in from their revels. 'What!' said the Earl of Rochester, 'doest thou stand here to — Time?' Dash they set to work.'

Song 1 — 'Love and Life, a Song', Wilmot, p. 65.

'Song' ('By all Loves soft, yet mighty Pow'rs'), ibid, p. 67.

'Appetite'/'Aversion': Hobbes, Book 1, Ch. VI.

Song 2 — 'The Mock Song', Wilmot, p. 69.

'Satyr', ibid., p. 6.

Song 3 — 'Satyr', Wilmot, p. 6.

Letter to Rochester from Savile, Treglown, p. 62.

Mrs Frances Stewart became Britannia on coins of the realm, but the point is more general.

'Incorporeal body': Hobbes, Book 1.

Song 4 — The suggestive impression in the grass I owe to Charles II's poem to Frances Stewart: 'I pass all my time in a shady old grove'.

References to 'leading the coranto' and 'Mercury's frauds' are lost; probably Rochester's letters, or Hobbes?

'Dowry snatches': At one level, Rochester's abduction of Elizabeth Malet; Adlard, p. 33. Both Aubrey and Pepys record the affront.

'Shutters, mid-stage.// She spreads her fan.' See Etherege, particularly Act Three, Scene 1. The character Dorimont was modelled either upon Rochester or upon a model of Rochester.

Song 5 — 'External things', 'running over an alphabet/ to start a rhyme', Hobbes, Book 1.

'Tarse' (penis) 'arse', as in 'In the Fields of Lincoln Inns' (possibly by Sedley), Wilmot, p. 53.

Song 6 — Letter from Rochester to Savile, Treglown, p. 66.

'Bougre': Letter from Rochester to Savile, ibid, p. 158.

The bugger who suggested the description was Titus Oates; see also letter from Rochester to Savile, ibid, p. 232.

Resources

Adlard, J (ed.) 1974, *The Debt to Pleasure, John Wilmot, the Earl of Rochester*, Carcanet: Manchester.

Etherege, G. *The Man of Mode*, in Gosse (ed.) 1964, *Restoration Plays*, Dent: Herts.

Hobbes, T. 1651 (1962) *Leviathan*, Fontana: Glasgow.

Treglown, J. (ed.) 1980, *The Letters of John Wilmot, Earl of Rochester*, Basil Blackwell: Oxford.

Wilmot, J. Earl of Rochester, 1680 (?), *Poems on Several Occasions*, Antwerpen (sic).

1994

24 Empty Diaries

The twelves, twenty-fours and thousands of its numbering relate to the measures both within and between texts in this work. The measures relate to mechanical measurements of human time. Word count (by line, poem, sequence, part) follows this numerical rule closely. Parts one, three and four are each a thousand words long. Part two (the first to be composed) escapes this organisation, since some texts are organised by syllabics, and there is no overall word count for it.

Blues 24 was announced as a numbering for the Stride volume *Empty Diaries* (1998), as 'Flashlight Sonata 2', and is used here again to arrange the 'Empty Diaries' 1901–1990 by year, as did the book, not by chronology of composition. Blues 16 was originally placed between 'Empty Diary 1987'and 'Empty Diary 1988' in the Stride volume.

1998/2007

26 Living Daylights

Living Daylights belongs to a self-involved category of work called a 'Remode' which consists of the 'remo(ul)ding' of a text into another form, to give a *version* of it, in this case through a fairly improvisatory versioning.

My entry into a number of years' experimentation with isoverbalist structures (particularly in *Empty Diaries* and *The Lores*) meant that when the remoding of three texts from *Daylight Robbery* (Stride, 1990) was carried out, I was obsessed with number as form, and imposed these new structures upon the looser work of the late 1980s. The fact that the 1980s texts, particularly 'Daylight Robbery' (remoded here as 'From the Stolen Book') were themselves acts of semantic translation, rhyme, and transformation seemed appropriate. 'Untitled for Patricia Farrell' becomes 'Working the Golden Book Number Two'; and 'Voices Under

Occupation' is transformed into 'Empty Diary 1941, Number Two'.

Remoding into isoverbal form was effected by taking the word patterning of another poem in *Daylight Robbery*, 'Swift Nudes', and using the first 3 of its 4 parts as a stanza form for the three remodes (slightly altered in the case of the third to make a sonnet-like form).

24 MAY 1998 (abridged 2005)

28 The Book of British Soil

'The Book of British Soil' was written specifically for the large scale live art piece *Weightless Witnesses*, devised by Jo Blowers. (See 'A Note on Performances' above.) This text was written to contrast with the central 'Killing Boxes' section (i.e., 5). While 'Killing Boxes' represents a violent involution of the anti-language of the Gulf War, which I generally read fast, the prose of 'The Book' was performed hesitantly. While it can be read sequentially as a prose text (as printed here) it is capable of further dispersal. The text has a definite beginning and an end (the first and last paragraphs) but the |paragraphs| in between may be read once or more than once, in direct response to the improvisations of dancers and/or musicians.

OCTOBER 1995

30 The Lores

The Lores started with a question: Is there civic — even revolutionary — potential in pitching the lores against The Laws? I had in mind the concrete example of the way that individuals physically negotiate a crowded urban street without bumping into one another. Could this be a model for political interaction? The text's poetic focus is the relationship of fascism to micro-fascism and the matching resistances to that at both the Grand Level and at ground level, street level. Transacting the anagram: 'lores' and 'rôles'. These matters are dispersed across the book, according to the poetics outlined in Sheppard 1999 below, in a mode of 'creative linkage' which I partly defined (in a note of 1995 accompanying the publication of Book 8) as 'a general and technical term for the aesthetic and ethical enterprise of linking the unlinkable. Such links can be articulated on a surface which is like the skin of delirium, with simultaneously *more* disruption than would be connoted by the term "juxtaposition" — and also *less*. The links, melted into the materials, disappear. Discontinuity worked to make new continuities.' However, certain foci are present in particular books, and between the paired books of its mirrored structure.

For example, Book 1 introduces the thematics of the work, and a darker second voice, while Book 12 traces whether there might be some hope of man dwelling in vectoral dispersion amid evident despair, but sets this against the fractures and schisms of various civil wars. The title comes from a damaged offshoot of one of Robert Motherwell's 'Elegies to the Spanish Republic'. See Elam (1991).

The various word counts for the poem *The Lores* derive from Plato's *The Laws*, in which 5040 is considered the ideal number of citizens for his second Republic because it is a number divisible by most numbers, and is therefore useful for the raising of taxes and militia, and — doubtless — for surveillance.

The following texts and images, in a variety of ways, and to a greater or lesser extent, informed the writing of *The Lores*. A few are quoted directly, while others provided images or attitudes. A number left an unpleasant after-taste.

Athol, Duchess of, *Searchlight on Spain*, Penguin, 1938.

BBC Radio 4 news: interview with the first British Army officer to enter Belsen.

BBC2 TV: programme on The Battle of Cable St. (1936).

Bird, ed. et al, *Mapping the Futures*, Routledge, 1993.

Blake, William, *The Book of Urizen*, 1795.

Bourdieu, Pierre, *The Field of Cultural Production*, Blackwell, 1993.

Carr, Raymond, *Images of the Spanish Civil War*, Unwin Hyman, 1986.

Deleuze, Gilles, and Guattari, Félix, *What is Philosophy?* Verso, 1994.

Derrida, Jacques, 'The Deconstruction of Actuality', *Radical Philosophy 68*, 1994.

Elam, Jack, *Motherwell*, Phaidon, 1991.

Enzensberger, Hans Magnus, *Civil War*, Granta Books, 1994.

Guattari, Félix, 'The Micro-Politics of Fascism', *Molecular Revolution*, Peregrine, 1984.

Hadfield, Heywood: to whom I owe the narrative of the talking fish of Juba, Sudan.

Lewis, DS, *Illusions of Grandeur*, Manchester University Press, 1987.

Logsdon, Guy, 'Woody Guthrie and the Dust Bowl', accompanying *Woody Guthrie*, RCA PL 12099.

Lyotard, Jean-François, 'Discussions, or phrasing "after Auschwitz"', (with comments by Derrida), ed. Benjamin, *The Lyotard Reader*, Blackwell, 1989.

Middleton Murray, John, *Europe in Travail*, The Sheldon Press, 1940.

Monaghan, Terry, 'D for Deleted', *Casablanca*, Summer 1994.

Mosley, Oswald, *My Life*, Nelson, 1968.

Newspapers, various: December 1989, December 1994.

New Statesman, 1968, 1988.

Niethammer, Lutz, *Posthistorie*, Verso 1992 (and through this book, Brecht, Benjamin, Hegel and others).

Osbourne, Peter, 'The Politics of Time', *Radical Philosophy* 68, 1994.

Plato, *The Laws*, Penguin, 1970.

Rudolf, Anthony, ed., *I'm Not Even a Grownup: the Diary of Jerzy Feliks Urman*, Menard/King's College, 1991.

_____, *Wine from Two Glasses*, King's/Adam, 1991.

Selwyn, Francis, *Hitler's Englishman*, Penguin, 1987.

Sheppard, Robert, 'Linking the Unlinkable', in *Far Language*, Stride, 1999.

Speer, Albert, *Spandau*, Fontana, 1977.

Thatcher, Margaret, *The Downing Street Years* (a condensation [thank God] of the book) in *Today's Best Nonfiction* [sic], Reader's Digest, 1994 — a volume I found lying outside my front gate during the summer of 1994, a veritable found text.

Virilio, Paul, *Speed and Politics* (and through this book Goebbels and others), Semiotext(e), 1986

West, Rebecca, *The Meaning of Treason*, Pan, 1956.

1997/2006

31 History or Sleep

The epigraph to 'History or Sleep' is drawn from Rudolf above (*Wine* . . .) and is echoed throughout the text. The reference to the Yaake ceremonies makes use of images found in Fisher, Angela, *Africa Adorned*, Collins, 1984.

1997

33 'Some Words of George Oppen'

adapts some words of George Oppen to be found in the interview with him, conducted by Kevin Power, in *Saturday Morning* 3, 1977.

1997

37 Neutral Drums

These texts were composed as exercises in Oulipean formalism, with sestinas arranged in isoverbalist (word-count) structures, with teleutons (repeating end-words) derived from 'Empty Diaries' for the years 1991–1996. Being as much a Tinguely as a Queneau ensured that the texts thus achieved were subject to an unsustainedness, dispersion, fracturing, and explosion that knocked them well out of shape and knocked that kind of formalism out of me, possibly forever! Further knockings out of, and into, shape were undertaken in 2005, necessitating the introduction of another 'remode'.

2005

38 Report on Seaport

As I describe it in 'Thelma' (unpublished):

'Writing *Report on Seaport* I aligned myself with the Mass Observation movement of the 1930s, the flip-side of surrealism. "Seaport" (with a nod to Robert Hampson's poem of that title) my answer to their "Worktown". Cris cheek had asked me (and others) for our observations of "everyday life" on General Election Day 1997. Mayday. It promised much.'

2005

41 Private Numbers

'Coming Down from St George's Hill'

The title refers to Gerrard Winstanley's 1649 community on St George's Hill, Weybridge.

'His Furious Skip'

'A falsely figural text of his phantasies': J-F Lyotard, 'The Critical Function of the Work of Art', *Driftworks* (Semiotexte, 1983).

'Hofmann': Hans Hoffman (1880–1966), painter and teacher.

'Dense oddities': Peter Porter, *The Observer*, 22 January 1989.

'Desire must compromise': Félix Guattari, *Molecular Revolution* (Penguin, 1984).

'Something we want mankind to be': George Oppen, UEA Interview (on
www.robertsheppard.blogspot.com).

'Who will recognise/ Thought was to one side or not real': Tom Raworth,
City Limits, 19 February 1989.

1990

62, 29, 67 Wayne Pratt: Watering the Cactus

I have decided to group the 'Pratt' texts together. I offer here an assessment
of his works and days, composed by one who knew him better than he
knew himself.

Wayne Pratt died in October 1998. He had been ill for many years.

It is the sudden surprise of Pratt's work, as in others' to have emerged
since the 1970s, that is so arresting. A simple trip to the dentist is
imaged so vividly that we feel we are there under the 'interrogating
bulls-eyes' of the dentist who 'garottes/ My gaping tooth with a clamp'.
Admiration of Pratt can easily degenerate into enumeration of apposite
images, or of his fearless entertainment of abstractions, as when he
writes of 'the boots of experience splashed at the/ Urinal of time'. His
poetry can be best read as a weird stain upon the silence of history: 'The
zeppelin of your tongue entered/ The moist hangar of my mouth/ And
burst into flames, an Hindenburg furnace'. Who has not caught his or
her breath at the particular and unique transexual accuracy of his
depiction of his post-orgasmic (?) female lover: 'Mustachioed with sperm
you lay'. Or empathise when sexuality is reduced, as so often in middle
age, to 'hanging, a vasectomised nothing, not THE FUTURE OF BRITAIN/
that smug loo graffitists apostrophise . . .'. And once read, who could
forget, in *Leather's Imperial Cousins*, his postcolonialist masterpiece,
how the nuns chant, 'Thank you for your magnificent erections!' to the
bare-chested native tent makers.

Pratt is aware of his position at the posterior of the century. Post-
modernist in content — remember that dentist: 'He scribbles master
hieroglyphs/ in the tomb of my mouth' — his work is crafted in post-
Movement traditionalism, but is a precursor of the celebrated mingled-
ness of the 1990s. Each poem is a narrative of lyrical experience, speech
levelled by device: 'Watching each other's food:/ Stirring each other's
tea!' We are with Pratt on his journeys 'Selecting a seat, not too near/
The back or front, lost up a branch line/ In my hiking boots'. Yet, so typi-
cally of his restless postmodernity, he dreams of the 'pornographic incu-
bator' of his mistress's laundry basket back in the city, with its masterly
rhyme on that justly famous expression.

Yet finally it is Pratt's compassion that we remember; it led him to
write of the partial demolition of the Brighton B Power Station and
become a Betjeman of the power stack! We see not only the tragedy of

an abandoned half-demolished, monument to the coal industry (and here we may intuit Pratt's left of centre political leanings) but also a residual sympathy for the unfortunate crippled of the human world: 'This plaintive monopede, stark against/ The evening sky;/ How can I, forlorn, alone,/ Ever salve its crumbled stump of stone?'

Even in his children's works, the evergreen classic *Lionel the Urinal* and his celebrated pop up book on immunology, *Maxine the Vaccine Fights Cyrus the Virus*, he bubbles with wit. The work dedicated to Mr Harwood of Hove, *Postcards of Coastguards*, and its follow-up, *Postcards of Lifeguards*, though somewhat differing in tone, attest to his range. Who has not tapped his foot along to the jaunty settings of his verse on Lounge Wizard's cult CD *Music to Eat Cheese By*, (Slugwash Records WP1) which was only unhappily released after his untimely death? And, as Pratt's first wife, Wendy Pratt-Sidebottom (as she is now), whom he once dubbed 'the thinking man's Petula Clark', says in her surprisingly upbeat memoir of her life with Pratt, *Tickling the Kipper*, 'It couldn't go on. . . .' [here the manuscript ends, defeated].

JUSTIN SIDEBOTTOM 1999

63 The End of the Twentieth Century

This 'text for readers and writers' was written on 1 May 1999 to be read at the English Research Day, Edge Hill University (then College of Higher Education), in announcement of the expiry of *Twentieth Century Blues* at the end of that year. It also formed part of a Talk at Birkbeck College organised by Robert Hampson in October 2001, and another at the University of East Anglia, organised by Victor Sage in February 2007.

2002–2007

74
Links in Ink

Poetic Sequencing and the New 3

Numb Numbers; Or: You're Never Alone with a Strand

[This note was released by email to mark the completion of the project.]

The work indexed in its final form here in such detail is not a 'long poem' in the sense of assuming a possible reading linear passage from its *Preface* to its 75th part. There is nothing wrong with such a passage (it will follow the aesthetic push and pull I think I can identify as my chronological progression, reacting against this style and then against that) but it is not recommended, let alone assumed. It will also get you into knots as the links of the numbering double back on themselves. [Note 2007: I am aware that this is more or less the arrangement of this 'complete' edition, which I explain in my 'Introductory Note'.]

Twentieth Century Blues is a network (or 'net/(k)not- work(s)' as I called it) of texts that are interrelated by multilinear 'strands'. That the project would seem open to the technology of hyperlinks has not passed me by, and I would like to utilise this in future presentations, although I conceived of the network's design before this possibility, or its now apposite metaphor, became available. [Note 2007: Although I imagined it as a hypertext, the time-based nature of the project—the year 2000 as its limit—imposed a forward trajectory on its links which, it strikes me now, is alien to the multi-directionality of the hyperlink, which is why I call the work a 'pseudo-hypertext' in my 'Introductory Note'.]

The strands are not sequences of poems in the usual sense and I doubt if they present interesting continua. (I've avoided constructing publications or poetry readings around such a scheme, except in the case of the 'Killing Boxes' strand, which was conceived and largely written as a performance work, in parts.) In any case, very few of the texts are only in a single strand, so to read through the strands would be as repetitive as reading the Blues in order. Strands are deliberately constructed or retrospectively discovered (dis)continuities between texts that I sensed as instructive. I hope a reader will consider them as part of the vast dialogic intratext of the project, but will not be over-directed by them. In fact, a few of the strands, as this full index shows, stretch back to texts written before *Twentieth Century Blues*. Their entanglements are part of the plot, as it were.

My plot, though, it is worth confessing. It has worried me at times that I have dictated connections between texts; it seems contrary, or at least resistant, to my aesthetic education, which emphasised the rôle of the reader in creating meaning within and between texts. However, I have enough respect for readers and their productive powers to know they *cannot* be prevented from making other connections; they might be encouraged by the beginnings I have made, which in some cases acknowledge the return of certain poetic foci, materials, techniques or forms.

Indeed to limit my rôle in this process is part of the relevance of choosing today, 28 December 1999 (a decade after writing the *Preface*), as the date on which the strand connections are 'frozen', to stop myself adding strands or making fresh connections at future dates. [Note 2007: The only strand continuing from *Twentieth Century Blues* to date is 'Killing Boxes' which extends its consideration of the Gulf War to the second such war and its circumstances, and which establishes a single link between this network and my later long work *Warrant Error*. Also 37 part 2 received a posthumous overhaul which affected the index.]

It was always intended that the project was to be time-based, as in the mode of certain performance events, of which I regard *Twentieth Century Blues* the textual equivalent. Earlier this year (see 63) I decided upon Noon Today as the time and date to consolidate the project, yet to leave one important hinge flapping: a final 'Empty Diary for the year 2000' [75], to be written, like the other post-1990 'Diaries' *during* the year it names, the year I still doggedly regard as the last of the twentieth century! So it's not over yet.

This point about time-based writing brings me to my final and most important negative. *Twentieth Century Blues* was conceived as the potentiality of a network to be stretched by writing through time towards a deadline. The title, kitschy and catchy, was originally chosen to impose a temporal limit. That parts of the text (the pre-1991 'Empty

Diaries' in particular) have taken on a historical perspective should not detract from the parts that haven't; I believe the title itself suggested that material now and then, rather than the other way round.

Completed 11.50: 28 December 1999; revised 2007

Index of *Twentieth Century Blues*

An Index of Strands through and out of *Twentieth Century Blues*

The following index lists the strands running through *Twentieth Century Blues*. In some cases this means that texts are linked with texts published outside of the project, mostly before. These publications are indicated by title. Otherwise the index refers to the numbering of the Blues and the page number where the work or notes about the work may be found in the present edition.

Lightning Source UK Ltd.
Milton Keynes UK
UKOW01f1506061016

284632UK00002B/57/P